Breakthroughs

An Integrated Advanced English Program

Teacher's Book

Marina Engelking

Gloria McPherson-Ramirez

OXFORD

UNIVERSITY PRESS

MW00905140

OXFORD
UNIVERSITY PRESS

70 Wynford Drive, Don Mills, Ontario M3C 1J9
www.oup.com/ca

Oxford University Press is a department of the University of Oxford.
It furthers the University's objective of excellence in research, scholarship,
and education by publishing worldwide in

Oxford New York
Auckland Cape Town Dar es Salaam Hong Kong Karachi
Kuala Lumpur Madrid Melbourne Mexico City Nairobi
New Delhi Shanghai Taipei Toronto

With offices in
Argentina Austria Brazil Chile Czech Republic France Greece
Guatemala Hungary Italy Japan Poland Portugal Singapore
South Korea Switzerland Thailand Turkey Ukraine Vietnam

Oxford is a trademark of Oxford University Press

This book is printed on permanent (acid-free) paper ∞.

Canadian Cataloguing in Publication Data

Engelking, Marina, 1959-
   Breakthroughs: an integrated advanced English program.
Teacher's book

ISBN–10: 0-19-541253-2   ISBN-13: 978-0-19-541253-6

1. Language arts. 2. English language- Study and teaching.
1. McPherson-Ramirez, Gloria, 1963- , II. Title.

PE1112.E54 1997 Suppl. 1   428   C97-932172-7

Cover art: Susan Leopold

Printed and bound in Canada

7 8 9 – 08 07 06

Contents

Introduction   v

Unit-by-Unit Teaching Notes

Unit 1   The Calm Before the Storm   1

Unit 2   Strange But True   10

Unit 3   The Road Less Travelled   20

Unit 4   That's Not What I Meant   28

Unit 5   The Cutting Edge   38

Unit 6   It Stands to Reason   45

Unit 7   All the Rage   55

Unit 8   It's How You Play the Game   64

Unit 9   Food For Thought   73

Unit 10   The Circle of Life   83

Reproducibles

1.1   Venn Diagram: Newspaper vs. Journal Articles   97

1.2   Designing a Disaster Shelter   98

1.3   Passive Sentence Game   99

2.1   Strip Story   100

2.2   Prefix Memory Game   101

3.1   A Travel Fair   102

4.1   Interpreting Body Language Game   103

4.2   Role Play — Cards   105

4.3   Role Play — Questions and Summary   106

4.4   Conversation Management   107

5.1   Inventors and Inventions   108

5.2   Creating Hybrids   109

6.1   Word Quiz   110

7.1   Survey: What's Hot and What's Cool   111

7.2   Mystery Word Game   112

8.1   Sports Categories Game   114

9.1   Healthy Eating   115

9.2   World Committee on Initiatives for Better Nutrition   116

10.1   The Seasons of Life   117

10.2   Composing a Prose Poem   118

Unit Quizzes/Mid- and Final Term Assessments

Unit Quizzes   120

Oral Evaluations (by unit)   130

Oral Evaluation Grading Criteria   135

Unit Quiz Notes/Answers   136

Mid-Term Assessment Notes   141

Mid-Term Assessment (reproducible pages)   142

Final Term Assessment (reproducible pages)   145

Final Term Assessment Notes   148

Tapescript   149

Introduction

Welcome to *Breakthroughs*, an advanced, integrated-skills English language program for adults and young adults. In this introduction we will familiarize you with the approach, components, and structure of the program and provide you with some tips for teaching the skills. We will also guide you through the skills development process implicit in this course text.

Approach

The *Breakthroughs* program is based on the premise that language is a system for communication. The goal of the program is to develop communicative competence in English at an advanced level. As a communicative program, the course focuses on both semantic notions and social/applied functions. The skill areas (speaking, listening, reading, and writing) are taught and practised in a balanced, integrated manner because that is how *real* communication works. Students must become active, engaged learners if they are to improve their communicative competence. The program fosters cooperation and provides ample opportunities for student interaction with the learning materials, the instructor, fellow students, and the language community. Risk-taking is encouraged because language learning is a process of discovery. Only by *breaking through* the restrictions of artificially defined rules can students hope to attain advanced level fluency.

Where possible, we have chosen authentic materials to reflect real-life demands and situations. Activities encourage and promote problem-solving and negotiation of meaning as reflected in genuine communication. One of the unique features of the *Breakthroughs* approach is the development and expression of critical thought in English. Students at the advanced level are often more frustrated by their inability to express critical thought than by their inability to master the linguistic details of the language. The instructor's role is to guide students through the process of active meaning construction, fostering independent, self-directed learning. The students' language skill development will continue beyond this course. Students must, therefore, develop strategies and skills for learning language that they can apply beyond the classroom.

The *Breakthroughs* program consists of four components.

STUDENT BOOK (SB)

Four-colour, 161-page main course text divided into ten themed units. Contains scope and sequence for the *Breakthroughs* program on introductory pages. Includes reading, writing, listening, speaking, vocabulary, and grammar activities in each unit. Grammar Focus pages are printed on a coloured background for easy identification and reference. Appendixes include Selected Answers (non-language related) to Quizzes, and Grammar Appendix (including verb tense review chart).

WORKBOOK (WB)

Black and white, 115-page Workbook divided into ten units (corresponding to SB) providing further practice in and expansion of vocabulary and grammar items in SB. Also contains process writing program with writing checklists students can use as guides and editing tools. Includes complete answer key to WB activities.

TEACHER'S BOOK (TB)

Black and white, 160-page Teacher's Book divided into ten units (corresponding to SB). Provides complete answer key to SB exercises, teaching guidelines, additional expansion activities including reproducible activities, lists of helpful Internet resources, unit quizzes (written and oral), a mid-term and final term assessment, suggestions for evaluation, and complete tapescript of material on the audio cassette. Cross-references to Workbook activities and tapescripts allow teachers to easily integrate the components of the program.

AUDIO CASSETTE (AC)

18 listening activities recorded with a variety of male and female voices of varying accents and ages. Materials range from interviews and political speeches to literary excerpts and popular songs.

The total SB program can be completed in about 60 hours, but can be shortened or extended to cover a shorter or longer period. The units are designed to be independent, allowing manipulation in the order and inclusion of the syllabus components. Only units 7, 8, and 9 must be completed in sequence if you are working with the Grammar Focus components since the grammar items in these units (verbals: *to + base, -ing,* and *d/t/n*) build upon each other. The process writing program in the WB follows a sequential approach, using the unit themes in application of the principles. The principles, however, can be adapted to any theme, allowing teachers to manipulate the order of the SB units while maintaining the order of the process writing program.

The Advanced Level

Students beginning the *Breakthroughs* program should be at an early advanced level of English communication. In speaking, these students are able to communicate fairly effectively in some unpredictable contexts, and function independently in most familiar situations. They understand and use vocabulary, idioms, and colloquial expressions to follow and relate stories of general and popular interest. In writing, students are able to write coherently at the paragraph level on familiar and relevant topics, yet they lack the ability to communicate independently and accurately in unpredictable contexts. Although clear in ideas, their writing contains errors in accuracy and lexical collocations. In reading, students are able to read 3–4 pages within an unfamiliar and only partially predictable context of daily social, educational, and work-related life experience. Students are able to deal with the ambiguity of texts containing a range of complex structures and unfamiliar vocabulary with teacher guidance. Students can understand meaning that reflects attitudes and opinion, although they often require re-reading and clarification of parts with general-use idioms and various culturally dependent implications and references. They can use a unilingual dictionary for general vocabulary building. These descriptions correspond to language learners at levels 8/9 of the *Canadian Language Benchmarks* (1996).

Unit Design

Student Book (SB)

The **opening pages** of each unit in the SB begin with visuals and accompanying discussion activities (photos, comics, sketches, puzzles, quizzes) that introduce the unit theme. These are designed to stimulate interest, to motivate students to want to interact with the materials, and to elicit prior knowledge and theme-related vocabulary.

Activities that practise and develop **skills** in reading, listening, writing, and speaking (as well as vocabulary and grammar sections) follow in varying order and level of difficulty. Within each skill focus, exercises proceed from controlled to communicative practice. Varying the skill focus of activities helps maintain a high interest level and offers variety in the types of activities learners encounter. It also facilitates the integration and balance of skills. Varying the skill focus within a constant theme helps build overall communicative competence, since each activity provides the student with more information, vocabulary, language functions, and strategies to communicate within that theme. Although the unit activities have been organized under the headings of Speaking, Writing, Vocabulary, and so on, this classification is somewhat artificial as many of the activities are in themselves integrated: one learner's speaking is another learner's listening. The heading is an organizing and focusing tool. It is not intended to suggest that only a single skill is developed or practised.

Each listening and reading activity has three components: **pre-, during, and post-listening/reading exercises**. The pre-activity exercises elicit students' prior knowledge and relevant vocabulary, motivate students to engage in the activity, and allow you to anticipate and address difficulties and unfamiliar vocabulary. The post-activity exercises allow students to review content and address bottom-up reading and listening in grammar, vocabulary, and discourse features. These activities thus encourage students to react to the reading or listening activity through reflection, application of content, questioning, elaboration, extension, and critical thinking.

It is not always necessary to do all three components (pre-, during, and post-) with every reading or listening. Try varying your approach. Reduce the number of pre- and post- exercises or the questions within them. Experiment. Have half the class complete the pre-activity exercises while the other half abstains. Determine if there is a difference in performance between the two groups. Have students discuss these results. Learning strategies are as important for students as language strategies. Let students become aware of learning strategies they can apply to other courses.

Each unit includes a highlighted **Grammar Focus** section covering a grammar point relevant to the unit topic. Grammar is not meant to be the driving force of the unit. Brief explanations, examples, and structured exercises all lead to applied communicative activities titled Grammar In Use. The goal is to help students improve their communicative competence by understanding and using structures appropriately and easily in a social/applied context.

One Step Beyond activities, a unique feature of the program, focus on the development and expression of critical thought. These activities encourage students to practise the higher level thinking skills of analysis, synthesis, and evaluation.

Each unit also contains **themed visuals** throughout to maintain a high interest level and to help students remain focused. Teachers can actively use these visuals and in some cases lexical presentations to generate discussion and encourage student response to the theme in both in-class work and in testing situations.

Finally, each unit ends with a **Unit Reflection** that summarizes and completes the unit. These activities ask students to reflect, assimilate, apply, and evaluate the unit content.

Workbook (WB)

The WB is divided into the same themed units as the SB and offers further practice in and expansion of the vocabulary and grammar. The WB maintains the same activity headings as the SB for easy reference. Thus, further practice of the vocabulary introduced in Vocabulary 2 in Unit 3 of the SB is found in Unit 3 of the WB under the heading Vocabulary 2. The WB activities can be completed in class, but are also ideal for homework assignments, as most of them are individual student activities. The WB activities provide the teacher with the flexibility to reinforce specific items in the syllabus and to provide individual students having difficulty in a particular area with additional practice. A complete answer key for all WB activities at the back of the book also allows students to use the WB for self-study.

The One Step Beyond (OSB) activities in the WB differ slightly from those in the SB. Although both stimulate critical thinking, in the WB the OSB activities challenge students to design their own vocabulary or grammar exercises that are reviewed and exchanged with peers, thus increasing the difficulty of the learning task. In addition, the WB includes a process writing program to be used optionally in classes where academic writing is a focus. Found at the end of each unit, the program builds writing skills from prewriting to paragraph and essay writing for specific purposes. A targeted writing checklist is found at the close of each process writing section, providing students with a useful guide and editing tool.

Teacher's Book (TB)

The main focus of the TB is to assist teachers in their lesson planning and to facilitate the teaching. The notes and additional activities provide for variety in the learning materials, assist in anticipating student difficulties and confusing grammar points, and clarify the purpose of each activity. Each unit corresponds to a unit in the SB and WB. Clear cross-references in the TB make it easy for teachers to integrate the WB and audio cassette components of the *Breakthroughs* program.

The TB unit opening page provides a quick overview of the unit, outlining the theme and specific topics, the unit vocabulary, grammatical items, and the process writing focus. This is followed by a Getting Started section that suggests a closed book activity to prepare

students for the theme. Teachers are then directed to the opening pages of the unit in the SB.

Each activity of the SB is then presented in order, listing the aims/skills of the activity, notes the teacher should consider before introducing the activity (One Step Ahead), an answer key, and cross-references to practice and expansion WB activities where appropriate. Suggestions for altering or expanding activities as well as additional Expansion activities including project work and games are also featured. A number of Expansion activities are provided on reproducible sheets. The unit ends with a list of Helpful Internet Resources suitable for accessing additional information on the unit theme and assigning project work to students.

The TB also includes reproducible written and oral Unit Quizzes, and a mid-term and final term assessment (with answer keys, notes, and suggested evaluation criteria), allowing for review of the unit materials and evaluation of oral proficiency achievement.

The final section of the TB is the transcript for all the listening material on the audio cassette.

The Skills

Reading, writing, listening, and speaking are inseparable skills. However, we address them here under separate headings for utility.

Reading

Philosophy/Approach: *Breakthroughs* promotes an interactive model of reading. Reading is both a bottom-up and top-down activity. Students build sounds and letters into words, phrases, and then patterns of meaning. But they also predict meaning as they read and match their own knowledge to the reading's content. Students approach reading with personal and cultural attitudes, values, and beliefs.

Tips: It is critical to engage your students actively in any reading. We have included many reading strategies in this program and each reading requires students to apply at least one strategy. Although the readings in the SB provide practice for applying reading strategies, they are also designed to contribute information to the unit theme. The unit shouldn't revolve around the readings. You will notice that in most cases the unit vocabulary was not selected from the readings. Rather, the vocabulary relates to the theme. Let the theme be the driving force of the unit. You may even wish to ask students to find examples of other readings that could be included in the theme.

A glossary has been included for some readings where needed. In some instances you may want to review the glossary terms before students read, but this is not always necessary. At the advanced level it is important to encourage students to guess meaning from context.

Unlike the readings in the SB, the readings in the WB contain the unit vocabulary or grammatical items. There are many activities you can do with readings, but take care not to over analyze a reading. Aim to keep students interested, to provide variety, and to get students to interact with the readings.

Identifying culturally dependent references and implications in readings is a difficult but necessary skill for students at the advanced level. Students will become better at this as they become more familiar with the target culture. Wherever possible, include discussions about cultural references in writing and show examples. The first step is for students to be aware that cultural references in writing exist. From your examples, you can begin to classify high frequency references into thematic categories such as political, religious, and social references. Comics are a good place to start as they often contain cultural references.

Listening

Philosophy/Approach: Developing listening skills is often neglected in the integrated language class. It is assumed that students will passively learn to listen. We believe that the skill of listening must be actively taught — both transactional and interactional listening. Transactional listening involves listening for a message. Interactional listening involves listening for communicative inter-action: this is the listening and speaking we do to build relationships. For example, when we hear the morning greeting ritual in an office we are engaging in interactional listening. You can model interactional speaking through informal teacher chat on personal topics or topical issues such as who won the baseball game.

Actively, developing listening skills goes far beyond completing audio cassette activities, although these are useful for targeted practice and provide variety. At the advanced level, listening practice should reflect listening as it is encountered in the real world. Students must be encouraged to listen for more than the meaning of words and phrases: they must be able to make affective inter-pretations by listening to linguistic (word choice and grammatical choice), paralinguistic (tone, stress, rhythm, intonation), and extralinguistic (body language) elements. In other words, students must interpret what is said, how it's said, and what is done as it's being said. An effective listening activity allows for transferability: the skills students apply to the listening activity should also be applicable in the language community outside the classroom.

Tips: Use every opportunity you can to develop listening skills. This is easy to do when so many activities have an oral component. Don't limit students to the listening activities on the audio cassette. One excellent way to foster effective listening skills is by incorporating more specific listening tasks into formal and impromptu oral presentations, speeches, and narratives. Make students aware that they can listen for a variety of specific language elements. These include listening for attitude, interaction, information, and to get things done. In addition, they can listen for conversational gambits and identify conversational strategies. For example, you can have them listen and observe English speakers on the radio, on television, in movies, and in the community to identify how speakers express agreement/disagreement, pleasure, surprise, hope, and disappointment. Ironically, observing others in natural conversation is effective in drawing students' attention to how the speaking/listening interaction works. Have students observe how speakers express logical conclusions, obligation, approval/disapproval, and so on, noting the specific conversational and behavioural markers used to express meaning in a given social and cultural context. A field study project wherein students observe English speakers at a mall, in a large store, or at the library, and record and present their findings to the class can reveal important information about how fluent English speakers really communicate.

In the classroom, give listeners a reason to listen. Listeners often play a passive role during oral interaction, especially during presentations. One technique using small groups involves having the speaker pause at given time periods during the presentation to facilitate a question/answer period, confirming that the listeners have understood the main ideas to that point. Each listener in the group (a limit of about six works best) asks one question about what was presented so far. The question/answer routine continues until both listener and speaker are satisfied that meaning has been negotiated. In large group presentations this question/answer routine can be varied. Prepare and hand out question cards to each listener in the group. Immediately, each member in the audience has a reason to listen. Questions are designed to ask for specific functions. For example:

Function	Question
1. Asking for repetition	Could you repeat the point you made about . . .?
2. Asking for restatement	Could you explain what you mean by . . .?
	I don't understand what you mean when you said . . .?
3. Asking for clarification	Could you give us an (another) example of . . .?
	Could you give more details about . . .?
4. Asking for application	How would this affect . . .?
5. Asking for more information	Could you say more about . . .?

Over time, you can stop giving students the specific questions and give them cards with only the function, letting them formulate appropriate questions for that function. Finally, in fostering true independence, tell students to listen and be prepared to ask one question. Eventually, students will learn that this is an effective strategy that will help them to listen actively. Use this approach frequently throughout your course for best results.

Speaking

Philosophy/Approach: In *Breakthroughs* the speaking focus is on fluency and communicative effectiveness. While we strongly believe that it is beneficial to teach and learn grammatical structure, we believe that the purpose of learning grammar in the context of speaking is to improve communicative competence. Oral communicative competence, however, involves much more than knowledge and formulation of grammar structures. It requires knowledge of the socio-cultural rules that determine appropriate use of words, registers, and grammar structures. It requires students to be able to sustain discourse and to ensure that communication is understood. The goal of teaching speaking in the *Breakthroughs* program is to encourage patterns of language interaction that mirror as closely as possible those used by competent speakers in the language community. The teacher can encourage informal, unrehearsed speech and provide significant opportunity for students to engage in a variety of real communication activities. In addition to providing semi-controlled speaking activities, students have to engage in communication activities that require and encourage a holistic approach to the communication process. Students must be able to speak about what is real and interesting, both in concrete and abstract terms. This was the major criteria for selecting the *Breakthroughs* unit themes and topics.

Tips: Task-based activities such as role plays, dramas, problem-solving, debates, team presentations, project work, and other activities that require pre-planning are rich in group interaction and provide excellent opportunities for natural, meaningful oral communication. To encourage more active participation in discussions, you may want to hold student-led discussion sessions. Have the student leader select a topic, write or find a short article, and design questions to facilitate the discussion. The student can begin with a brief introduction and should end the session by summing up the discussion highlights. Many of the activities that promote active listening, such as the field observation described in the previous section, are also useful in developing effective speaking skills.

Writing

Philosophy/Approach: Although an academic process writing program is included in the WB, it is not the main focus in the *Breakthroughs* program. The activities in the SB encourage students to write for a variety of reasons by providing a range of writing tasks that are practical and creative. The goal is to improve individual student progress in writing proficiency. Students should be encouraged to become independent readers of their own work with the ability to create, revise, and reshape their writing to meet the tasks at hand. The writing "product" is important. Attention to grammar and mechanics is essential, particularly in the editing stage. In trying to foster accuracy in writing, however, teachers are sometimes tempted to control every aspect of the process which can result in artificial restrictions. In our view, writing is a process of discovery in which writers develop their thoughts during the writing process rather than before. Thus the writing process model should not be restrictive. On the other hand, a formal writing process model can be a useful focusing tool and guide to students as they develop their writing skills. As a result, process, content, and accuracy should be developed simultaneously.

Tips: Even if you are not using the process writing program in the WB, note that many of the strategies presented (especially the prewriting activities) can be applied to any type of writing. It is worthwhile to review these with your students. Provide opportunities for practical writing (letters, e-mails, reports, forms, surveys, outlines for presentations, lists, notes, and messages) and emotive writing (in journals, diaries, personal letters). Students need to write to improve their writing and while marking students' writing can be very time consuming, shorter, less formal writing tasks provide good writing practice yet need not take a long time to mark. In less formal writing activities students may be more likely to give and accept peer feedback. Use a variety of feedback strategies for writing, and note that not all writing needs to be marked. A 15-minute oral conference with a student or responding orally on audio tape may be less time consuming than detailed written remarks on a student paper.

Whatever your approach, ensure that there is clear teacher/student agreement on feedback and train students in what to do with the feedback. Before beginning a writing task, you may want to have students collaboratively design an editing checklist (provided one of the checklists in the WB is not suitable for the task) that they can use to edit their own work. Self-identification and correction of errors is a significant step towards improving writing. When evaluating a student's writing, we suggest you deal with communicated meaning first, then deal with grammar. On a first draft, mark only those errors that interfere with communicative competence. If you plan to use peer editing, make sure students clearly understand what aspects of the writing they should comment on. A peer-editing sheet can be a useful guiding tool. Peer editing seems to be more successful when it is restricted to non-expert, general reaction information such as identifying the purpose of the writing, listing one thing the peer really liked about the writing, asking a question the peer expected the writer to answer that wasn't answered, and so on. Alternately, consider having peers read only the introduction of a paper first, followed by a prediction about what the rest of the writing will discuss. Then the peer reviewer can continue reading and compare his or her predictions to what is found in the paper. Skim peer feedback sheets, at least periodically, to ensure applicability and appropriateness.

Grammar

Philosophy/Approach: Grammar is important, but it shouldn't be the driving force of a lesson. The goal in the *Breakthroughs* program is to improve communicative competence and that includes linguistic competence. Teaching grammar means enabling students to use linguistic forms accurately, meaningfully, and appropriately. While rules can be useful, learning rules alone does not improve grammar. It is helpful to view a grammatical item from three different perspectives: (1) the form or structure, (2) the meaning of the grammatical item, (3) the social context in which it is appropriately used.

Tips: While each unit has one or two Grammar Focus sections, students don't master grammatical structures one at a time. Grammar items need to be continuously reviewed and recycled. Students build on what they already know, especially at the advanced level, so it isn't necessary to teach every aspect of a new structure. Gauge what students already know and fill in the gaps. We have provided the rules and meanings of the grammatical items in the Grammar Focus of each unit. In the Grammar In Use activities, students practice the grammar in a real-life context. At the advanced level students have often already been exposed to the form and meaning of a grammar point, but still have difficulty using it appropriately in a consistent way. Help your students to develop the decision-making skills needed to judge what grammatical structures a given situation requires. Aim to make the activities real and useful. Integrate the grammar into all the skill areas.

Vocabulary

Philosophy/Approach: Teaching vocabulary is perhaps one of the most neglected areas in the language classroom. Many times teaching vocabulary doesn't go beyond writing a word on the blackboard and describing or discussing its meaning. Students should acquire some strategies to learn vocabulary beyond the classroom. To truly know a word, a student must interact with it to make it his or her own. A student must know its meaning (or various meanings), be able to manipulate its grammatical forms, understand any associated social and cultural connotations such as age (is it a word only teenagers use?), sex (is it a word women tend to use more frequently than men?), and region (is it a word used mainly in a specific region of the country?). A student needs to know about the word's frequency (is it a word used frequently?), lexical and grammatical collocations

(is it usually partnered with specific words?), and social context (is it a word used mainly in politics?). Clearly, knowing only the meaning of a word is not enough.

Tips: *Breakthroughs* engages students in a wide variety of vocabulary-building activities built around themed vocabulary. Nonetheless, there are opportunities to teach unplanned vocabulary as well. When doing so, try these three steps:

- convey meaning (through miming, visual representation, etc.)
- check understanding (sorting, classification, and "which word doesn't belong" activities, etc.)
- reinforce (use the word in a sentence, use these words in a story, role-play a situation where the word(s) would naturally occur, etc.).

Student Interaction

Student interaction is essential in the language classroom because language is interactive. *Breakthroughs* materials provide ample opportunity for active student interaction with the themes and topics, peers, and the language community. Reading and writing activities include opportunities to interact before and after the activity, and sometimes during the activity as well. In jigsaw reading, for example, students read different parts of a text and then join in teams (where each member has read a different part) to discuss and construct meaning. Some of the listening activities ask students to complete charts in pairs *during* the listening process.

Although some student interaction should be informal and non-structured (for example, chatting before or after class or during a break, chatting briefly about local issues, or engaging in interactional speaking), most interactive work needs to be structured. Some students (and some teachers) see group work as a waste of time and a source of frustration. Here are five keys to successful group interaction:

1. Students must understand the purpose of the interaction, either implicitly or explicitly. If they don't see the purpose, tell them.

2. Students have to know what they are supposed to do. It is critical to explain the task clearly and sufficiently. In an advanced class it is not always necessary to write instructions on the board, especially if the task is simple, but it is a good idea to confirm understanding. Try selecting a student to rephrase the steps involved in the task, especially in multi-phased tasks and with game instructions. You may also wish to assign roles in some cases to avoid single student-dominated discussions. Students can be assigned as timekeepers, recorders, presenters, and so on. Time spent on explaining and clarifying instructions at the start is time saved during the activity.

3. Students must be aware of how much time they have to complete the task, and should be reminded that time is coming to a close just before the task ends. The teacher should circulate around the room to ensure teams are on task, to gauge performance, and to offer guidance and feedback when needed. Pair and team activities should be wrapped up. It is very frustrating to work on or complete a team activity and then not take it up. Timing is very important. Allow enough time to complete pair and group work.

There are various ways to assign pairs and teams. Students can find their own partners or you can assign them. (They will generally choose their friends). Choosing their own partner gives students more control over their learning. You can assign partners according to the following criteria: geographically (work with those around you), by level (strong with strong / weak with strong), by interest (students who like baseball / students who like skiing), by sex (male / female), by language background (students of varying language backgrounds), and so on. Classroom dynamics, the task, and personal preference may influence how you set up your pairs and teams. Although you may wish to vary your approach, usually in the first few classes it is a good idea to assign partners and teams especially if students don't know each other.

Role Play

In a role play each person adopts the role of a character in a conversation or a situation. Students improvise speech, although usually with preparation. Role play is a fluency activity. While it is necessary to provide feedback, it is inappropriate to focus on grammatical errors beyond a severe, repeated error. Try not to interrupt during a role play unless communication has completely broken down. Give the audience a reason to listen.

Games

Students generally enjoy the fun aspect of playing games. It is very important, however, to make sure students know the purpose of playing the game, especially existing board games and other non-word games. Instructions for games are often more complex than activities. If instructions are written out, students can engage in a guided, pre-game activity to understand the instructions. Try to use the same types of games periodically, varying the level of difficulty perhaps. Once students are familiar with a game pattern, they tend to get into it more quickly and perform better.

Discussion

Guided discussions are extremely useful for student interaction and are easy to set up. The key to success however lies in the guidance. Discussions can easily go on for longer than desired and can get off track (although that has its merits at times). Another danger

with discussions is that they can turn into lectures. The teacher's role is to guide the topic and encourage participation. Finally, discussions are sometimes dominated by a small number of speakers. To ensure maximum participation, try having students discuss some aspects in small teams before holding a full class discussion. Another technique is to inform students of an upcoming discussion and assign certain topic responsibilities to different groups. For example, if you are discussing drugs at the Olympic games, ask one group of students to give some thought to Olympic committee rules about performance-enhancing drugs, while another group considers the athletes' perspective.

Encourage your students to interact with the language community. Assignments that involve going out into the community are very useful in modelling real communication. Watching or listening to (selected) television and radio programs is also useful. Where possible use realia in the classroom. The touch, feel, and look of a real magazine, newspaper, letter, chart, map, or prop is much more interesting and beneficial to work with than a copy.

Using the Internet

The Teacher's Book includes some helpful Internet sites at the end of each unit that relate to the unit theme. These sites can be used by the teacher for background information, or by students for project work, research, or reading and writing language practice. The amount of information on the Internet can be overwhelming. The key is knowing how to search for information. If your students have access to the Internet and you plan to have them use it, it is worthwhile to give a short lesson on how to search for information. There are several good resources to help you. In *The Internet Guide for English Language Teachers* (1997), Dave Sperling devotes the first three chapters to using the Internet.

Note that the Internet is not regulated. Not only might students be able to access inappropriate materials, but the information they do find may not be completely accurate. We have listed what we consider to be reliable sources (government agencies, reputable media sources, etc.) in providing you with Internet sites, but the reliability and biases in information on the Internet may be a useful discussion for your students. The Internet is also a commercial tool. Caution students not to give out personal information or credit card numbers. In searching for sites on the paranormal in Unit 7, we found a large number of sites that ask for payment for psychic services.

We have taken care to provide accurate and current information. However, the Internet is a rapidly changing environment. Information may be in one place today and in another tomorrow. New sites come on the Internet daily, others disappear. Therefore, in addition to listing

Internet addresses, we have also provided key words for searching purposes. With appropriate use and common sense, the Internet is a wonderful tool for connecting your students to the language community.

Evaluation

The assessment tools in the *Breakthroughs* program go beyond testing the students' ability to recount the vocabulary, grammar, and informational content of the units. They assess whether students can actually apply listening, speaking, reading and writing strategies to communicate competently in English, in performing complex communication tasks.

The TB includes a variety of reproducible assessment tools that evaluate students' progress

A. Unit Quizzes: A written (30 minutes) and oral (15 minutes) quiz have been designed for each unit. Both quizzes are based on the content and theme of the unit.

Written: To accommodate time constraints and increase utility, the written quiz is designed more as a review tool than an assessment of students' ability to apply the strategies and content learned. As such, the skills are not assessed in an integrated manner, but rather as discrete items. The quiz consists of three sections: a) Vocabulary — a controlled or semi-controlled activity that tests the students' ability to retain the unit vocabulary; b) Grammar — a controlled activity designed to test students' ability to produce the grammar items of the unit's Grammar Focus; c) Writing (optional) — a theme-based communicative activity that requires students to apply the learned vocabulary and grammar. Notes, answers, and a marking scheme are provided for each written quiz.

Oral: The oral quiz is a task-based quiz, done in pairs. It is a communicative assessment, consisting of three parts: a) an interactive activity in which students ask and respond to each other's questions; b) a communicative activity in which each student must expresses his or her own ideas and thoughts clearly and articulately; c) an interactive activity that requires students to discuss an aspect of the unit theme, usually prompted by a visual. An oral grading criteria guideline sheet can be found on page 135 of the TB. This grading tool can be applied to all oral assessments, including the mid-term and final oral assessments.

B. Mid-Term Assessment: The mid-term assessment is a one-hour, task-based, integrated-skills communicative assessment that requires students to apply communication strategies developed in the *Breakthroughs* program to complete a task. The task is not related to the unit themes, so the assessment can be done after completing four, five, or six of the *Breakthroughs* units. (We recommend completing at least three of the units before

giving the mid-term assessment). Students work in teams of three or four to complete the task while the teacher circulates from team to team assessing each member's ability to handle the task.

C. Final Term Assessment: The final term assessment consists of a written (2 hours) and oral (10 minutes) component.

Written Assessment: This assessment requires students to read an article on the development of the English language and answer questions that assess comprehension of content and contextual vocabulary. Students then write a paragraph in response to the reading. The paragraph allows teachers to assess students' grammar competence and ability to use appropriate vocabulary. Teachers can also evaluate students' ability to express ideas clearly and accurately in writing. A marking scheme is provided.

Oral Assessment: Subsequently, students work in pairs to apply and expand on what they've read in a discussion about the future of the English language.

Invitation to Comment

We welcome your suggestions and comments on any of the materials in the *Breakthroughs* Integrated Advanced English Program. Please write to us.

Marina Engelking, Gloria McPherson-Ramirez
c/o ESL Department
Oxford University Press Canada
70 Wynford Drive
Don Mills, Ontario
Canada M3C 1J9

SYMBOLS USED IN THIS BOOK:

 Closed book activity

 Open book activity

 Answer key

UNIT 1
The Calm Before the Storm

Getting Started

The following activity can be used to introduce the unit. Copy the following word parts onto cards: *earth, quake, vol, cano, tor, nado, flood, water, after, shock, ava, lanche, tidal, wave, bliz, zard, hurri, cane, cy, clone, ty, phoon, land, slide*. Give each student in the class one card. If the class is an uneven number, take one card yourself. Instruct the students to mingle and find a partner whose card, when combined with their own, forms a word or phrase. Once students have found their pairs, have them form teams of six to determine what their words have in common and what the topic of the unit might be.

Unit Opening Pages (SB p. 1)

ONE STEP AHEAD

The quiz "Would you survive?" could be timed. Give students 2–3 minutes to complete it, simulating the reaction time available when a natural disaster occurs. The quiz can be done individually or in pairs. Allow at least 15 minutes for a class discussion of the answers.

The following are some basic facts you might like to know before starting this quiz.

Earthquake: During an earthquake you should stay indoors to avoid falling debris. Avoid standing next to heavy objects such as bookcases that may tip over. Move away from glass doors and windows that might shatter. Stand in a door frame as long as there isn't a door that can slam shut on you. The best tip is to *duck, cover, and hold* — get under a heavy table or desk and hang on. If outdoors, stay away from brick walls, chimneys, power lines, and trees.

Floodwater: Small cars can be swept away in as little as 30 cm of water; any other vehicle in 60 cm of water. A person can be knocked down by as little as 15 cm of rushing water. Stay away from power lines and electrical sources.

Hurricanes: Wind speed is measured on the Beaufort scale from 1 (calm) to 12 (hurricane). Hurricanes are most common between June and November. The centre of the hurricane is called the eye. One of the major impacts of a hurricane is flooding.

Tornado: A tornado is a column of air spinning in a counterclockwise direction. It is associated with dark skies (sometimes an emerald green sky), strong winds, lightning, thunder, and heavy rain or hail. It strikes quickly and randomly with little or no warning. The pressure inside the funnel can be 90% lower than normal atmospheric pressure, which creates a suction allowing the funnel to easily pick up heavy objects.

Tsunami: A tsunami is a huge ocean wave caused by an earthquake or volcano. Wave speeds can reach over 800 km/h. In deep water the wave can be less than 1 m high, but in shallow water or bays the water forms a destructive wall. In 1964, a 6 m high wave hit the coast of Vancouver causing millions of dollars in damages.

Volcanic Eruption: Lava flows and burning hot projectiles will be evident in the immediate vicinity. Mudflows and clouds of volcanic ash can follow rivers and valleys and go for hundreds of kilometres, sweeping away everything in their path. When fleeing the scene, wear long sleeves to protect from falling ash and cover your mouth and nose to aid in breathing.

Lightning: Lightning is a flash of brilliant light in the sky caused by the production of natural electricity as clouds collide. Lightning can be zigzagged or sheet lightning.

For some helpful Internet sites, see p. 9.

V ocabulary 1 (SB p. 2)

Aims/Skills
- categorize themed vocabulary according to types of disasters
- identify parts of speech

🔑 Answer Key

1. Below are a number of words associated with natural disasters. Use your dictionary to check the meanings of any words you are not familiar with, and then copy the chart below and write the words in the appropriate colums.

Earthquake	Hurricane	Volcano
epicentre (n)	torrential (adj)	eruption (n)
trembling (adj/verb)	rain (n)	lava (n)
aftershocks (n)	eye (n)	poisonous (adj)
fissures (n)		gases (n)
		spew (v)

Flood	Tornado	Blizzard
deluge (n/v)	funnel (n)	whiteout (n/adj)
floodwater (n)	twister (n)	blinding (adj)

Workbook Practice and Expansion:
Vocabulary 1 Exercises A and B (WB p. 1)
Vocabulary Expansion Exercise C (adj.-noun collocations) and Exercise D (WB p. 2)

R eading 1 (SB pp. 2–4)

Aims/Skills
- read for meaning
- define vocabulary from context
- read tables of statistics
- develop scanning skills

🔑 Scanning (SB p. 2)

Quickly scan the text to find the following information.

1. When did disaster strike in Bangladesh? *April 1991*
2. Where were the wildfires located? *California and Australia*
3. What is the world population expected to be by the middle of the next century? *10 billion*
4. How many people were killed by flood and by famine? *flood = 304 870   famine = 605 832*
5. Words matched with definitions:

line 33 exacerbate	a) *to make worse*
line 8 unprecedented	e) *never having occurred before*
line 20 propagation	j) *spreading*
line 1 menaced	g) *threatened*
line 3 recurring	c) *happening again and again*
line 13 perennial	f) *occurring every year*
line 13 havoc	h) *great destruction or disorder*
line 12 droughts	i) *long periods of time with little or no rain*
line 13 scourge	d) *something that causes great suffering*
line 24 adversely	b) *unfavourably*

Reading for Information (SB p. 4)

Now read the text to find the answers to these questions.

1. There are six natural disasters discussed. What are they? *cyclones, earthquakes, floods, droughts, volcano, wildfires*

2. Where are risks of disasters greatest? *river valleys and coastal plains*

3. What natural hazards do we face in the future and why? *threat to freshwater availability, floods, radioactive and chemical releases in atmosphere due to the changing climate, human, and environmental factors*

4. What type of natural disaster killed the most people from 1967–1991? *drought (from Table 1)*

5. *Note: The answer for the second part of the question is not found directly in the reading.*
   How many deaths have insect infestations caused? *0*
   Could there be indirect deaths as a result of these infestations? *Yes, starvation if crops are destroyed.*

One Step Beyond (SB p. 4)

Some possible suggestions of human activities that may be drastically affecting the environment and contributing to natural disasters: carbon emissions, clear-cutting of forests, freon gas from air conditioners and refrigerators, and other pollution.

Expansion

A. Focus on Table/Statistics Reading

Have students focus on the table (SB p. 3) and then ask them these questions.

1. List the five top causes of death. *drought, cyclone, earthquake, famine, flood*

2. What years do the statistics cover? *1967–1991*

3. Approximately how many people were killed by meteorological and hydrological events from 1967–1991? *about 3.5 million*

4. What weather event caused the fewest deaths? *cold and heat wave*

5. Which geological event caused the fewest deaths? *tsunami*

B. Chart Making

Have students create three pie charts, one for each category in the table: weather events, associated with weather events, geological.

1. Total the number of deaths reported in each category.

2. Divide the total deaths for each type of disaster by the total for the whole category and multiply by 100 to determine the percentages. *Note: As a result of rounding off numbers, the percentages added together may not equal 100.*

3. Draw a circle and divide it into slices which represent the percentages. The slices can be colour coded for easy identification.

4. Label the slices with the names of the disasters and the percentages.

5. Add a title, labels, and dates.

Answer Key:
Deaths by Natural Disasters 1967-1991 (percentages)

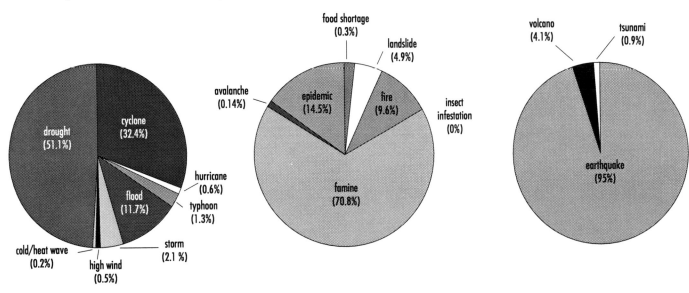

Weather Events   **Associated with Weather Events**   **Geological**

Grammar Focus 1 (SB pp. 4–6)

Exercise A (SB pp. 4–5)

Identify the subject (agent) and the object (receiver of the action) in the following sentences. Some sentences may not have an object. Determine if the sentences can be changed to the passive voice and then rewrite them.

Note: Ask students to underline the subject and circle the object.

EXAMPLE: Forest fires destroyed (thousands of hectares of) (valuable timber.)

SUBJECT: forest fires   OBJECT: timber

PASSIVE: Thousands of hectares of valuable timber were destroyed by forest fires.

1. The geologist found (volcanic glass) from an eruption 2000 years ago.
   Volcanic glass from an eruption 2000 years ago was found by the geologist.

2. The sudden blizzard stranded (people) in their cars along the highway.
   People were stranded in their cars along the highway by the sudden blizzard.

3. Meteorologists predict a (hurricane) in the Caribbean next week.
   A hurricane is predicted in the Caribbean next week by meteorologists.

4. The weather forecaster goes to the station twice a day.
   Passive voice not possible.
   Note: The object in this sentence is the object of the preposition.

5. The tornado destroyed the (town.)
   The town was destroyed by the tornado.

6. The avalanche occurred on Whistler Mountain.
   Passive voice not possible.

7. The avalanche buried (three skiers) alive.
   Three skiers were buried alive by the avalanche.

8. There will be many monsoons in Japan during the rainy season.
   Passive voice is not possible.

9. The tornado picked up the (car) and deposited it in a tree.
   The car was picked up and deposited in a tree by the tornado.

10. The flood caused (millions of dollars in damages.)
    Millions of dollars in damages were caused by the flood.

Exercise B (SB p. 5)

Use the following words to create passive sentences. Use the "by" phrase if it is important to know who or what was responsible for the action.

EXAMPLE: floodwaters / town / flood
         The town was completely flooded.

In this example, it is obvious that the town was flooded by floodwaters so there is no need to state the obvious in a "by" phrase.

EXAMPLE: suspect \ people \ several tenants \ kill \ blast
         People suspect that several tenants were killed in the blast.
                            OR
         Several tenants were killed in the blast.

When the subject of the active sentence is "people," it is often omitted in the passive voice.

1. village / bury / volcanic ash
   The village was buried by volcanic ash.

2. survivors / rescue / passing ship / lifeboats
   The survivors in lifeboats were rescued by a passing ship.

3. snow / travellers / snowed-in
   The travellers were snowed-in.

4. burn / fire / forest
   The forest was burned.

5. trap / rubble / earthquake / people
   People were trapped by rubble from the earthquake.

6. operate / rescue equipment / trained specialist
   Rescue equipment is operated by a trained specialist.

7. find / wreckage / passing plane
   The wreckage was found by a passing plane.

8. town / tornado / destroy
   The town was destroyed by a tornado.

9. 3 a.m. / strike / island / tidal wave
   The island was struck by a tidal wave at 3 a.m.

10. announce / prime minister / disaster relief plan
    The disaster relief plan was announced by the prime minister.

Grammar In Use (SB p. 6)

1. It is common to find the passive voice used extensively in newspaper reports. Reporters generally take "poetic licence" with the language, however, and leave out the *be* form of the verb.

   Look at the following newspaper headlines and expand them. Then rewrite them in the active voice.

   EXAMPLE: Hundreds feared dead as volcano buries village

   EXPANDED HEADLINE: Hundreds of people are feared dead as volcanic eruption buries village

   ACTIVE VOICE: We fear that hundreds of people are dead due to a volcanic eruption that buried the village.

a) Island "totally destroyed" by hurricane
   The island was totally destroyed by a hurricane.
   A hurricane totally destroyed the island.

b) 180 000 left homeless in southern Florida
   180 000 people were left homeless in southern Florida
   Disaster left 180 000 homeless in southern Florida.

c) Death toll expected to top 5000
   The death toll is expected to top 5000.
   They expect the death toll to top 5000.

d) Death toll rises as boats tossed onto sidewalks
   The death toll rises as boats are tossed onto sidewalks.
   A hurricane tossed boats onto sidewalks, causing the death toll to rise.

e) Hundreds swept to their deaths as tsunami hits coast
   Hundreds are swept to their deaths as a tsunami hits the coast.
   A tsunami hits the coast sweeping hundreds to their deaths.

Workbook Practice: Grammar Focus 1 Exercises A–E (WB pp. 2–3)

Writing (SB p. 6)

Aims/Skills
- write a newspaper article
- write a journal article
- use passive voice appropriately in writing
- use logical sequencing
- practise description

ONE STEP AHEAD

It is very important to model writing for students. Either have students bring in examples of newspaper articles and journal articles or provide samples of each for students to analyze in terms of content and style.

Expansion

Pre-Writing (Reproducible 1.1)
After exposing students to examples of both newspaper and journal writing, have them work in small teams to complete the photocopiable VENN diagram (Reproducible 1.1). They need to determine which points describe features of newspaper writing, which describe features of journal writing, and which are common to both.

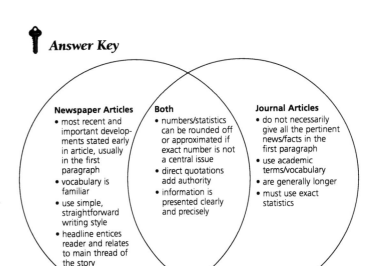

Answer Key

Newspaper Articles
- most recent and important developments stated early in article, usually in the first paragraph
- vocabulary is familiar
- use simple, straightforward writing style
- headline entices reader and relates to main thread of the story

Both
- numbers/statistics can be rounded off or approximated if exact number is not a central issue
- direct quotations add authority
- information is presented clearly and precisely

Journal Articles
- do not necessarily give all the pertinent news/facts in the first paragraph
- use academic terms/vocabulary
- are generally longer
- must use exact statistics

Speaking (SB p. 6)

Aims/Skills
- give step-by-step instructions on the phone
- speak clearly and concisely
- focus on telephoning
- clarify information

ONE STEP AHEAD

Not all natural disasters will work well for this activity because there must be some warning period. Tornado, hurricane, earthquake, and flood would work well. Have students give instructions about what their younger brother or sister should do 1) before the disaster (e.g., items to gather), 2) during, and 3) after. How will he or she contact you after the event?

Give students 10 minutes to present their dialogues in pairs. Then have students analyze the effectiveness of the techniques each team has used to make its message clear. If two teams give information about the same disaster, have the class determine which set of instructions was more useful and why.

Listening 1 (SB pp. 6–7)

See Tapescript 1.a

Aim/Skill
- listen for details

Focused Listening (SB p. 6)

You will hear different individuals telling you how they predict certain weather patterns. Listen for the answers to these questions.

1. What does it mean if the salt stays dry on the onion? *The month that the onion represents will be dry.*

2. Which way does a swan usually fly? *with the wind*

3. What colour of the sky indicates danger? *emerald green*

4. What is the significance of a groundhog seeing its shadow? *Winter will continue another six weeks.*

5. How do pets indicate an earthquake is about to happen? *They begin to behave strangely.*

Note: The folk ways of predicting the weather are recorded by speakers from different areas of the world. Have students identify which parts of the world the speakers may be from. The first is from France, the second from the Caribbean, the third and fourth from Canada or the United States, and the last from an oriental country.

One Step Beyond (SB p. 7)

As an alternative to this activity and one that involves research, report writing, and a full presentation, see the project option below.

> **Expansion**

Project Option (Reproducible 1.2)

Aims/Skills
- research
- practise diagramming
- present information clearly

Photocopy enough assignment/grading sheets (Reproducible 1.2) for each member of the class. Students work in teams to develop a family shelter for protection from a natural disaster of their choosing. They should use at least three different sources in their research. They will then hand in a written report and present their findings to the class. Their presentation should include appropriate visuals such as diagrams and flow charts.

> **ONE STEP AHEAD**
>
> Proverbs are short sentences or phrases that state a general truth or give advice. They come from a rich oral tradition and generally rhyme to make them easy to remember. In this exercise, it is not important for the students to know the proverbs or remember them. They should be using contextual clues and rhyming to complete the sayings. Before beginning the exercise, discuss what a proverb is with the class.
>
> *Note:* Sometimes poetic licence is used in proverbs. Grammatically, 3 Down should be fishes' **mouthes**, but this wouldn't rhyme and it would not be as effective to have the wind blow the bait into only one fish's mouth.

♦ *Answer Key*

When the wind is in the east,
'Tis neither good for man nor beast, *(1 Across)*
When the wind is in the north,
The skillful fisher goes not forth; *(2 Across)*
When the wind is in the south,
It blows the bait in the fishes' mouth; *(3 Down)*
When the wind is in the west,
Then 'tis at the very best. *(1 Down)*

When the dew is on the grass,
Rain will never come to pass. *(3 Across)*

Red sky at night,
Sailors delight. *(4 Down)*
Red sky in morning,
Sailors take warning. *(2 Down)*

> **Workbook Expansion:** Vocabulary 2 Expansion (additional proverbs and idioms) Exercises A and B (WB p. 4)

Vocabulary 2 (SB p. 7)

Aims/Skills
- use rhyming and contextual clues to complete proverbs
- understand what a proverb is and its role in language

Speaking (SB p. 7)

Aims/Skills
- listen for weather information
- become familiar with common weather terms
- practise using precise weather forecast-related vocabulary

Expansion

Pre-Activity

Give each pair of students a photocopy of a weather map from a local newspaper. Have students explain what the different symbols represent and let them describe the weather in various locations. They should use vocabulary such as partly sunny/cloudy, cloud, sun, rain, cold front, warm front, etc.

Culture Note

Being familiar with weather terms and being able to discuss the weather is very important since our climate influences our lives greatly and therefore forms a major part of small talk in North America. Some weather terms you might wish to discuss with students:

chinook, snow squalls, flurries, showers, drizzle, fog, humidex, UV index, wind chill factor, sleet, hail.

 **Reading 2 (SB pp. 8–12)**

Aims/Skills
- summarize
- retell a story
- understand the role of images in mythology

Language Note

Various terms are used to describe Native peoples. These include Native peoples, Aboriginal peoples, First Nations, and Indians (which has fallen out of favour because it was an inaccurate description by Columbus). Students will hear all terms used, as well as Métis to describe people of mixed heritage and Inuit (Eskimo is no longer commonly used).

Expansion

Pre-reading

Ask students to look at the paintings on p. 8 of the Student Book and present their interpretation. Compare the different responses. The following are some springboard discussion questions.

1. How do we communicate through art?
2. What characteristics make native art distinctive?
3. Describe native cultural art from your original country.
4. Discuss native people's relationship with nature.

Project Option

Have students do a presentation on a native artist from their culture. They can explore galleries on the Internet, or do research in encyclopedias and at local libraries.

 ## Comprehension Check (SB p. 10)

Ga-oh, Spirit of the Winds

1. Which wind is responsible for the beautiful weather of spring and summer? *Fawn (south wind)*
2. Who causes hurricanes and tidal waves when angry? *Ga-oh unbinding Bear*
3. Which animal is associated with the east wind? *Moose*
4. What would happen if Ga-oh were to get loose? *He would tear the heavens into fragments.*
5. Answers will vary.

 ## Comprehension Check (SB p. 11)

How the World Was Made

1. Where did everyone and everything live before the Earth was formed? *in Gălŭñ'lătĭ, beyond the arch*
2. Which animal was responsible for forming the Earth? *waterbeetle*
3. How were the valleys formed in Cherokee country? *When the Great Buzzard flew over the Earth his wings struck the ground and formed the valleys.*
4. How will the world end? *The cords holding the four cardinal points will break and the Earth will fall into the ocean.*
5. Answers will vary.

Comprehension Check (SB p. 12)

The Story of Corn

1. Who did Masswaweinini meet on the prairie? *Wagemena*
2. What was the origin of the corn? *It came from the transformation of Wagemena into an ear of corn and Masswaweinini scattered the kernels over the ground.*
3. How long did it take for the corn to grow? *One month (moon) to sprout and one summer to grow to full ears.*
4. Answers will vary.

 **Writing (SB p. 12)**

Aim/Skill
- practise narrative writing

Alternative Activity

Have teams of two or three students illustrate one myth / legend or make a collage of what the myth / legend represents for them. Alternatively, teams can make up their own legend.

Grammar Focus 2 (SB pp. 12–13)

Exercise A (SB p.13)

Identify the tense of the verbs in the following passive sentences.

1. The corn was nurtured by the women. *(simple past)*
2. The winds are being confined by Ga-oh. *(present continuous)*
3. Native myths are passed down orally. *(simple present)*
4. Native history would not have been written down thousands of years ago. *(perfect conditional — refer to chart SB p. 12)*
5. Appreciation of native culture is being encouraged through educational programs. *(present continuous)*

Exercise B (SB p. 13)

Read the following passage identifying the sentences in passive voice and the tense of the passive verbs. Then rewrite the passage using only active voice.

Global warming could have catastrophic effects for our planet. The impending doom of planet Earth due to our continued abuses has been predicted *(present perfect)* by scientists over the last decade. Heat from the sun is being trapped *(present continuous)* by gases such as carbon dioxide causing a gradual rise in world temperatures. Carbon dioxide is formed *(simple present)* by burning fossil fuels which people find difficult to do without. Future generations will be affected *(simple future)* by our refusal to radically change how we live. Scientists predict that if current patterns continue, low-lying coastal land will be submerged *(simple future)* by rising sea levels. Warmer winters and increased hot spells will be experienced *(simple future)* by people all over the world. Increased flooding and droughts will occur in many areas. Temperature and rainfall patterns will be shifted *(simple future)* in unpredictable ways by global warming. Scientists believe that it is virtually impossible for nations to work cooperatively to save our planet and that we should in fact be spending our research dollars on strategies to deal with the unavoidable consequences of global warming.

Active Passage

Global warming could have catastrophic effects for our planet. Over the past decade scientists have predicted the impending doom of planet Earth due to our continued abuses. Gases such as carbon dioxide are trapping heat from the sun causing a gradual rise in world temperatures. Burning fossil fuels, which people find difficult to do without, forms carbon dioxide. Our refusal to radically change how we live will affect future generations. Scientists predict that if current patterns

continue, rising sea levels will submerge low-lying coastal land. People all over the world will experience warmer winters and increased hot spells. Increased flooding and droughts will occur in many areas. Global warming will shift temperature and rainfall patterns in unpredictable ways. Scientists believe that it is virtually impossible for nations to work cooperatively to save our planet and that we should in fact be spending our research dollars on strategies to deal with the unavoidable consequences of global warming.

> **Workbook Practice and Expansion:** Grammar Focus 2 Exercises A–D (WB pp. 4–6) and Grammar Expansion (use of "get" in the passive) Exercises E–G (WB p. 6)

Expansion

Grammar Game (Reproducible 1.3)

Cut the page (Reproducible 1.3) into strips and place them in a pile. Divide the class into two teams. One person from each team comes to the front and takes a strip from the pile. The student who is able to use all of the images on the strip in a passive sentence correctly gets a point for his or her team.

EXAMPLE:

The fish was tossed into the rowboat by the twister as it crossed over the lake.

Alternatively, individual students could select a strip from the pile and write an imaginative story linking the three objects together.

Listening 2 (SB p. 14)

See Tapescript 1.b

Aims/Skills
• listen for main ideas in interviews
• interpret meaning of comments

ONE STEP AHEAD

Farley Mowat is a controversial Canadian author. Many of his books such as *People of the Deer* deal with the problems of misunderstanding and exploitation of both nature and native peoples such as the Inuit. His passionate stories attract either bitter attacks or prolific praise. He has written over 26 books and is Canada's most widely read author.

David Suzuki is a Canadian geneticist and broadcaster. He is convinced that public awareness of science contributes to both better science policies and an enriched culture. He is best known for his long running TV series *The Nature of Things* and his special *A Planet for the Taking*. He has also written an autobiography *Metamorphosis* (1987) and a number of other books including *Time to Change* (1994).

As a warm-up activity before the listening, ask students if they know or have heard of these two people. If not, give them some background and have them think about the direction the discussion between these two men might take.

Language Note

Students will hear David Suzuki use the term "man" in the generic sense of "people" ("It's the arrogance of modern man to think that we . . ."). Farley Mowat also uses the term in the quotation SB p. 14 Before You Listen #1 "Modern man is such an arrogant cement head . . ." "Man" used in this sense is increasingly being replaced with "humans," "humanity,"or "humankind" which are considered non-sexist. Students will still encounter materials that use "man" in the generic sense, but it should be pointed out that the language is changing.

Comprehension Check (SB p. 14)

1. What does Farley Mowat mean when he says that we can only know nature by becoming part of it?
   We need to learn from our ancestors and the survivors of the hunter/gatherer tribes who use nature only for their basic existence and live in harmony with it; they do not try to control nature or distance themselves from it.

2. According to David Suzuki, what is modern human's relationship with nature? Give an example.
   Modern humans think that nature can be dominated and directed. An example of this is the clear-cutting of forests, which destroys old-growth watersheds. Suzuki maintains that these forests and watersheds cannot be replaced.

3. According to David Suzuki, what have been the two most significant changes in our relationship with nature since the beginning of human existence? Why do these changes pose a serious danger?
   The two most significant changes are the population explosion and advances in technology. These pose a serious threat because we now have unprecedented power, but not the wisdom to use it properly.

Process Writing (WB pp. 6–9)

The Workbook introduces process writing with exercises focusing on prewriting (freewriting, cluster map, star map), identifying the audience, narrowing the topic, and effective topic sentences.

Unit Reflection (SB p. 14)

If students are unable to come up with other sayings/idioms, provide categories or words to use as springboards (water, wind, etc.). Once students have a list of five sayings, ask them to discuss their meanings and categorize them according to whether they apply to emotions, general truths, or some other category.

Some other possible expressions are:
as the crow flies
fly by night
second wind
it's a breeze
ebb and flow
breezy attitude
tip of the iceberg
moving mountains
to go out on a limb
to nip something in the bud
feast or famine
cream of the crop
when it rains, it pours
to be afraid of your own shadow

Helpful Internet Resources

Information about natural disasters and preparing yourself to survive these disasters can be found on the internet.

Key word search: natural disaster preparedness

The following sites are great resources:
http://hoshi.cic.sfu.ca/~pep/link_EMR1_frame.html
A Canadian site giving information on all types of natural disasters.

http://ltpwww.gsfc.nasa.gov/ndrd/disaster/
A site with hot links to all the best information about natural disasters.

http://www.usace.mil/spd-q/brochure.html
A brochure about earthquake preparedness

http://www.state.sd.us/state/executive/governor/checklist.htm
Information about floods

UNIT 2
Strange But True

OVERVIEW

Theme: The Supernatural

Topics:
- supernatural phenomena SB pp. 15–16
- dreams (Listening 1) SB p. 17
- out-of-body experience (Reading 1) SB pp. 17–20
- guardian angels or spirits (Reading) WB pp. 14–15
- apparitions (Listening 2) SB p. 25–27
- astrology (Reading 2) SB pp. 28–29

Vocabulary:

Student Book
astrology
clairvoyance
curse
levitation
medium
numerology
omen
poltergeist
premonition
psychic
psychokinesis
reincarnation
seance
shaman
subconscious
telepathy
voodoo

Workbook
apparitions
demean
demystify
discredited
dissatisfied
malediction
malicious
monotheistic
monotonous
posthumously
posthypnotic
transmit
transcend

Student Book Prefixes
para-   pre-   sub-   super-   syn-   tele-

Workbook Prefixes
de-   dis-   mal-   mono-   post-   re-   trans-

Grammar:
Reported Speech – Statements (SB pp. 20–24)

Reported Speech – Questions (SB pp. 26–27)

Reported Speech – Commands/Requests/Advice (WB p. 16)

Process Writing:
Narrative Paragraphs (WB pp. 16–18)

Getting Started

A strip story activity (Reproducible 2.1) can work as a way to generate discussion about the paranormal. Have students work in pairs or teams of three. Copy the story (one for each team) and cut it into strips. Shuffle the order of the strips. Give students ten minutes to sequence the strips and rebuild the story.

Then ask students these questions:
Where did the story take place?
When did it happen?
What happened in the story?
Who was in this story?
Why did Charlie suddenly start whining?
What explanations can you offer for what happened?

The last question will lead to a discussion about the paranormal.

Unit Opening Page (SB p. 15)

The unit cover page highlights some symbols of the paranormal (palmistry, crystal ball, tarot cards) and Albert Einstein's quote about the mysterious. The purpose is not so much to identify the symbols as to encourage students to think critically about the supernatural and accepted beliefs. The concept of the supernatural is usually presented as religious, nonsensical, or at least "unscientific." Without imposing any specific view on the subject, ask students to reflect on the message this unit cover page sends. Why is this visual presented with the Einstein quote?

Expansion

Cover Page Design
Have students create or design a new unit cover page that gets across the same or a similar message.

---

ocabulary 1 (SB p. 16)

Aim/Skill
• match meanings with themed vocabulary

Answer Key
Match the words to the meanings below. Use a dictionary to help you.

1. A level of thoughts and memories just below the surface of the conscious mind. *d. subconscious*

2. A sign that heralds either good or bad luck to the one who sees it. *k. omen*

3. A feeling, dream, or vision about something which will happen in the future. *c. premonition*

4. The ability to move objects through mind power. *e. psychokinesis*

5. Rising off the ground in defiance of gravity. *j. levitation*

6. The belief that numbers have meaning and can be used to read a person's character and future. *g. numerology*

7. A spiritualist cult based in Haiti; called Hoodoo in parts of America. *q. voodoo*

8. The study of how the planets influence the character and future of people. *a. astrology*

9. A meeting led by a medium in which spirits of the dead are contacted. *n. seance*

10. The power to see clearly in the mind images or events that are happening out of sight or in the future. *f. clairvoyance*

11. Someone who, for some reason, can be used as a go-between or a "telephone line" between this world and the "next." *b. medium*

12. A "noisy ghost" often associated with children and thought to be either a manifestation of psychokinesis (PK) or a troublesome spirit. *m. poltergeist*

13. The rebirth of the soul, usually as another person, but sometimes as an animal or a demon. *l. reincarnation*

14. Spiritual leader of tribal communities, including North American Native communities, who can communicate with the spirit world, cure illnesses, etc. *p. shaman*

15. An appeal to a supernatural power for harm to come to a person or group of people. Also called malediction or hex. *i. curse*

16. The ability to communicate by thought alone. *o. telepathy*

17. Sensitivity to forces outside the natural laws of science, or someone with this sensitivity. *h. psychic*

Workbook Practice: Vocabulary 1 Exercises A–C (WB pp. 10–11)

Listening 1 (SB p. 17)

See Tapescript 2.a

Aims/Skills
• listen for supporting ideas
• listen for specific information
• take notes
• infer meaning and draw conclusions from facts

ONE STEP AHEAD

Have students look at the vocabulary words on p. 16 and identify which words could be associated with the "dream state" (e.g., subconscious, premonition, clairvoyance, medium, seance). Use this as a lead-in to the discussion of dreams and the pre-listening questions.

Focused Listening (SB p. 17)

ONE STEP AHEAD

Review the basics of taking notes before your students begin. If you wish students to listen more than once, have them listen first only for answers to general W5H questions. Then assign the focused listening.

 Answer Key

Listen to the account and list all of the facts supporting the idea that this house was the house of Harry's dreams.

1. *The house in Italy had an olive tree orchard behind it. The house in Harry's dreams had an orchard with vegetation unfamiliar to Canada.*

2. *Harry recognized the house in Italy from the outside as the one in his dreams. The houses looked the same.*

3. *The house in Italy was the same inside as the one in his dreams. He recognized all the rooms except the secret compartment.*

4. *Harry expected to see a secret room in the house in Italy. When it wasn't there, he searched for it and found it behind a fake wall.*

5. *In both the house in Italy and the house of Harry's dreams, the secret room had been used to hide things.*

For Discussion (SB p. 17)

1. Harry Stevens asks: "Had I lived in that house in some previous life, before being reincarnated to a Canadian life?" What evidence is there that makes him consider this alternative?
He believes he had been at the house in Italy before for two reasons: 1) He found he could speak Italian while in Italy although he had never learned it formally. Perhaps he had spoken it once. 2) The house in his dreams actually existed though he had never been there before in his current life. Perhaps he had seen the house in another time.

2. He also wonders whether some mysterious soul from the past had been put to rest by his finding that house. What does Harry say at the end of his story that suggests this might be true?
He never had the dream again after he found the house in Italy.

One Step Beyond (SB p. 17)

> ### ONE STEP AHEAD
> This question challenges students to critically examine what appears to be evidence that this was a paranormal experience. Some of the facts in the account may have another explanation. Encourage students to raise questions of their own. To help them focus, copy the tapescript at the back of this book (p. 150) and have them concentrate their discussion around the questions Harry asks himself.
> Ask students:
>
> Why does Harry ask himself these questions?
>
> What implication, if any, lies in each question?
>
> What additional questions can students pose that either support or refute the fact that this occurrence was in the realm of the supernatural?
>
> What possible explanations for the account can students offer?

 Answer Key
1. What possible explanations can you offer for this occurrence?

Here are some curious facts:
Harry forgot most of his Italian after he left Italy. Is this really so unusual? Many soldiers learn to speak other languages while stationed overseas and then forget them when they stop having to use them. This fact doesn't prove anything.

Harry implies that his never having the dream again after he visited the house in Italy might indicate that some mysterious soul may have been put to rest by his finding the house. In fact, he only had the dream when he was a child of about 8 or 12. Why didn't he continue to have the dream into his teens and early adulthood until he visited the house?

Perhaps he had seen the house as a child in a magazine or had heard a story about a house with a secret room for toys, and then had dreamt about it because it somehow made an impression on him. Perhaps he had even visited the house as an infant and had somehow remembered it.

 **Reading 1 (SB pp. 17–19)**

Aims/Skills
• apply meaning through context
• read for details
• paraphrase sentences
• infer meaning
• analyze symbols
• analyze how style and structure contribute to mood and persuasiveness

 Applying Meaning Through Context (SB pp. 17–18)

You will read an account of a near-death experience from the journals of the famous psychiatrist Carl Gustav Jung. The account describes the experience of one of Jung's patients. Some of the sentences have been left out. Read the passage and insert the sentences listed on the next page where you think they fit.

1. e) *She tried to answer, but couldn't.*
2. c) *She was not in the least frightened.*
3. a) *It gave her the impression of a clearing in the forest, never yet trodden by the foot of man.*
4. d) *That was why she found the agitation of the doctor and the distress of her relatives stupid and out of place.*
5. b) *The nurse energetically denied this criticism in the belief that the patient had been completely unconscious at the time and could therefore have known nothing of the scene.*

 Comprehension Check (SB p. 18)

Are the following statements true (T) or false (F)?
1. **F** *The patient died.*
2. **T** *(line 55–56) The woman had been unconscious for about half an hour.*
3. **F** *The patient thought her relatives were stupid.*
Note: The patient thought the actions of her relatives and the fact that they thought she was going to die were "stupid" (in this context meaning "foolish" because she knew she wasn't going to die). She did not think her relatives themselves were stupid, which would be derogatory. [See culture note below.]
4. **F or NA** *(no answer) The patient delivered her baby in spring.*

Note: The reading does not state or imply that the baby was delivered in spring. In fact, there is nothing in the reading that indicates when she delivered the baby. The purpose of the question is to gauge if the students believe she delivered in the spring because the park-like description appears to be spring-like. Give students who identify that the statement is neither true nor false extra praise. They have understood a challenging question.

5. **F** *The woman felt tempted to gaze at a picture on the wall.*

6. **T** *(line 3) The woman was in labour for more than twenty hours.*

Culture Note

In North American culture, especially in Canada, people are very conscious about being polite and respectful when speaking to others. Consequently, we often use grammar and conversational strategies to remove the "personal" aspect from our comments when they are negative. For example, a conversational technique a parent might use with a child is to say, "What you did was stupid," but not "You are stupid," which would be derogatory. We manipulate grammatical stuctures in a similar way. For example, in an office, a supervisor is more likely to say, "Why wasn't this report handed in last week?" rather than "Why didn't you hand in this report last week?" thus not accusing the writer of the report directly. Passive voice structures are commonly used this way in speaking. Similarly, if I don't like your suggestion, rather than saying, "I don't like your suggestion" or "It's not a good idea," I'm more likely to make an alternate suggestion such as, "Why don't we do this instead?" Some cultures are much more direct and aggressive in their speech, and this often meets with negative reactions from North American English speakers.

Sentence Meanings (SB p. 19)

Find the sentences in the reading that mean the same as the sentences below.

1. The woman had been in labour for a long time without results. The doctor decided to intervene.
   (lines 3–5) After thirty hours of fruitless labour the doctor considered that a forceps delivery was indicated.

2. The patient felt as though she were falling.
   (lines 11–13) She had the feeling that she was sinking through the bed into a bottomless void.

3. The patient concluded from the nurse's reaction that her pulse was barely noticeable.
   (lines 14–16) From the way she moved her fingers to and fro the patient thought it must have been almost imperceptible.

4. The woman had an out-of-body experience and could see everything happening in the room.
   (lines 20–24) The next thing she was aware of was that, without feeling her body and its position, she was looking down from a point in the ceiling and could see everything going on in the room below her...

5. The landscape she saw was bright and the colours were extremely beautiful.
   Note: Two answers are possible, although the sentence on lines 40–41 is preferable.
   (lines 40–41) The whole demesne sparkled in the sunlight, and all the colours were of an indescribable splendour.
   (alternately lines 33–37) All this time she knew that behind her was a glorious, park-like landscape shining in the brightest colours, and in particular an emerald green meadow with short grass, which sloped gently upwards beyond a wrought-iron gate leading into the park.

6. Confident that the patient was unaware of what had happened, the nurse covered up for the doctor's inappropriate behaviour by claiming it didn't happen.
   Note: This sentence is the one inserted from b) in Applying Meaning Through Context.
   (line 60) The nurse energetically denied this criticism in the belief that the patient had been completely unconscious at the time and could therefore have known nothing of the scene.

Discuss the Reading (SB p. 19)

1. Why did Jung believe the patient's version of the experience?
   Jung believed the patient's version because he had no reason to doubt her reliability and truthfulness. Also, the patient had suffered a genuine heart collapse, was in a true coma, and therefore, should have had a complete psychic black-out.

2. Why was the patient not afraid?
   She knew she wasn't going to die.

3. The woman describes the park-like landscape as "a clearing in the forest, never yet trodden by the foot of man." What do you think she means by this?
   A place in the natural world undisturbed by the presence of humans. We might speculate that it is a kind of otherworldly paradise.

One Step Beyond (SB p. 19)

1. What about this reading makes it believable?
   - *a world-famous, qualified medical doctor and psychiatrist is telling the story and believes it*
   - *it is written in an objective tone, without value judgements inserted by the writer*
   - *the vocabulary is sophisticated and scientific (e.g., conjecture, psychogenic twilight state, heart collapse, etc.)*
   - *the writer offers a medical/scientific explanation of why this experience should not have been possible*

2. What significance does the "gate" have in the woman's vision?
   The gate is a symbol of a "crossing over" from one world to the next.

3. What makes the description of the landscape so appealing?
   - *the writer uses interpretive adjectives such as glorious, gay, and indescribable (splendour)*
   - *the description is full of beautiful colours and light (e.g., emerald green, sparkle, sunlight)*
   - *the image of the park is recognizable as an other-worldly paradise of indescribable beauty*

Expansion

Discussion

You may wish to discuss how culture is reflected in literature, storytelling, and art. There is a possible Christian interpretation of the park-like scene in the woman's dream: the description of the park has similarities with the Garden of Eden image, and the gates to the park could be interpreted as the "pearly gates" to heaven. Hold a brief discussion about whether these or similar images exist in non-Christian cultures.

Alternately, ask students to discuss or write about their own culture's beliefs about what happens after death. They could also do an illustration.

A sample chart might look like this:

	patient	nurse	husband	mother	physician
relationship of the character to the action					
background of the character in relation to the event					
worries of the character in relation to the event					
feelings of the character in relation to the event					
responsibilities of that character in the situation					
what the character actually saw happening					
actions of that character in the situation					

If having your students design the chart isn't appropriate to your teaching situation, design it yourself and give each team a photocopy to focus and guide them in the storytelling.

Speaking (SB p. 20)

Aims/Skills
- describe details accurately
- sequence information appropriately
- offer other character's perspectives
- use reported speech
- add logical details

ONE STEP AHEAD

To help your students focus and evaluate their peers' performances effectively, have them design a chart that outlines what they need to consider when telling the story from a different perspective. Inform students that they'll have to fill in extra information and background to tell their stories. Anything is acceptable, as long as it makes sense. For example, when telling the story from the perspective of the husband, a student might say, "My wife and I had been looking so forward to the birth of our first child. I had been worrying about the delivery though because my sister had died in childbirth." Although this information isn't given in the story, it's completely believable for this character.

Writing (SB p. 20)

Aim/Skill
- write a narrative paragraph

(See also narrative paragraph writing in the Workbook pp. 16–18)

ONE STEP AHEAD

If you have the time, select a movie or television episode about the paranormal to show in class as a precursor to the activity. Or, just assign watching one outside of class time. To heighten interest, have students work in teams after watching the film or episode to design a list of criteria they would use to judge the effectiveness of a movie or television show about the paranormal. You can also have students develop the list before watching and then ask them to evaluate their show or film using these criteria. Students sometimes have difficulty thinking about criteria, however, without having something concrete to refer to such as a recently-viewed film or show.

Grammar Focus 1 (SB pp. 20–24)

Exercise A (SB p. 22)

Convert the quoted speech into reported speech changing the tenses as required.

1. The psychiatrist said, "The patient's dream is quite revealing."
   The psychiatrist said that the patient's dream was quite revealing.

2. The counsellor said, "The patient has experimented with psychokinetic powers."
   The counsellor said that the patient had experimented with psychokinetic powers.

3. The psychiatrist said, "The patient has been having premonitions."
   The psychiatrist said that the patient had been having premonitions.

4. The counsellor said, "The patient won't remember the strange event."
   The counsellor said that the patient wouldn't remember the strange event.

5. The psychiatrist said, "Mrs. Acker will never forget the experience."
   The psychiatrist said that Mrs. Acker would never forget the experience.

Exercise B (SB p. 23)

Change the quoted speech to reported speech.

1. The young woman said, "I floated out of my body and looked down on the scene below me".
   The young woman said she had floated out of her body and had looked down on the scene below her.

2. The young man said, "I floated out of my body and looked down on the scene below me."
   The young man said he had floated out of his body and had looked down on the scene below him.

3. The young man said to me, "I will show you the place where I saw the beast."
   The young man said he would show me the place where he had seen the beast."

4. The young woman said to us, "I will show you the place where I saw the beast."
   The young woman said she would show us the place where she had seen the beast.

5. The young children said to their grandfather, "We will show you the place where we saw the beast."
   The young children said they would show him the place where they had seen the beast.

Exercise C (SB p. 23)

Look at the quoted speech below. Then report the speech from the different time perspectives given. In your answers, include the time when Madame Girard made the announcement.

QUOTED SPEECH: On Wednesday morning Madame Girard announces to her class: "Next week, we will begin our study of the paranormal."

1. On Wednesday afternoon, Jocelyn reports to a classmate who was absent in the morning: This morning Madame Girard told us that . . . (what? when?)
   This morning Madame Girard told us that we would/will begin our study of the paranormal next week.

2. On Thursday, Jocelyn reports to a classmate who was absent:
   Yesterday morning Madame Girard told us that we would/will begin our study of the paranormal next week.

3. On Monday, Jocelyn reports to a classmate who has been absent for a few days:
   Last Wednesday Madame Girard told us that we would/will begin our study of the paranormal this week.

4. One week later on Thursday, Jocelyn reports to a classmate who was absent all week:
   A week ago Wednesday (the Wednesday before last) Madame Girard told us we would begin our study of the paranormal this week.

Exercise D (SB p. 24)

What did the original speaker say? Change the reported speech to quoted speech.

1. He said that he didn't understand what had just happened there.
   "I don't understand what has just happened (or what just happened) here."

2. The little boy said that he had seen soldiers marching in battle.
   "I saw soldiers marching in battle."

3. The doctor insisted he didn't believe in the paranormal.
   "I don't believe in the paranormal."

4. The woman informed the police that her son had been captured by aliens.
"My son has been captured by aliens."

Workbook Practice: Grammar Focus 1 Exercises A and B (WB pp. 12–13)

Expansion

Grammar Game

This game gives students practice changing sentence parts in reported speech. Make a set of five "change cards" as follows: tense, noun, verb, adjectives, pronouns. Divide the class into two teams. Write a sentence in reported speech on the blackboard (make sure it has an adjective, a noun, and a pronoun). Place the "change cards" face down on a table at the front of the room. Two members, one from each team, come to the front of the class. Alternately each team member turns over one card and announces it to the class. The aim is to change that grammatical marker of the sentence. Any member of either team can shout out an appropriate change (you can ask students to go in turn if you want to ensure that everyone gets a turn). If the change is correct, that team gets a point. If it is incorrect, a point gets deducted from that team's score.

For example, a sentence might change like this:
The psychic said I would meet the tall woman of my dreams. (change tense)
The psychic said I had met the tall woman of my dreams. (change noun)
The barber said I had met the tall woman of my dreams
OR
The psychic said I had met the tall man of my dreams.
OR
The psychic said I had met the tall woman of my nightmares. (change adjective)
The psychic said I had met the frightening woman of my nightmares. And so on.

Rule: No sentence part can be changed back to a previously used word.

ocabulary 2 (SB p. 21)

Aims/Skills
• understand the meaning of prefixes from understanding the word
• use the meaning of prefixes to guess the meanings of words

🔑 *Answer Key*
1. Discuss the meaning of the following words. Look in a dictionary if necessary. Then, explain the meaning of the underlined prefixes.
Meanings of prefixes: pre = before, sub = under or below, para = above or beyond, super = above or over, syn = common or same, tele = far or over a long distance

Workbook Practice and Expansion: Vocabulary 2 Expansion Exercises A–C (WB pp. 11–12)

Expansion

A. Prefix Memory Game (Reproducible 2.2)
The aim of this game is to match a prefix with its appropriate meaning. Students play in small teams. Photocopy one set of cards for each team (Reproducible 2.2). Cut out the cards and shuffle them. Have students spread out the cards face down on a table in a large square or rectangle (choose any irregular shape to make the game more difficult). One team member turns over two cards. If one card has a prefix and the other card has the corresponding meaning, then the student keeps the two cards and goes again. If not, the student turns the unmatched cards over again, keeping them in their original position. All team members should try to remember the words or prefixes on the cards as well as their positions. The next team member (clockwise) now turns over one card. It can be the same one just seen or any other card. He or she then tries to find the corresponding match. The game continues until all the cards have been matched. To increase the difficulty, ask students to provide a word with the prefix and/or use it correctly in a sentence.

Note: Some of the meanings cards can fit with more than one prefix, e.g., *opposite of* can be matched with *de-*, or *dis-*. Any appropriate match is acceptable.

B. Wordbuilding Game
The purpose of this game is to make as many words as possible with specified prefixes. Divide the class into small teams. On the blackboard, write a prefix. Give teams 2 to 3 minutes to write as many words as possible with that prefix. Then take up the list and give teams one point for each word they have that no other team has. Don't deduct a point for a non-existent word, as this might deter students from taking risks. In fact, have teams challenge words they think might not exist. If no one challenges a word, it counts for a point. If a word is challenged yet exists, then the challenging team loses a point.

Speaking (SB p. 24)

Aims/Skills
• narrate a story
• create suspense in a story
• use paranormal-related vocabulary

Listening 2 (SB p. 25)

See Tapescript 2.b

Aims/Skills
- listen for specific information (details)
- listen to sequence events
- infer meaning from direct statements

❦ Focused Listening (SB p. 25)

Read the questions below. Then listen to the account and choose the correct answers.

Note: Answers are circled.

1. This incident took place in the summer of
   a) 1988.
   b) 1976.
   c) 1966.
   d) 1978.
2. Dr. Muckle was _____ when the sighting happened.
   a) sitting on an easy chair in the living room
   b) sitting in a garden chair on the lawn
   c) sitting in an easy chair on the verandah
   d) standing by the front door of his small bungalow
3. The apparition of the cat
   a) looked completely normal but walked about a foot and a half above the floor.
   b) was surrounded by a glow and walked about a foot and a half above the floor.
   c) had a dark aura.
   d) looked ghost-like and floated through the air.

4. Immediately after seeing the apparition, Dr. Muckle
   a) called two of his children to give him a hand to see if they could find any cat anywhere in or near the bungalow.
   b) called his children and his wife to tell them of the experience.
   c) went inside the bungalow to see if by chance it could have been some sort of optical illusion.
   d) got up and tried to follow the apparition.
5. Two and a half hours later,
   a) Dr. Muckle telephoned his neighbour to see if his cat was alright.
   b) Dr. Muckle received a message that his neighbour had called.
   c) Dr. Muckle had a strong feeling that his cat had died.
   d) Dr. Muckle's wife informed him that their cat had died three hours earlier.

❦ For Discussion (SB p. 25)

1. How did Dr. Muckle feel when he saw the apparition?
   He wasn't frightened. He felt normal.
2. What did Dr. Muckle do to confirm that he had indeed seen an apparition?
   He went into the room to check if it could have been an optical illusion. He also checked around outside for a cat.
3. Dr. Muckle says, "I immediately wondered whether I would have seen the apparition had the cat died instantly — the implication I trust is obvious." What does he mean by this?
   He assumes the cat "travelled" to the resort before it died to say goodbye. If the cat had died instantly, he may not have seen its apparition.

❦ One Step Beyond (SB p. 25)

Why do you think Dr. Muckle adds at the end that this was the only experience he had had with the paranormal?
To make his story more believable. He was, after all, a doctor and may not wish to be seen as someone who supports non-scientific phenomena.

❦ Sequencing Events (SB pp. 25–26)

Immediately after the experience, Dr. Muckle may have written down a few key points to help him remember the sequence of events. The points on the next page are not in the correct order. Put them in the correct order. Then listen to the story again to check your answers.

a) **3** *suddenly, see pet cat walking calmly across room*

b) **4** *cat walked across room above floor level and, before reached other wall, disappeared*

c) **6** *experience was not frightening*

d) **1** *several days after arriving, sitting on bungalow verandah in afternoon, reading book*

e) **5** *other than walking above floor level, nothing strange about cat*

f) **2** *chair sideways, so could see living room through door from corner of eye.*

Expansion

Arguments and Evidence

After listening to the account, ask students to list what they would consider convincing arguments or evidence that supports the existence of the paranormal. Try to elicit concepts such as witnesses, objectivity, seriousness with which the account is treated, believability of the storyteller, and so on.

Grammar Focus 2 (SB pp. 26–27)

 Exercise A (SB p. 27)

Change the quoted speech to reported speech.

1. "How did I know there would be a secret room?" Henry asked himself.
   Henry asked himself how he had known there would be a secret room.

2. Turning to the patient, the nurse said, "Do you want anything before I go for supper?"
   Turning to the patient, the nurse asked if the patient (she) wanted anything before she (the nurse) went for supper.

3. Henry asked himself, "Has some mysterious soul been put to rest by my finding the house?"
   Henry asked himself if some mysterious soul had been put to rest by his finding the house.

4. "Was someone sending me messages through mental telepathy?" wondered Henry.
   Henry wondered if someone had been sending him messages through mental telepathy.

5. Dr. Muckle wondered, "Why would our neighbours phone us here?"
   Dr. Muckle wondered why his neighbours would phone them there.

Workbook Practice: Grammar Focus 2 Exercise A (Questions), Exercise B (Statements and Questions) with Reading "A Cradle of Love," and Exercise C (WB pp. 14–16) Grammar Expansion (Commands/Requests/Advice) Exercises D–E (WB p. 16)

Writing (SB p. 27)

Aims/Skills
- write letters using reported speech
- write to maintain a storyline, tone, and style
- edit for grammatical errors

Writing in the round: This activity works best if it is timed. All students must exchange papers simultaneously. An alternative approach to beginning this activity is to provide students with a common first paragraph that has been written by the teacher or another student. Students may also write their introductory paragraphs as a homework assignment before continuing with the activity in class.

Reading 2 (SB pp. 28–29)

Aims/Skills
- read for clues
- understand how illustrations contribute to meaning
- use process of elimination to find answers

ONE STEP AHEAD

This is a light, fun reading activity. Introduce it with a fun activity. Copy your local newspaper's horoscope section the day before you present this in class. White out the zodiac signs and dates and make enough copies for each student. Have students read all the horoscopes and choose the one they think applied to them yesterday. They can explain why they chose this horoscope. Then provide the answers. Finally, have students examine how similar or different each prediction is, and discuss the validity of horoscope predictions.

Culture Note

Many North Americans enjoy reading their daily horoscopes in the newspaper and sometimes in books. Some people visit psychics occasionally to have their futures told. In this regard, the paranormal is viewed as a form of entertainment. Over the last several years, however, more and more people are experimenting with "New Age" philosophy, which acknowledges the existence of the supernatural and aims to connect a person more deeply with a cosmic spirituality. A smaller contingent of people take supernatural phenomena very seriously. Discuss how other cultures view the supernatural. What role does the paranormal play in the daily lives of people in various cultures?

Project Option
Hold a psychic fair. Have students research, write about, and prepare displays and presentations on one aspect of the paranormal. Topics can include palmistry, tarot card readings, tea leaf readings, numerology, astrology, or a paranormal activity from their native culture.

Process Writing (WB pp. 16–18)

The Workbook provides an explanation and exercises focusing on writing narrative paragraphs, a natural extension of the emphasis on storytelling and anecdotes in this unit. The exercises include practice with sequencing events, writing using a series of illustrations, and editing.

Unit Reflection (SB p. 29)

This activity can be done in writing, but try presenting it in a debate format.

Note: Please alert your students that many sites for "psychics" are commercial sites and require payment. Avoid these sites. There are numerous non-commercial sites of interest, depending on which area of the paranormal you are interested in.

Key word search: paranormal, parapsychology, psychic, astrology, ghosts, UFOs

http://www.yahoo.com/Science/Alternative/Paranormal_Phenomena
A useful search page that allows access to many categories of other paranormal sites.

http://www2.clearlight.com/~oddsend/paranorm.htm
Known as the "Paranormal Palor," this site also allows access to many other interesting categories of the paranormal from "skeptics" to "ghosts."

http://www.tenthmuse.com/paranormal/index.html
This site has some interesting articles and images on the paranormal. Students can complete a survey and ask questions at this site.

UNIT 3
The Road Less Travelled

OVERVIEW

Theme: Travel and exploration

Topics:
- travel and sightseeing
  SB pp. 30–33
- adventure travel autobiography
  (Reading 1)
  SB pp. 36–38
- famous women explorers
  (Listening 1) SB p. 39
- pioneer experiences
  (Reading 2) SB pp. 43–45
- space exploration
  (Listening 2) SB pp. 45–46

Vocabulary:
Student Book
adventurous
brave
courageous
dedicated
inspirational
persevering

Workbook (Idiomatic Expressions)
different strokes for different folks
to be on one's last legs
to blow it
to give it one's best shot
to play it by ear
to put something on the line

Grammar:
Adjective Order in Descriptions
  (SB pp. 34–35)
Relative Clauses (SB pp. 40–43)
Grammar Expansion – Relative
  Clauses (WB pp. 24–26)

Process Writing:
Descriptive Paragraphs
  (WB pp. 27–30)

Getting Started

The following activity can be used to introduce the unit. Have students write their names on pieces of paper to enter in a draw. Draw for the following prizes:

1) an all-expenses paid trip to the destination of your choice
2) use of a time machine to accompany an explorer on a journey into the past or future
3) an all-expenses paid weekend to a Canadian tourist attraction

Announce the prizes before having the draw. Let each student identify which prize he or she would like to win and why. Once the draw has taken place, have the winners describe where they will go.

Travel Quiz (SB pp. 32–33)

Where in the World is Marco?

1. My best friend Marco is travelling around the world. He sends me postcards telling me all about the wonderful sites he's seen and the things he's done, but he never tells me exactly where he is. I always have to guess from his descriptions. Working with a partner, read his postcards to see if you can identify where he's been.

ONE STEP AHEAD

You may want to do the first part of this quiz (#1) as a closed book activity. Divide the class into two teams. Challenge a representative of each team to listen to you read Marco's postcards and guess the locations. The first person to guess the location gets a point for his or her team. Students could then open their books, look at the photographs, and discuss what is appealing about each location.

2. Marco had an around-the-world ticket that allowed him to make as many stops as he wanted as long as he continued to travel in the same direction without backtracking. Assume that he started from where you are. Once you have determined from where he has sent the postcards, put them in order of his destinations.

Start at your location and then follow the shortest possible route from one place to another. For example, if starting from Toronto, the order would be: New York, Prince Edward Island, Venezuela, England, Italy, Egypt, India, China, Australia, Arizona.

Note: Around-the-world tickets work by longitude. Please also note that although at one time visitors could climb to the torch of the Statue of Liberty, today visitors can climb only to the crown.

A. Where in the World Am I?

Have each student write a short description of a reasonably well-known tourist destination on a piece of paper. Gather the descriptions and divide the class into two teams. Select a player from each team and read them a description. The first player to correctly identify the location gets a point for his or her team. If a player guesses incorrectly, the team loses a point. Select two other players and continue the game until all of the descriptions have been read.

B. Riddle

The following is just a short, fun activity. It can be done any time during the unit when you have 5 to 10 minutes. Read the following instructions to the students:

1) Pick a number between 1 and 9.
2) Subtract 5.
3) Multiply by 3.
4) Square the number (multiply by same number).
5) Add the digits until you get a single digit. (e.g., 64 = 6 + 4 = 10 = 1 + 0 = 1)
6) If the number is less than 5, add 5, otherwise subtract 4.
7) Multiply by 2.
8) Subtract 6.
9) Match each digit to a letter of the alphabet (1 = A, 2 = B, etc.).
10) Pick a name of a country that begins with that letter.
11) Take the second letter of the country and pick a mammal beginning with that letter.
12) Think of the colour of that mammal.

Here it comes: *You have a grey elephant from Denmark.*

Language Note

Canada follows the international metric system for all weights, measures, and numbers although students will still come across some use of imperial measures and some variations in styles of metric usage. (The United States follows imperial measures.) Canadian school textbooks, technical and scientific materials, and government publications follow standard metric guidelines most closely (e.g., spaces rather than commas between digits in large numbers – 30 000 rather than 30,000; no periods in abbreviations – km not km.). In informal writing and in many newspapers, magazines, novels, etc., students will come across variations in styles. Most of these publications still use the comma rather than the space in large numbers. Marco's postcards in this unit reflect this common informal usage, while the journal article from the American Meteorological Society in Unit 1 (p. 3) follows the more formal metric style. Expressions such as "give them an inch," "go for miles," etc. are also still common though based on imperial measures. In Unit 2, Listening 2 the speaker still talks about the cat as being "a foot and a half above the floor."

Grammar Focus 1 (SB pp. 34–35)

ONE STEP AHEAD

It is very rare to string together more than three adjectives in speech or writing. Two adjectives are most common. Depending on the grammar book that you use as a reference, you may find slight variations in the order of adjectives. For example, another order could be *determiner / opinion / size / shape / condition / age / colour / origin / noun*. The order charts should serve only as a general guideline since students may hear other orders in natural speech.

Exercise A (SB p. 34)

Write descriptive phrases by putting the following adjectives in appropriate order.

EXAMPLE: Chinese / warriors / 1.8 metre tall / distinctive / terracotta / thousands
thousands of 1.8 metre tall distinctive terracotta Chinese warriors

1. tropical / multi-coloured / schools / fish / salt water / small
schools of small, multi-coloured, tropical salt water fish

2. sandy / clean / kilometres / beaches / white
kilometres of clean, white, sandy beaches

3. stone / winding / wall / man-made / long
long, winding, man-made stone wall

4. oriental / intriguing / ancient / culture / colourful
colourful, intriguing, ancient oriental culture

5. people / friendly / enthusiastic / nature-loving
friendly, enthusiastic, nature-loving people

Exercise B (SB p. 34)

Refer back to Marco's postcards. Identify the descriptive words or phrases and the type of adjectives used in the postcards.

EXAMPLE: great stone slabs
size / material / noun

1. *N.A.*
2. *one man-made thing — determiner / (origin or general description) / noun*
3. *white marble edifice — colour / material / noun*
4. *elaborate burial places — general description / purpose / noun*
5. *thick tropical rain forest — general description / origin / noun*
6. *great stone slabs — size / material / noun*
7. *one of the most widely recognized symbols — determiner / general description / noun*
8. *little nine-seater — size / noun*

9. *it's a lot taller and steeper than it looks* — *determiner / size / size*

10. *simple white and green farmhouse* — *general desription / colour / colour / noun*
   fictitious red-haired, pigtailed, lovable child — *general description / general description / general description / general description / noun*

Grammar in Use (SB p. 34)

ONE STEP AHEAD

It is important for students to write naturally rather than try to string together as many adjectives as possible. Model examples of good descriptive writing by bringing in some travel brochures and descriptive paragraphs. Have students identify the descriptive phrases and determine the average number of adjectives used to describe the nouns. If possible, bring in some examples of extremely flowery descriptions and discuss the difference in tone created between natural usage of adjectives and extensive, formal usage.

Expansion

Determining Sources
Provide short descriptive passages taken from a number of sources such as poetry, literature, newpapers, journals, scientific reports, etc. Have students work in teams of two or three to determine the possible sources of the passages and then have the teams give reasons for their decisions.

Workbook Practice and Expansion: Grammar Focus 1 Exercises A–F (WB pp. 19–21)

Reading 1 (SB pp. 36–38)

Aims/Skills
- read for comprehension
- infer meaning
- read maps

Comprehension Check (SB p. 38)

1. Why did the Starkells choose to paddle around the cays even though they were located far from the shoreline? *the water around the cays was calmer*

2. What were the major factors that determined how far they would paddle that day? *hunger and tiredness*

3. Approximately how wide was the island? *approx. 30 m (line 30)*

4. What are some key descriptive words that the writer uses to create a picture of how poorly constructed the shack was? *ramshackle, grim shape, flimsy shelter, crude siding, plywood siding, stilts*

5. Make a list of the damage caused by the storm. *siding pulled away from walls, plywood siding ripped off, canoe and boxes full of water*

One Step Beyond (SB p. 38)

1. Why was the radio going silent a signal of approaching disaster? *the electrical storm interfered with the radio signals*

2. Was the shack used frequently? *probably not because it was very dirty and in poor shape*

3. Why was the shack built on stilts? *because if storms hit and waves washed over the island, the shack would remain standing*

4. The writer recognizes that his readers may be unfamiliar with the area he is describing in this journal entry. What evidence is there in the passage to support this? *he defines some unfamiliar terms such as cays; the writer wouldn't do this if writing only for himself*

5. Why did the Starkells consider their survival, and the survival of their canoe, as such a miracle? *the storm was very fierce; their canoe wasn't sheltered from the storm and could easily have been shredded on the coral reef; they could easily have been swept away if the shelter had collapsed*

Speaking (SB p. 38)

Aims/Skills
- formulate questions
- use contextual cues
- ask for tourist information

Answer Key
The following is a list of reponses he [Don Starkell] would have received if he had called the tourist board before departing. What are the questions that he might have asked to get these responses?

EXAMPLE:
Response: It takes place in February. Mardi Gras attracts tourists from all over the world.
Question: When is Mardi Gras?

1. Response: Of course, Mardi Gras is just one of the annual attractions; however, there are many other attractions that are open all year round.
   Question: Are there other attractions besides Mardi Gras?

2. a) Response: One thing you certainly don't want to miss is the Audubon Zoo. It has a Louisiana swamp exhibit that lets you wander through a cypress swamp and view a rare white alligator. It also has a show of robotic prehistoric animals.
   Question: What attractions do you recommend?

b) Response: You can either take a streetcar or get there by boat from the French Quarter.
Question: *How do I get there?*

3. a) Response: The most unique thing to see is probably the Voodoo museum.
Question: *What is the most unique thing to see in New Orleans?*

b) Response: It's located at 724 Dumaine.
Question: *Where is that located?*

4. Response: The French Quarter is filled with unique shops as well as the best restaurants and hotels. It's alive with street tap-dancers, musicians, mimes, and portrait artists. You simply can't visit New Orleans without visiting the French Quarter.
Question: *I've heard of the French Quarter. What is it?*

5. Response: The Prince Conti is located in the French Quarter. It's a European-style hotel that has 50 guest rooms filled with antiques. I would also recommend Place D'Armes located at Jackson Square — it's classic yet casual.
Question: *That sounds nice. What are the good hotels in that area?*

6. Response: We're open from 9 a.m. to 5 p.m. If you think of any other questions, give us a call or visit our web site.
Question: *What are your hours?*

Now role play the telephone conversation with a partner. Then select another tourist destination and create a dialogue in which one person asks for specific information about the area and the other person provides it. Present the dialogue to the class.

Expansion

Project Option (Reproducible 3.1)
Give students a copy of Reproducible 3.1. Have students put on a travel fair where they are all travel representatives trying to attract tourists to their travel destinations. If another class is available, they can be invited to come and shop for their dream vacation.

Listening 1 (SB p. 39)

See Tapescript 3.a

Aims/Skills
- listen for specific information
- complete a chart

> **ONE STEP AHEAD**
>
> When students listen for information to complete the chart, have them fill out only the types of travellers before the 19th century. Also, it isn't important for students to know how to write/spell the names of the explorers (e.g., Etheria or Sacagawea), they can just write in the types of explorers (e.g., nun, guide/interpreter, etc.).

 Focused Listening (SB pp. 38–39)

You will hear a brief lecture about historic women travellers and their contributions. As you listen, complete the following chart.

Types of travellers	Examples/Names	Places explored	Contribution
religious pilgrims	Etheria (Egeria) (a nun from southern Spain or France)	Jerusalem and Egypt	wrote brief account of journey to guide other pilgrims, earliest piece of travel writing by a woman
guides and interpreters who accompanied foreign explorers	Sacagawea, guide and interpreter	western North America to the Pacific Ocean	communicating with the Shoshone people so that they helped Lewis and Clark and treated them as friends
travellers through family relationships	wives, sisters, daughters of soldiers and diplomats, Emily Eden	India	wrote *Up the Country*
emigrants	Susanna Moodie	backwoods Ontario	wrote *Roughing it in the Bush, Or Life in Canada*

🔑 Comprehension Check (SB p. 39)

Based on the lecture, complete the following sentences.
Possible answers:

1. Women emigrants *left their homelands behind to move to an unfamiliar country.*
2. Religion prompted *travellers to venture far from home to visit shrines and holy places.*
3. Women travellers of the 19th century prepared the way *for the later achievements of women in many other fields.*
4. Women travelled to accompany *their menfolk.*
5. Women did not have the same *rights and responsibilities as men.*
6. In the 19th century women travelled to *please themselves.*
7. Women served *as role models for future generations.*

> ### Expansion

Presentation/Writing
Have students do a short presentation or write a narrative paragraph about a female explorer or key female achiever in their culture (past or present) e.g., Aung San Suu Kyi (Burmese woman who won Nobel Peace Prize), Golda Meir, Rigoberta Menchu, Benazir Bhutto, Indira Gandhi, Mother Teresa, Svetlana Savitskaya, Japanese women who climbed Mt. Everest, etc.

Vocabulary 1 (SB p. 40)

Aims/Skills
* unscramble adjectives from context
* brainstorm precise descriptive words

🔑 *Answer Key*

1. Unscramble the adjectives in the following sentences. Use the context to help you.

   a) Mary Kingsley was a (vaber) *brave* woman who travelled in Africa through the unknown country of the Fang people.

   b) Marguerite Baker Harrison was a (gcrououesa) *courageous*, (vatruodneus) *adventurous* woman who served her country as a spy.

   c) The (dddeteaci) *dedicated* Japanese women's climbing expedition reached the summit of Mt. Everest.

   d) Svetlana Savitskaya, a truly (patlanosiniri) *inspirational* woman, was the first woman to walk in space.

---

e) The (srpreegniver) *persevering* Naomi Jones sailed around the world alone in nine months in 1977/78.

2. Below are four rather general descriptive words. Brainstorm with a partner to find at least eight other words you could use in their place that would be more precise or descriptive. Think of appropriate nouns some of your new adjectives could describe and share your descriptions with other teams.

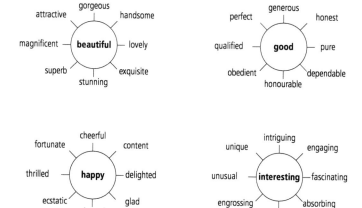

> **Workbook Practice and Expansion:** Vocabulary 1 Exercises A–C (WB pp. 21–22)
> Vocabulary Expansion (adjective/adverb intensifiers) Exercise D (WB p. 22)

Writing (SB p. 40)

Aims/Skills
* use descriptive phrases
* write a journal article

> ### ONE STEP AHEAD
> If students have difficulty getting focused on a topic, a documentary from National Geographic or pictures from the magazine could be shown.

Grammar Focus 2 (SB pp. 40–43)

🔑 Exercise A (SB p. 40)

1. Read the following passage and underline the relative clauses.

   Isabella Bird, whose married name was Bishop, was born in 1831 in Yorkshire, England. This was a time in history when religion played a very important part

---

in people's lives. Under the influence of her father, who was a clergyman, she became a devout member of the Church of England. She believed that religions which differed from her own were based on harmful superstitions. As a youngster, Bird had extremely poor health that sometimes prevented her from getting out of bed. A doctor recommended travel to perk up her spirits. In 1854 she set out by steamship to visit Canada where her cousin lived.

During the trip her health improved tremendously. For the first time in her life she was on her own. This was a liberating experience for a Victorian woman. After visiting with her cousin a short while, she set off on a three-month tour that took her to Montreal, Toronto, Chicago, and New England. She travelled by train and by stagecoach along bumpy and rutted roads. Her family really enjoyed her lively and colourful letters, which described why she found her travels so inspirational. When she came home, she decided to turn her letters into a book, which was published in 1856.

2. Now based on your analysis of the passage, answer these questions.
   a) Is each relative clause subordinate or independent? That is, can the relative clause stand on its own as a complete sentence or does it need to be attached to another clause for meaning? *all clauses are subordinate*
   b) Which words at the beginning of a relative clause are used to describe people, objects/conditions, possession, location, and time? *people — who; objects/conditions — that, which; possession — whose; location — where; time — when*
   c) Why are some relative clauses set off by commas while others are not? Do the clauses set off by commas provide essential information? *the commas surround non-essential information (non-restrictive relative clauses)*

Exercise B (SB p. 42)

Identify the relative clauses in the following sentences and determine whether the relative pronoun is acting as the subject, object, or possessive.

1. The backpacker *that we gave a ride to* is from Australia. *that = object relative pronoun*
2. *Paddle to the Amazon* is about a man and his son who canoe from Winnipeg to the Amazon. *who = subject relative pronoun*
3. Marco is the person whose postcards we read. *whose = possessive relative pronoun*
4. Isabella Bird sold the stories which she wrote. *which = object relative pronoun*
5. Have you visited the woman whom you met on your trip to France? *whom = object relative pronoun*
6. The travel magazine, the title of which I can't remember, provides useful information. *of which = possessive relative pronoun (object of preposition)*

Exercise C (SB p. 42)

Working in pairs, determine whether the clauses in the following sentences are restrictive (R) or non-restrictive (NR). If they are non-restrictive, add appropriate punctuation.

1. In the 1800s only a few Europeans managed to explore Tibet, which is located on a high isolated plateau between China and India. (*NR*)
2. Tibet's religion, Buddhism, was ruled by a caste of high priests, who were called lamas. (*NR*)
3. In 1892, the English missionary Annie Taylor, who lived and worked in China, (*NR*) was the first Western woman to visit Little Tibet, which was located on the southwestern border of Tibet proper. (*NR*)
4. Alexandra David-Neel was the first Western woman to reach Lhasa. Reaching Lhasa, which was both a geographical achievement and a spiritual adventure, (*NR*) was accomplished in 1924.
5. In 1927, Alexandra David-Neel wrote a book that gained her recognition as the world's leading authority on Tibet. (*R*) The book was called *My Journey to Lhasa*.

Exercise D (SB pp. 42–43)

Combine the following sentences using relative clauses.

1. Fanny Bullock Workman made several cycling journeys through India and Southeast Asia. The bicycle journeys totalled 22 400 km.
   Fanny Bullock Workman made several cycling journeys, which totalled 22 400 km, through India and Southeast Asia.
2. In 1893 Mary Kingsley travelled to West Africa. She collected river fish there.
   In 1893 Mary Kingsley travelled to West Africa where she collected river fish.
3. From 1931–1938, Louise Arnor Boyd led four expeditions to East Greenland. The expeditions were undertaken to make maps, take photographs, and collect plant specimens.
   From 1931–1938, Louise Arnor Boyd led four expeditions to East Greenland that were undertaken to make maps, take photographs, and collect plant specimens.
4. In 1975, a climbing expedition reached the summit of Mt. Everest. The expedition consisted of only Japanese women.
   In 1975, a climbing expedition that consisted of only Japanese women reached the summit of Mt. Everest.
5. In 1979, Sylvia Earle reached the record breaking depth of 380 m beneath the sea's surface. She was an American scientist and diver.
   In 1979, Sylvia Earle, who was an American scientist and diver, reached the record breaking depth of 380 m beneath the sea's surface.

Reading 2 (SB pp. 43–45)

Aims/Skills
- read for information
- use descriptive words and phrases to create images
- make inferences
- adjust formality registers
- use appropriate descriptive phrases to organize ideas spatially

Comprehension Check (SB p. 44)

Susanna Moodie's language is extremely rich with description. Each sentence is carefully crafted to evoke detailed pictures in the reader's mind. Match the descriptive phrases Susanna Moodie has used in Column 1 with the plainer and less formal descriptions in Column 2.

1. received the impress of civilization ·

2. the forest has never yet echoed to the woodman's axe

3. scarcely surpassed by anything

4. long range of lofty mountains

5. sprinkled over with neat cottages

6. covered with flocks and herds

7. diversified with islands of every shape and size

8. adorned with orchards and white farmhouses

9. strangely novel and imposing

g) touched by people

e) no trees have ever been cut down in that forest

f) hardly anything is better

a) a bunch of high mountains

h) small cottages are scattered

c) there were many sheep and cattle

b) there were several different-sized islands in the river

i) covered with orchards and farmhouses

d) interesting and memorable

Culture/Language Note

Students may not be familiar with the word *habitants* (line 2) in the reading, the term for early French Canadian settlers. Also, it may be worth noting that Susanna Moodie's description is coloured by her familiarity with the cultivated landscape of England from where she came — thus descriptions such as *neat cottages, green slopes, covered with flocks and herds,* and her astonishment at the beauty, silence, and solitude of the contrasting untouched wilderness in Canada. England had no such wilderness.

For Discussion (SB p. 45)

1. In teams of three or four reread the passage, substituting the simpler phrases from Column 2. (You may have to change them slightly to fit grammatically.) Discuss the effect this has on the description.

Reworked passage:

Eastward, the view down the St. Lawrence towards the Gulf is the finest of all, *hardly anything is better.* Your eyes follow *a bunch of high mountains* until their blue summits are blended and lost in the blue of the sky. *Small cottages are scattered* over some of these, partially cleared round the base, and *there are many sheep and cattle* on the green slopes. *There are several different-sized islands in the river,* some in wood, others partially cleared, and *covered with orchards and farmhouses.* As the early sun streams upon the most prominent of these, leaving the others in deep shade, the effect is *interesting and memorable.* In more remote regions, *where no trees have ever been cut down in the forest, and where the landscape has never been touched by people,* the first approach to the shore inspires a melancholy awe which becomes painful in its intensity.

The substitutions make the description less formal and flowery.

2. What words or phrases has Susanna Moodie used to indicate that her description is following a specific sequence, that is, left to right or top to bottom, etc.?
eastward, the view down the St. Lawrence toward the Gulf . . .
your eyes follow the long range of lofty mountains
. . . their blue summits
. . . cleared round the base
. . . green slopes that spread around them
. . . surface of the river
In more remote regions, . . .

One Step Beyond (SB p. 45)

1. Susanna Moodie ends the description with a poem. Why? What effect does it have on the reader?
She is inspired by the untouched wilderness around her which fills her with an intense melancholy awe and leads to the poem. She may have felt the poem was a better form in which to express these intense emotions.

2. In what types of writing would richly descriptive language like Susanna Moodie's be appropriate? In what types of writing would it be inappropriate?
It would be appropriate in formal, literary forms but inappropriate in any informal writing, in scientific reports or journal articles, and in newspaper articles where information/facts must be presented clearly, concisely, accurately, and objectively.

3. Why is it important to use spatial descriptors when describing a scene?
The descriptors help to organize the information logically so that the reader can clearly follow the description without becoming confused or disoriented. The aim is to recreate the scene clearly in the reader's mind.

Listening 2 (SB p. 45)

See Tapescript 3.b

Aims/Skills
• listen for specific information
• anticipate dialogue changes based on context

 For Discussion

After listening to the interview, discuss the following questions in teams.

1. Who might Peter Pan be? Why is this an appropriate example to use with a group of 10-year-olds?
Peter Pan is a mythical boy who can fly. Children find his carefree lifestyle very attractive. Most North American children read about Peter Pan as children.

2. What impact did seeing Earth from space have on Dr. Bondar?
It filled her with a sense of protection towards the Earth. It helped her feel closer to the people on Earth and made her realize that there were no borders in the world.

3. Dr. Bondar is asked a question about God at the end of the interview that she doesn't want to answer. How does she handle this?
She avoids answering the question by focusing on something common to everyone (the spirit in all people) and expands on that.

Speaking (SB p. 46)

Aims/Skills
• describe a location
• use precise descriptive words and phrases
• use spatial indicators in a description
• practise presentation skills

Writing (SB p. 46)

Aims/Skills
• write a short descriptive essay
• use comparison/contrast techniques in writing

You may wish to take students through the Process Writing practice in the Workbook outlined below before they complete this writing activity.

Process Writing (WB pp. 27–30)

The process writing section in the Workbook focuses on descriptive paragraphs. It includes key elements in a good descriptive paragraph plus exercises on selecting appropriate sentences for a descriptive paragraph, writing a paragraph from an outline and photograph, and writing from the imagination.

Unit Reflection (SB p. 46)

If students have problems with this, have them focus on the word "road" as in "the road to freedom" and what that means to them. It isn't a physical journey and will encourage them to think abstractly. They could also focus on words such as "journey," "path," etc.

Helpful Internet Resources

Key word search: travel and city/country name

The following are some helpful sites:

http://www.travel-library.com/europe/
Travelogues and information about European countries

http://www.chinavista.com/trave/virtualtours.html
China Virtual Tours: information and images from China's most famous tourist and scenic attractions

http://www.city.net/
Easy access to information about cities all around the world

http://www.search.com/Single/0,7,0-300458,0200.html
Fodor's trip planner

UNIT 4
That's Not What I Meant

OVERVIEW

Theme: Communication Barriers

Topics:
- cartoons about communication SB p. 47, p. 59
- conversational styles of men and women (Listening 1) SB pp. 48–50
- cross-cultural communication (Reading 1) SB pp. 53–55
- active listening (Reading 2) SB pp. 58–61
- communication styles in the workplace WB pp. 33–35

Vocabulary:

Student Book

Idioms:
to beat around the bush
to get off track/to get sidetracked
to get to the point (of)
to miss the point (of)
to hear (it) through the grapevine
to pin (someone) down (on something)

Other:
barriers
concise
cue
feedback
gestures
interaction
interpersonal
message
perception
vague

Workbook

Idioms and phrasal verbs:
to bite one's tongue
to blurt out
to broach the subject
to catch someone's drift
to cut off
to listen up
to mark someone's words
mum's the word
to rattle on (about)
to tune in (to)
to tune out

Other:
buzz-word
to grasp

Grammar:
Conjunctions and Prepositions of Contrast (SB pp. 51–52)

Transition Words and Phrases of Contrast (SB pp. 56–58)

Process Writing:
Paragraphs that Compare and Contrast (WB pp. 37–38)

Getting Started (Reproducible 4.1)

 Play a matching game. Copy the shaded Body Movement (BM) cards and matching white Message Cards (MC) from Reproducible 4.1. Divide the class into two groups. Give one group BM cards and the other group matching MC cards (one card to each student). Allow MC students to clarify any unknown vocabulary in their group without letting the BM group hear their messages. Give the BM students time to understand their body movements. Then have students find the person with their matching BM or MC card. If you have time, repeat the exercise giving the BM group MC cards and the MC group BM cards. Follow the game with a demonstration of the body movements and their message, and a discussion about interpreting North American body language. If appropriate, ask students how the same messages are communicated in their native culture.

Answer Key

1. Put the palm of one or both of your hands flat against your cheek(s) and tighten your face muscles. *Embarrassment*

2. Stand holding your arms crossed over your chest with hands gripping the upper part of the opposite arm. *Defensiveness*

3. Stroke your chin, moving your head slightly up and down. *Thinking or evaluating*

4. Shuffle across the room with your hands hanging limp at your sides and your head bent forward. *Dejection*

5. Stand straight with the tips of your fingers on your left hand pressed against those of your right hand in a steeple position. *Confidence*

6. Open your eyes and mouth wide and cover your mouth with the palm of your hand. *Astonishment*

7. Pat someone on the arm or back and smile. *Everything will be fine.*

8. Widen your eyes and rub your hands in front of you in anticipation of a treat and smile. *Expectation*

9. Shrug your shoulders and hold your hands out, palms up, in front of you. *What do you want from me?*

10. Lower your head slightly, close your eyes, pinch the bridge of your nose, and take a deep breath. *A tough decision*

11. Raise your hand to head level and cross your fingers. *Hoping for good luck*

12. With your head slightly bent down and to the side, peek at the audience and then turn your eyes away while smiling and drawing in your bottom lip.
Shyness

Alternative: Rather than having students find their matching partner, divide the class into two teams. Have one student perform the body movement for the class. Students from either team can try to guess the message. Write the possible messages on the blackboard or have students guess at large. Give the team with the correct answer a point. Continue until all the body movements have been performed. Then do the follow-up discussion as above.

Unit Opening Page (SB p. 47)

The cover page demonstrates miscommunication and communication barriers in a humorous way, and invites discussion about communication barriers.

Begin with the Dennis The Menace cartoon if you have completed the Closed Book activity above since the cartoon also deals with reading body language.

Vocabulary 1 (SB p. 48)

Aims/Skills
• match meanings with communication-related idioms
• select appropriate idioms based on context

Answer Key
1. The idioms below are all associated with communication. Match those in Column A with their meanings in Column B.

Column A	Column B
a) to get to the point (of)	6. *to say what is most important*
b) to miss the point (of)	3. *to not understand the specific idea expressed*
c) to get off track / to get sidetracked	2. *to start talking about a topic that is different from the original purpose or subject of conversation*
d) to beat around the bush	5. *to avoid making a direct (clear) statement*
e) to pin (someone) down (on) (something)	1. *to force or pressure someone to provide details*
f) to hear (it) through the grapevine **or** to hear through the grapevine that . . .	4. *to hear (something) from someone who heard it from someone else*

2. Fill in the blanks with an appropriate form of the idiom. Pay attention to the required tense.

GIRLFRIEND: Honey, you're not listening to me again.

BOYFRIEND: I am listening, but you're just going on and on. Why don't you just *get to the point?*

GIRLFRIEND: Alright! Alright! I'm just trying to *pin you down* on your plans for the future as far as it concerns us.

BOYFRIEND: You're *beating around the bush* again. Why don't you just come out and ask. You want to know if I'm going to marry you.

GIRLFRIEND: Okay. Do you want to marry me?

BOYFRIEND: Look. Neither of us is settled into a secure job yet and I'm a little unsure about my future. And what about you? Didn't you want to go to graduate school? By the way, have you heard anything yet about getting accepted?

GIRLFRIEND: Forget about that. Let's not *get sidetracked (or) get off track.* I asked you specifically if you want to get married.

BOYFRIEND: It's not that I don't want to marry you. It's just that this isn't the right time. Listen. I've *heard through the grapevine* that Professor Stanson may be leaving the department. I think I have a good chance to get his job. If I do get the job, it'll mean a lot of work in the beginning. So this just isn't a good time to think of marriage. Do you get my point?

GIRLFRIEND: Oh I get your point. But you've *missed my point.* I want to settle down and start a family. We've been dating for six years already and I'm not willing to wait another five years.

Workbook Practice and Expansion: Vocabulary 1 Exercise A (WB p. 31)
Vocabulary Expansion (additional idioms) Exercise B (WB pp. 31-32)

Listening 1 (SB pp. 48–50)

See Tapescript 4.a

Excerpt 1 (SB p. 49)
Aims/Skills
• listen for details
• interpret underlying meaning behind words
• relate communication styles to personal experience

Focused Listening (SB p. 49)

Listen to this conversation between Maureen and Philip who are trying to set a date for a dinner party. Then answer the questions.

1. What happens on the weekend of October 10 that influences the decision about the date of the dinner party?
The weekend of October 10 is the opening of the hunting season.

2. Why does Maureen ask Philip whether he wouldn't want to hunt later on the Saturday, after he has just agreed to setting the date of the party on the Saturday?
She asks him this because he hasn't given a reason for his suggestion. Without an explanation, she assumes that the point is still negotiable. She also says she is trying to be considerate of him.

3. Why does her question annoy Philip?
Philip finds her question intrusive. He feels he has clearly stated his preference and shouldn't have to explain his decision. He sees having to explain his decision as a threat to his independence.

 One Step Beyond (SB p. 49)

1. What causes the argument?
Each partner misunderstands the motives behind what the other says. Maureen takes Philip's statement that they should set the party for Saturday as a suggestion, whereas Philip thinks of it as a statement of fact. Because she interprets his comment as a suggestion, she feels the topic is still open for discussion. Because he feels he has stated his preference as a fact, he regards her questioning as a threat to his statement.

2. Compare what happens in this conversation to what happened in the argument you discussed earlier. Describe the similarities and differences between this argument and the one you had.
Answers will vary.

Excerpt 2 (SB p. 49)

Aims/Skills
- listen for descriptive details
- listen for differences in self-descriptions
- listen for paralanguage cues
- infer meaning from conversational markers
- relate communication styles to personal experience

Focused Listening (SB p. 49)

 Answer Key

Listen to this fictional dialogue which illustrates another difference in how men and women communicate. Then answer the questions.

1. What do you know about Johan based on his description of himself?
extremely intelligent, successful, youthful, well-balanced, sexy, a man with a world conscience, well-read, a good mixer, friendly, likes sports, is a good family man, good son, has no debts, pays his taxes

2. What do you know about Marianne based on her description of herself?
married to Johann for 10 years, has two daughters named Karin and Eva, thinks Johan is nice, likes her life

One Step Beyond (SB p. 49)

1. What were some of the obvious differences between how Johan and Marianne answered the interviewer's questions?
Johan — boastful, says a lot, focuses on himself, describes himself on his own merits
Marianne — insecure, says little, focuses on family (husband and children), describes herself through others

2. Who do you think is the dominant partner in this relationship? Give reasons for your answers.
Johan is the dominant partner. He talks a lot more than Marianne. He is more confident than she is. He interrupts her when she is speaking, suggesting that she can't express herself and that she has little to say of value. He belittles her by poking fun at her comments, interjecting silly remarks, and by commenting on her figure, an inappropriate sexual reference that suggests her value as a person lies in her appearance.

3. Why do you think Marianne has such a difficult time describing herself?
She may be insecure or shy, may not want to be seen as boasting, may not have a strong sense of her own value.

4. What is your impression of Johan's character?
   Answer will vary.

5. This is a fictional conversation from a movie. Do you think it bears any relation to the way men and women communicate in reality? If so, how? If not, why not?
   Answer will vary.

Expansion

Self-Perceptions
On small scraps of paper, have students quickly write down three attributes that make them a wonderful person. Give them only 60 seconds. Collect only the completed lists (a completed list must have three attributes) from the men. Put them aside. Then do the same for the women. Count how many papers you collected from each group and calculate the percentage returned. Discuss the results in terms of gender perceptions and, if applicable, cultural perceptions. You may also wish to discuss other factors that may influence a person's ability to complete this task.

Excerpt 3 (SB p. 50)

Aims/Skills
- listen for details
- listen to complete a chart
- listen for specific information
- apply information to other contexts

Focused Listening (SB p. 50)

ONE STEP AHEAD
Have students try to answer the Focused Listening questions and complete the chart on p. 50 before listening. This will gauge how much they know or what they think about the topic. Then have them listen for confirmation, discussing how their pre-listening responses compare to their post-listening responses.

Some answers in the chart must be inferred from the listening, they are not directly stated. If your students completed the chart as a pre-listening task, they may find it easier to do the Focused Listening. If not, have students individually try to complete the chart after one or two listenings, then work in pairs or groups to flush out their answers. A final listening will help them confirm that they have understood the main ideas.

Answer Key
Listen to this excerpt which describes research on how men and women learn different ways of speaking even in early childhood. Then answer these questions.

1. What evidence is there to support the idea that children learn to talk not only from their parents but also from their peers?
   Children of parents with foreign accents do not speak with their parents' accents. They have the pronunciation of the region where they live.

2. How are boys' games organized?
   Boys' games are usually played outdoors in large groups and are hierarchical in structure. The games have a lot of rules and challenging or arguing about the rules is an important part of the game. The games have a leader and participants win or lose.

3. How are girls' games organized?
   Girls' games are usually played in small groups or with a partner. They are not hierarchical and often there is no leader. Everyone gets a turn and there are often no winners or losers.

4. Listen again and complete the following chart comparing specific aspects of boys' and girls' games.

	Boys	*Girls*
What is most important in their games?	Boys' games are all about jockeying for status.	Girls' games are all about creating friends.
How do they achieve status?	Boys achieve status by giving orders and making them stick, challenging each other, taking centre stage, and proving who is best.	Girls don't officially jockey for status in games. However, girls get unofficial status by being liked. They are liked when they don't boast, appear fair to others, and have close relationships with the other girls.
How do they communicate in their games?	Boys give orders, such as "Get outa here!" (Get out of here) or "Gimme that!"(Give me that).	Girls make suggestions such as "Let's . . ." and "How about . . .?" to avoid sounding bossy. Suggestions are more likely to be accepted by the other girls.

Grammar Focus 1 (SB pp. 51–52)

✦ Exercise A (SB p. 51)

Complete the following sentences using coordinating conjunctions of contrast.

Possible answers:

1. Boys and girls grow up in the same neighbourhoods,
   but they learn to communicate differently.
   yet they grow up in different worlds of words.

2. Parents speak to both their sons and daughters,
   but not in the same ways.
   yet they expect and accept different ways of speaking from each.

3. Gender stereotypes are still evident today,
   but they are being challenged more and more.
   yet there are many examples of individuals who don't fit the stereotypes.

✦ Exercise B (SB p. 52)

The following list of gender talk differences has been researched and compiled by Lillian Glass in her book *He Says, She Says*. Use the information in the list to write sentences that show contrast. Try to use different subordinate conjunctions. (You may also get into a lively discussion about whether you agree or disagree with these statements!)

ONE STEP AHEAD

Students may try to combine #1 under Women with #1 under Men etc. but this pattern won't work in all cases. Model the concept for students by providing some sample answers.

Possible answers:

a) *Men stretch their arms and legs out away from their bodies when sitting, while women direct their arms and legs toward their bodies.*

b) *Men gesture away from the body whereas women gesture toward the body.*

c) *Although women tend to look more directly at another person and have better eye contact than men, they don't touch others as often.*

d) *Women provide more listener feedback through their body language although they tend to beat around the bush more often.*

e) *In spite of the fact that men provide less listener feedback through their body language than women, they tend to touch others more in conversation.*

f) *In spite of the fact that men talk at a slower rate of speech, they mumble words more and have sloppier pronunciation.*

g) *Although women talk at a faster rate of speech, they tend to beat around the bush more often.*

h) *Men get to the point more quickly whereas women tend to beat around the bush.*

i) *Even though men use more slang words and jargon, they tend to get to the point faster than women.*

j) *Even though women use quicker and more precise articulation and better pronunciation, they tend to beat around the bush more often.*

k) *Although women use fewer slang words and jargon, they tend to beat around the bush more often.*

l) *In spite of the fact that women laugh and giggle more than men, they use little sarcasm and teasing to show affection.*

m) *Men use more teasing and sarcasm to show affection, though they laugh and giggle less.*

n) *Men talk more about themselves and their accomplishments, while women talk more about other people's accomplishments and minimize their own.*

o) *Men see time as having a beginning, a middle, and an end, while women see time as flowing more continuously.*

p) *Although women gossip more than men, they are more likely to apologize after a confrontation.*

q) *Men do not often apologize after a confrontation whereas women often do.*

✦ Exercise C (SB p. 52)

Possible answers:

1. *Despite providing less listener feedback through their body language, men touch others more often.*

2. *Women tend to beat around the bush more often in spite of talking at a faster rate of speech.*

3. *Men get to the point more quickly despite talking at a slower rate of speech.*

4. *In spite of gossiping more, women still talk more about other people's accomplishments.*

5. *Despite sloppier pronunciation and a slower rate of speech, men get to the point more quickly.*

Speaking (SB p. 53)

Aims/Skills
• understand messages in cartoons
• brainstorm ideas

As a follow-up to this activity, assign students the task of finding other examples of miscommunication in newspaper cartoons. Alternately, have students create their own cartoons.

Workbook Practice: Grammar Focus 1 Exercises A–B (WB p. 32)

Vocabulary 2 (SB p. 53)

Aims/Skills
- match words with meanings
- match nouns with appropriate prepositions

Answer Key

1. Match the words in Column A with their definitions in Column B.

Column A	Column B
a) interaction	10. *communication or dealings between people*
b) barriers	7. *problems or obstacles*
c) feedback	5. *a response with your opinion*
d) interpersonal	6. *between people*
e) gestures	1. *body movements*
f) perception	3. *interpretation of an idea*
g) vague	2. *not clearly expressed*
h) message	8. *information sent to a person, group, etc.*
i) cue	9. *signal*
j) concise	4. *expressed clearly and with few words*

2. Match each word in the list below with a preposition that is often used with it. You may use a preposition more than once. Then write a sentence for each word and preposition combination. Check your answers with a partner.

interaction between

barriers to   *barriers between*

feedback to   *feedback on*

perception of

Workbook Practice: Vocabulary 2 Exercise A (WB pp. 32–33)

Expansion

Role Play (Reproducibles 4.2 and 4.3)

Aims/Skills
- practise using verbal and non-verbal cues to communicate messages
- practise reading verbal and non-verbal cues to interpret messages
- compare how communication styles between individuals differ

This role play involves two characters, a customer and a bank teller (customer service representative). Have two pairs of students prepare the role play to perform for the class. In one pair assign the role of customer to a female, in the other to a male. The role of teller can be assigned to either a male or female. Have one pair leave the room while the other is performing its role play. Role cards, questions, and a chart to fill in are on Reproducibles 4.2 and 4.3 on pages 105 and 106. After the first role play, take up the answers to the questions. After the second pair performs its role play, ask the class to contrast and compare how the characters in the two role plays communicated their messages and have students complete the chart. Note: In this role play, finding a solution to the problem is not as important as the process of complaining and resolving complaints, although the role cards advise the customer not to leave the bank until a solution is found.

Follow-up: Take up the answers in the chart. Ask if students noticed any differences in communication based on gender or culture (if applicable). Discuss any miscommunication between the two roles. At this point you can have the actors read out the role play cards. Discuss appropriate ways to complain, express frustration, handle conflict and problems, emphasizing the North American approach to conflict resolution, problem-solving, and customer service. A discussion of aggressive/assertive behaviour, eye contact, etc. may be appropriate. To practise some grammar, you could have students write sentences or a comparison/contrast paragraph based on what they observed.

Reading 1 (SB pp. 53–55)

Aims/Skills
- anticipate information
- read for details
- guess meanings of words from context
- understand the main point
- read for structural cues
- understand the function of anecdotes in readings

Note: Answers to the discussion questions in each section will vary.

Paragraph 2: Comprehension Check (SB p. 54)

1. In the village where Hoa grew up, what happened once boys and girls reached the age of ten?
   They were not allowed to play with each other.

2. What was the punishment in Hoa's village for girls who violated these social rules?

They were forced to kneel down on the ground so villagers could spit and throw rocks at them.

3. What do you think is the meaning of the phrase "accepting them as merely perfunctory acts" in the last paragraph? *accepting them as habitual actions that had no ulterior motive*

🔑 Paragraph 4: Comprehension Check (SB p. 54)

1. What aspects of culture affect how we communicate? *language, beliefs, rules, customs, myths, family patterns, political and economic systems influence how we communicate verbally and non-verbally*

2. What sentence in this section gives a clue about what you will read in the next section? *the final sentence: "With such a diversity in beliefs, customs, and social systems, it is not difficult to understand that how people use body language to communicate will vary from one culture to another."*

🔑 Paragraph 5: Comprehension Check (SB p. 55)

1. Why is head touching taboo in Malaysia and other Islamic countries? *the head is believed to contain sacred spiritual and intellectual powers*

2. How is eye contact interpreted differently in Arab countries as compared to Japan? *In Arab countries extended eye contact is desirable because Arabs believe that the eyes reveal what's in the heart. Avoiding prolonged eye contact is considered impolite and suggests one is insincere. In Japan children are taught early not to look directly at someone with superior status such as a teacher.*

3. Why are Americans uncomfortable with prolonged eye contact? *In North America prolonged eye contact suggests an intimacy that is inappropriate in most social situations.*

🔑 Paragraph 6: Comprehension Check (SB p. 55)

1. What does it mean to learn to communicate in another language? *It means more than learning grammar; it means learning a range of communication signals, such as body language, in a cultural context.*

2. Which sentence in this section states the main point of this reading? *first sentence: "Just as Hoa and Tom's lack of understanding of what and how different cultures communicate through body language resulted in a communication blunder, our own lack of understanding can lead us to sometimes serious miscommunication."*

Note: You may wish to debate which sentence illustrates the main point because they are all important. While learning to communicate in another language does require more than learning grammar, this is not the main point of the reading. The reading focuses only on body language and culture, not other factors such as political and economic systems. The final sentence about the importance of learning how other cultures use body language is also important, and could, arguably, be the main idea. But the reading focuses more on how body language varies from culture to culture and how not understanding this can lead to miscommunication than how important it is for foreign learners of English to learn how body language is used in North America and vice versa.

🔑 One Step Beyond (SB p. 55)

1. What role does the anecdote about Hoa and Tom play in this reading? *It illustrates the main idea of the reading, and introduces the reading with a real-life situation the reader can relate to.*

2. How does the writer make the transition between the anecdote and the essay? *The writer poses a question that encourages the reader to analyze the communication problem described in the anecdote and then continues to explain the problem.*

3. How does the writer connect the anecdote at the beginning of the reading to the main point of the reading? *The writer reintroduces the anecdote at the beginning of the final paragraph (6), drawing an analogy between its lesson and our personal experience.*

Writing (SB p. 56)

Aims/Skills
- write an example paragraph from an outline
- write an anecdote
- write a comparison/contrast paragraph

Writing an anecdote: The critical point to emphasize is that an anecdote illustrates a main point. As an expansion activity and to illustrate the concept, ask students to identify the main points of some common fairy tales or folk tales. You could also give students some main points and ask them to "tell" stories that illustrate the points before they write an anecdote. Review the narrative paragraph format in Unit 2 of the Workbook (pp. 16–18). An anecdote is a narration.

Journal entry: Review the comparison/contrast paragraph format in Unit 4 of the Workbook (pp. 37–38) with students before they write this paragraph.

Speaking (SB p. 56)

Aim/Skill
- understand meaning from gestures and body language

> ### ONE STEP AHEAD
> If you want to make this activity more challenging, prepare cards with the phrases listed in the Student Book ahead of time. Then have students play the game with their books closed and without knowing what phrases they are choosing from.
>
> To heighten the fun, have a timekeeper time students on each team. The student who acts out his or her expressions in the shortest time wins.

Grammar Focus 2 (SB pp. 56–58)

Exercise A (SB p. 57)

> ### ONE STEP AHEAD
> The meanings of these transitional expressions vary only slightly. It is more important for students to know when each can be used than to write a definition. If looking the words up in a dictionary poses problems, have students write the sample sentences from the dictionary instead.
>
> Explain that expressions of contrast focus on "differences" of ideas. Concession and opposition are two ways to express differences of ideas. In a sentence expressing concession, the second idea is surprising or unexpected based on the information in the first idea. For example, "Although their first encounter was unpleasant, Hoa and Tom became good friends." Expressions of concession include: *but, although, despite, in spite of, however, nevertheless/nonetheless, even so,* and *still.* In a sentence expressing opposition, the second idea is different from the first but not surprisingly so. For example, "Men get to the point quickly in conversation, whereas women tend to beat around the bush more often." The two ideas are clearly different, but based on the first idea, there is no reason to be surprised about the second idea. Expressions of opposition include: *but, yet, whereas, while, on the other hand, in contrast,* and *on the contrary.*
>
> Have students write sentences using the expressions to guide them in their appropriate use.

Answer Key

however = *despite or nevertheless*
still = *even so or despite*
nevertheless = *despite what has just been said or referred to*
nonetheless = *same as nevertheless*
on the contrary = *the opposite of what has just been said*
even so = *despite this*

on the other hand = *comparison of two opposing opinions or two ways of thinking about the same thing, or used to mention two opposing groups in an argument*

Exercise B (SB p. 57)

Work with a partner. Join the ideas in the following pairs of sentences to clearly show a contrastive relationship. Try to use as many different contrastive conjunctions and expressions as possible.

Possible answers:

1. Many people believe that most of the impact of a message is conveyed through words. Research has shown that almost 97% of a message's impact is conveyed through non-verbal communication.
   Many people believe that most of the impact of a message is conveyed through words. **Yet,** *research has shown that almost 97% of a message's impact is conveyed through non-verbal communication.*

2. We don't know how much space any individual person needs to communicate comfortably. We do know what happens when this space is threatened.
   We don't know how much space any individual person needs to communicate comfortably. We do know, **though,** *what happens when this space is threatened.*

3. Girls are more likely to say, "I'm sorry" than boys. Some research suggests that they are often less sorry when they make a mistake.
   Girls are more likely to say, "I'm sorry" than boys; **nevertheless,** *some research suggests that they are often less sorry when they make a mistake.*

4. Her knowledge of English grammar was excellent. Her heavy accent remained a barrier to communication.
   Her knowledge of English grammar was excellent. **Even so,** *her heavy accent remained a barrier to communication.*

5. Technology hasn't made communicating easier. It has made it more difficult.
   Technology hasn't made communicating easier. **On the contrary,** *it has made it more difficult.*

6. Word processing lets you revise text more easily. It can't teach you how to write more effectively.
   Even though *word processing lets you revise text more easily, it can't teach you how to write more effectively.*

7. Technology doesn't mean an improvement in the quality of life. Sometimes it means a worse quality of life.
   Technology doesn't mean an improvement in the quality of life. **On the contrary,** *sometimes it means a worse quality of life.*

8. We may think we are good listeners. Most of us are poor listeners.
   We may think we are good listeners. **Still,** *most of us are in practice probably poor listeners.*

9. We usually think of communication as spoken messages. Experts divide communication into two categories: verbal and non-verbal communication.
*We usually think of communication as spoken messages. Experts, **on the other hand**, divide communication into two categories: verbal and non-verbal communication.*

10. Some experts question how effective technology has been in improving communication. One cannot argue that the way in which we communicate has changed significantly with the introduction of technologies such as cellular phones.
***In spite of the fact that** some experts question how effective technology has been in improving communication, one cannot argue that the way in which we communicate has changed significantly with the introduction of technologies such as cellular phones.*

Workbook Practice: Grammar Focus 2 Exercise A (WB p. 33)
Grammar Expansion (with reading "Communication and Success in the Workplace") Exercises B-F (WB pp. 33–36)

 Grammar in Use (SB pp. 57–58)

Read the two opposing opinions about the use of language in communication. Then write as many contrastive sentences as you can.

Possible answers:

1. *The structure of English is not based on an unchanging set of rules that must be followed. On the contrary, the structure of English continues to evolve as the global culture that influences it changes.*

2. *We have to understand that following the rules of grammar and spelling is important. On the other hand, we have to understand that grammar and spelling rules also change.*

3. *Language is alive in the sense that its grammar and spelling can change. Still, it is essential that we learn to express ourselves using current standard grammar and spelling.*

4. *Not accepting poorly written papers and not tolerating any spelling errors does not encourage freedom of expression. On the contrary, it discourages freedom of expression.*

5. *It is true that vocabulary changes, with new words coming into the language and some words falling out of favour. Nonethless, we still have to have a base of varied vocabulary to express thoughts accurately.*

Aims/Skills
- understand the underlying message in a cartoon
- read for specific information
- apply information from a reading to another task
- scan for information
- apply information from a reading to another context

ONE STEP AHEAD

After your students have completed the survey in "Before You Read" and the follow-up Discussion questions, spend a few minutes on the Calvin and Hobbes cartoon on p. 59. Ask students these questions:

1. Why is the cartoon funny?

2. Have you ever experienced a similar situation? (on the receiving or giving end)

3. What message about how we listen does the cartoon send?

Comprehension Check (SB p. 61)

1. In the anecdote that introduces the article, what example of a communication blunder do we see Linda S. making?
Linda S. doesn't listen as evidenced by her constant interruptions as others are speaking.

2. What example is given that illustrates how we can control the effect of interruptions?
Learn to bite your tongue until after the other person has finished speaking. The writer even suggests sitting on your hands to keep your gestures from speaking for you.

3. According to Dee Soder, why do many people interrupt?
They are bright, think they have grasped the point, and want to show off how much they know.

4. In what situation might the listener have to delve deeper and ask for more information?
When you suspect that a delicate or negative subject is being avoided

5. How can you show someone that you are listening?
Maintaining good eye contact and leaning slightly forward when someone else is speaking is one way.

6. How can we make sure we've understood what the speaker has said?
Clarify by saying something like "Let me make sure I understand what you're saying."

Workbook Practice: Vocabulary Expansion (using words from Reading 2) Exercises A and B (WB pp. 36–37)

Speaking (SB p. 61)

Aims/Skills
- debate an issue
- express an opinion
- paraphrase to clarify understanding
- report what someone has said

It is very important to model this activity so that students understand what to do.

Expansion

A. Conversation Management (Reproducible 4.4)
The following is an alternative or additional speaking activity. Put students into teams of four or five. Tell them they will have a 15-minute conversation in which they have to solve a problem. Assign each student a role card (Reproducible 4.4) that should not be shown to other team members. There are six role cards to choose from. You need not use all of them but be sure to include the task master and the expert. Give each team a problem card and have students discuss the topic while playing their roles.

B. Optional Project
Have your class design a large wall collage of images and quotes that illustrate various messages. Choose about five words (messages) from this unit that will become the headings for the collage. Tell students to look for communication tools such as photos, illustrations, advertisements, poems, or quotes that illustrate these messages in their minds. The meanings of the words you choose can be expanded beyond how they are used in this unit. For example, the word *interaction* could elicit a photo of a child and an older person holding hands. You can ask students to chose one message and look for all of the communication tools, or to choose several messages, but only choose one communication tool for each.

When the communication tools have been collected, have students present them to the class and explain why they chose those specific images or quotes and how they communicate the target message. Then assign teams to design and create the various "headings" of the collage. Encourage your students to be creative. By the end of the project, you should have a large wall collage with five headings and corresponding images and quotes. Suggested messages include: *barriers, perception, gestures, interaction, and listening.*

Unit Reflection (SB p. 61)

This activity can be very useful to students throughout their studies. If you wish to expand on this notion, hand out a one-page summary, prepare a short presentation, or have students prepare a short oral presentation on listening effectively to lectures. Some useful resources (not ESL materials) include:

Misener, Judi and Sandra Steele. *The Business of English.* Toronto: Oxford University Press Canada, 1994, pp. 72–100.

Nelson, Paul and Judy Pearson. *Confidence in Public Speaking.* Iowa, USA: WCB Brown & Benchmark Publishers, 1993, pp. 24–41.

Fleet, Joan, Fiona Goodchild, and Richard Zajchowski. *Learning For Success: Skills and Strategies for Canadian Students.* Toronto: Harcourt Brace & Company, Canada, 1994, p. 56 (contains a one-page summary for listening to lectures).

DeVito, Joseph A. Messages: *Building Interpersonal Communication Skills.* New York: HarperCollins College Publishers, 1996, pp. 78–105.

Helpful Internet Resources

Key word search: cross-cultural communications, socio-linguistics, ESL

http://www.worldculture.com/
A great starting point for access to various sites that deal with cross-cultural communications, from body language to information about currency, traditions, customs, and language.

http://transcript.simplenet.com/gototongue.htm
Home of Tongue, an on-line magazine for high school students that deals with various English communications issues. A new topic is featured monthly.

Process Writing (WB pp. 37–38)

Writing comparison and contrast paragraphs is a natural extension of the content and grammar in this unit. The Workbook includes explanations and exercises focusing on the point-by-point and block methods of organizing comparison and contrast paragraphs and provides a useful checklist.

UNIT 5
The Cutting Edge

Theme: Science and Technology

Topics:
- advances in science and technology SB pp. 62–63
- science fiction and Star Trek (Reading 1/Listening 1) SB pp. 64–66
- future predictions (Reading 2) SB pp. 69–71
- gene manipulation (Listening 2) SB pp. 73–74

Vocabulary:
Student Book
(Noun + Preposition Collocations)

a debate about / for / on
a degree in
an argument against / for / about
an analysis of
an example of
a reputation for
an experiment in
an observation about / of
an article about / for / on
an investigation of / into
an examination of
research in / into / on

Roots: astro- auto- bio-
          cyclo- dyn-   geo-
          -graph patho- poly-

Workbook
(Idiomatic Expressions)
to be under pressure
to burn the midnight oil
to figure out
to find out
in the nick of time
out of the blue
to roll up one's sleeve and dig in

Grammar:
Noun Clauses (SB pp. 67–68)

Functions of Noun Clauses (SB pp. 72–73)

Use of "so" replacing "that" in Noun Clauses to Answer Yes/No Questions (WB pp. 41–42)

Process Writing:
Expository Paragraphs (WB pp. 46–47)

Getting Started (Reproducible 5.1)

The following activity can be used to introduce the unit. Have students work in small teams to identify the inventions and inventors (where possible) based on the clue cards (Reproducible 5.1). Teams get one point for identifying the invention and an additional point for identifying the inventor. Students can discuss what their lives would be like if the invention had never been created. This discussion, as well as learning about the inventions and inventors, are the main purposes of this activity.

Answer Key

1. Drycleaning — Thomas L. Jennings
2. Electric telegraph system — Samuel F.B. Morse
3. Sewing machine — Elias Howe
4. Telephone — Alexander Graham Bell
5. Electricity — Thomas Edison
6. Wheel — ancient Sumerians
7. Dynamite — Alfred Nobel
8. Paper — the Chinese
9. Snowmobile — J. Armand Bombardier
10. Airplane — Wright brothers

Unit Opening Pages (SB pp. 62–63)

Da Vinci's sketches of future technological applications are amazingly accurate, yet at the time he was considered somewhat crazy for these wild notions. Ask students if they know of other remarkable people from their history or culture who have demonstrated such genius for predicting our scientific future.

Reading 1 (SB pp. 64–66)

Aims/Skills
- use clues such as titles and introductions to anticipate content
- find synonyms
- read for supporting evidence
- read for information
- identify audience and tone

Comprehension Check (SB p. 66)

Find words in the reading that are synonyms for the following words or that match the following definitions.

Paragraph 1:
- a) extraordinary — *fantastic*
- b) foreign — *alien*
- c) ridiculous — *nonsensical*

Paragraph 2:
- d) imagined — *conceived*
- e) changing from the natural condition — *distorting*
- f) state of being connected without break — *continuum*

Paragraph 3:
- g) put out — *extinguished*
- h) continue to live — *survive*
- i) replaced — *restored*

Paragraph 4:
- j) difficult — *rigorous*
- k) co-workers — *colleagues*
- l) shows (*n.*) — *series*

Paragraph 5:
- m) consisting of two parts — *binary*
- n) over-precise or picky about details — *persnickety*

Paragraph 6:
- o) something interesting because never experienced before — *novelty*
- p) increases — *expands*
- q) not based on reality — *fanciful*

> **Workbook Practice:** Vocabulary (from the reading "The Science of *Star Trek*") Exercises A–C (WB pp. 39–40)

Reading for Information (SB p. 66)

What evidence is there in the reading for the following statements?

1. *Star Trek* promotes science and technology.
   (lines 59–63): Star Trek attracts and excites generations of viewers about advanced science and engineering, and it's almost the only show that depicts scientists and engineers positively, as role models.

2. Roddenberry based his show on scientific facts; however, he took some liberties with scientific details in order to accommodate the reality of television programming.
   (lines 11–14): . . . writers of the show have started with science we know and s-t-r-e-t-c-h-e-d it to fit a framework of amazing inventions that support action-filled and

entertaining stories.
   (lines 16–19): . . . spaceships unable to travel faster than light would take decades to reach the stars, and that would be too boring for a one-hour show per week . . . so he introduced warp drives into the show

3. *Star Trek* attracts a diverse audience including well-educated people such as scientists.
   (lines 47–48): I'm a physicist and many of my colleagues watch Star Trek.
   (lines 85–86): . . . it's the only science fiction series that many scientists watch regularly.

4. Some of the science portrayed in the shows is not just stretched truth — it is inaccurate.
   (lines 33–34 and following paragraph): . . . they do sometimes get science details wrong (e.g., holding breath during decompression would kill a person)

One Step Beyond (SB p. 66)

> **ONE STEP AHEAD**
>
> Read a passage from "The Science of *Star Trek*" and then from "History of the Future" (SB pp. 70-71) aloud to the class and have students identify which passage they think was written by someone with a PhD. Then continue with the questions below.

1. This article was written by a man who has a PhD in physics. He has studied science at the university level for about ten years. With this fact in mind, is there anything unexpected about the vocabulary or tone used in the article?
   The tone is not formal or academic and vocabulary does not include scientific jargon. In fact, the tone is personal and conversational as shown in the first line with the phrase "just a lot of gee-whiz nonsensical Sci-Fi?" and with the use of contractions, questions, and exclamations.

2. Who is the intended audience for this article? What aspects of language and sentence structure support your opinion?
   The audience is anyone interested in science or science fiction — both fans and those who don't watch Star Trek. Tone and vocabulary as noted above are evidence of this.

Expansion

Project Option
The *Enterprise* needs a new commanding officer. Have students conduct an interstellar search to come up with the perfect candidate for the job. In teams of two or three, have them create a character, visually demonstrate what the character looks like, and write a point-form outline detailing the character's personality, any special abilities of his/her race, and specific skills. Once the characters have been created, have the class determine the necessary characteristics and skills of a commanding officer. Select the candidate that most closely matches the profile identified.

Speaking (SB p. 66)

Aims/Skills
- use descriptive language
- create an effective commercial

Writing (SB p. 66)

Aims/Skills
- write concise, informative descriptions
- use precise vocabulary
- create an effective and visually appealing brochure

> **ONE STEP AHEAD**
>
> Working in teams, have students look through magazines, newspapers, and brochures to pick out five advertisements that they find the most appealing. Students should identify the features of the advertisements that make them effective and then use these criteria as they create their own brochures.

Grammar Focus 1 (SB pp. 67–68)

> **ONE STEP AHEAD**
>
> Please note that there is a typing mistake in the first printing of the Student Book instructions for Exercise A. There are only four noun clauses in the paragraph.

Exercise A (SB p. 67)

1. Read the following paragraph and identify the four noun clauses.

   On *Star Trek: The Next Generation*, one of the ship's officers is an android named Lieutenant Commander Data. He is a human-looking robot whose actions indicate that he has all the capabilities of a self-aware super computer; however, he lacks human emotions. At a recent concert on cybernetics, the president of the American Association for Artificial Intelligence revealed that the creation of an android like Mr. Data is the ultimate goal of his field of technology. At this point, scientists are unable to say whether it can actually be done. Watching Commander Data weekly on television allows us to imagine what it might be like if we were to co-exist with androids in the future.

2. Examine the sentences that contain the noun clauses. What function does each noun clause have in the sentence?

   Each noun clause is subordinate and answers the question what?.

3. All the noun clauses in this paragraph function as *objects* in the sentences and answer the question *what?*

Exercise B (SB p. 68)

Change each question in parentheses to a noun clause.

EXAMPLES: (What are the real costs of technological advances?)
Many people do not know *what the real costs of technological advances are.*
(Will there be enough jobs for everyone in the future?)
No one can predict *whether there will be enough jobs for everyone in the future?*

1. (Which computer should he buy?) John doesn't understand *which computer he should buy.*
2. (Where will the jobs of the future be?) We can't imagine *where the jobs of the future will be.*
3. (Who is the best science fiction writer?) Liam asked *who the best science fiction writer is.*
4. (What career should they choose?) Many teenagers don't know *what career they should choose.*
5. (When will androids be possible?) Who knows *when androids will be possible.*
6. (Should all students learn to use computers?) Schools need to decide *if all students should learn to use computers.*
7. (Do you like to read science fiction?) I would like to know *if you like to read science fiction.*
8. (Is there any truth in science fiction?) Many people question *if there is any truth in science fiction.*
9. (Do we need to worry about the effects of technological advances?) I'm not really sure *whether we need to worry about the effects of technological advances.*
10. (Will people live on Mars some day?) I wonder *if people will live on Mars some day.*

Grammar In Use (SB p. 68)

Complete the following sentences with a noun clause.

EXAMPLE: Scientists observe . . .
Scientists observe *that some of the technological equipment featured on Star Trek is not feasible in the future.*

Possible answers:

1. The show's writers do their best to guarantee *that the scientific aspects of the show are as accurate as possible.*
2. Not all scientists agree *that the science errors in Star Trek are forgiveable for the sake of entertainment.*
3. In the future scientists will announce *how close they are to actually developing an android.*
4. Recent advances in computer technology mean *that micro-sized watch computers will soon be available.*

5. In the next 200 years, scientists will discover *that all diseases can be cured.*

6. As medical science makes new advances, many people assume *that their lives will be improved.*

7. In order to make the show work in a one-hour format, Roddenberry realized *that he had to take some liberties with real science.*

8. Many people fear *what the future holds.*

9. Educators recognize *that education is the key to unlocking the future.*

10. It's not too difficult to imagine *what numerous changes will affect our lives in the future.*

Workbook Practice: Grammar Focus 1 Exercises A–D (WB pp. 40–41)
Grammar Expansion (use of "so" replacing "that" in noun clause in response to yes/no questions) Exercises E and F (WB pp. 41–42)

Vocabulary 1 (SB p. 68)

Aims/Skills
- recognize common noun + preposition collocations
- identify common noun + preposition collocations found in scientific literature

Answer Key
1. When learning new vocabulary, it is important to learn words that often go together. Use a good dictionary to find the prepositions commonly used after the following nouns. You will come across these combinations often in scientific literature.

a) a debate *about / for / on*
b) a degree *in*
c) an argument *against / for / about*
d) an analysis *of*
e) an example *of*
f) a reputation *for*
g) an experiment *in*
h) an observation *about / of*
i) an article *about / for / on*
j) an investigation *of / into*
k) an examination *of*
l) research *in / into / on*

Workbook Practice: Vocabulary 1 Exercises A–B (WB p. 42)
Vocabulary Expansion (idiomatic expressions) Exercise C (WB p. 43)

Listening 1 (SB p. 69)

See Tapescript 5.a

Aims/Skills
- listen for specific information
- recognize expressions used to clarify, jump into a conversation, and show disagreement
- identify tone and vocabulary to determine the relationship among characters
- make inferences from details

Focused Listening (SB p. 69)

You will hear a conversation amongst three friends. During their lunch break, they are discussing what they did the previous evening. As you listen, put a checkmark beside any expressions you hear that you listed in your chart. Add any other expressions that you have not already listed.

Expressions from the conversation on the cassette:

Expressions to Clarify
So what you're saying is . . .
Are you saying . . .?
Let's put it this way . . .
Do you think . . .?
Actually . . .

Expressions to Jump into a Conversation
Wait a minute . . .
Now that's . . .
And the . . .
Stop right there . . .

Expressions to Show Disagreement
No. I don't like . . .
How can you say that?
Oh, come on.
You're wrong.
You don't really believe that do you?
You expect me to believe . . .

Expansion

Role Play
The expressions in the listening activity are all very informal due to the nature of the conversation. Have students come up with several formal expressions for each category, identify a situation where a conversation or discussion using those expressions might occur, write a dialogue, and then role play it for the class. Some suggestions might include a televised debate about the impact that shows like *Star Trek* have on young people, or a discussion panel of experts giving their informed opinions about different aspects of *Star Trek*.

R eading 2 (SB pp. 69–71)

Note-Taking (SB p. 69)

Read each paragraph in the excerpts and then write one or two sentences expressing the main idea of each paragraph in your own words.

Possible answers:

Excerpt 1

Paragraph 1. *We view the future as an extension of the present.*

Paragraph 2. *Although we base our future predictions on existing trends, the reality may be that the future is based on something else entirely.*

Paragraph 3. *Scientific advances in the future could have totally devastating effects.*

Paragraph 4. *Scientists' ability to manipulate genes and distort nature's course will change every aspect of nature. By controlling nature, we are ultimately defeating ourselves.*

Paragraph 5. *Changes in genetics will have a tremendous impact on our future. The future of diseases will also be affected by gene manipulation.*

Paragraph 6. *Trying to conquer nature forces us to be out of tune with it, resulting in diseases.*

Paragraph 7. *Prevention may be the answer, not cures.*

Excerpt 2

Paragraph 1. *In the 22nd century, we are driven to master nature for our own purposes.*

Paragraph 2. *Space travel may give us a better perspective on our planet.*

Paragraph 3. *Travel between Earth and Mars will be common in the next millennium.*

Paragraph 4. *The Martian Cycler will carry up to 52 people to recreational resorts.*

Paragraph 5. *We hold the power to shape the future in our hands.*

Expansion

Creating and Evaluating Inventions

Most inventions are actually improvements on items that already exist or they combine aspects of existing objects to create something new. Have students "build" on an existing object(s) to invent a new object that will greatly improve students' personal lifestyles. Have them present their ideas for inventions to the class. A panel from the class should act as judges who will give out funding for the creation of new inventions based on their usefulness and how they will impact individuals' lives.

To determine criteria for usefulness, have students identify the five objects (inventions) that they use the most in their lives and why these objects are very useful, (e.g., computer: written communications, accessing information easily and quickly, reasonably affordable, easily connects people, runs a variety of software packages, essential for work, etc.).

Discuss the Vocabulary (SB p. 71)

Reading from context, discuss the meaning of the following words:

millennium — *a period of 1000 years*
existential — *pertaining to human existence*
plethora — *large amount, excess*
adversary — *enemy*
cyclaport — *docking station*

Expansion

Creating Hybrids (Reproducible 5.2)

Cut up enough copies of Reproducible 5.2 so that each team of 3–4 students has a set. Have students turn the pictures face down in a pile. Each team acts as a group of genetic scientists who will create a cross-species or new hybrid of animal. Have teams draw sets of two animals from the pile and decide how they will combine the best aspects of both animals to create their hybrid. Each team can present its best "new creation" to the class, detailing the new animal's looks and characteristics.

W riting (SB p. 71)

Aims/Skills

- write a letter of inquiry
- write an expository paragraph

ONE STEP AHEAD

When writing a letter of request, suggest students adhere to the following guidelines:

1) make the specific request immediately

2) give any background information or ask any questions necessary to clarify the request

3) avoid wordiness

4) clearly identify what action the reader is to take and indicate appreciation for that action

Before having students write the expository paragraph, you may want to cover the section on expository paragraphs in the Workbook (pp. 46–47).

 Exercise A (SB p. 72)

Identify the noun clauses in the following sentences and determine their functions.

1. The belief is that we will have developed the capability to live on other planets in the next 200 years. *complement of verb "be"*

2. I would like to enquire about whether engineers really think scientists can recreate gravity. *after a preposition*

3. It's because of the dangers of overusing prescription drugs that many people are turning to alternative medicines. *with the subject "it"*

4. It seems that people will increasingly question the value of certain medical advances in the coming century. *with the subject "it"*

5. What the future will hold for our grandchildren is only speculation at this point. *as the subject of the sentence*

6. I was amazed that the authors thought we would have recreational sites in outer space. *after an adjective that expresses a feeling or attitude*

7. The fact that there is no gravity on other planets remains a challenge. *after a noun*

8. It is obvious that we are not satisfied to let nature rule. *with the subject "it"*

9. Have they reached a decision on who will govern Mars? *after a preposition*

10. Whether we will be able to live peacefully with nature remains to be seen. *as the subject of a sentence*

 Exercise B (SB pp. 72–73)

Write new sentences with noun clauses by matching the ideas in Column A with the appropriate sentences in Column B.

Column A	Column B
1. humankind is threatening its own existence	a) I believe it.
2. space travel to Mars will be possible	b) You may be sure of this.
3. a cure for cancer may be found	c) It seems possible.
4. many diseases are a result of human actions	d) We think so.
5. how their research will affect our future	e) Scientists show no concern about it.
6. the more we know, the less we know	f) We know that.
7. future medicine will focus on prevention	g) It is a well-known fact.

Possible answers:

We know that humankind is threatening its own existence.

We think that space travel to Mars will be possible.

It seems possible that a cure for cancer may be found.

It is a well-known fact that many diseases are a result of human actions.

Scientists show no concern for how their research will affect our future.

You may be sure that the more we know, the less we know.

I believe that future medicine will focus on prevention.

Workbook Practice: Grammar Focus 2 Exercises A–E (WB pp. 44–45)

Expansion

Grammar Application
Have students look at some science magazines and select a short article that interests them. They could identify all the noun clauses in the article and determine their functions.

Listening 2 (SB pp. 73-74)

See Tapescript 5.b

Aim/Skill
• listen for details

Focused Listening (SB p. 74)

Listen for the answers to the following questions.

1. By what "unusual method" was Dolly created?
   The scientists took a mammary gland cell and fused it to the egg of another sheep to produce an identical twin of the original sheep — that is, cloning.

2. What new scientific understanding have we gained through this experiment?
   The same technique could be used to copy humans.

3. Why might the researchers be afraid of being identified?
   They thought animal rights activists might want to seek revenge for the experiments with sheep.

4. Is Dr. Alan Colman sure that his research will have no negative impact on humankind?
   He acknowledged that it would be exceedingly difficult but technically possible for some tin-pot dictator to clone himself.

> **Expansion**

Debate
Have students divide into two teams to debate the pros and cons of genetic manipulation.

Aims/Skills
• determine the meaning of roots
• define words from context
• form words

Answer Key

A. Many scientific words in English have common roots which often originate from the Greek. With a partner, discuss the meanings of the italicized words in the following sentences. Then see if you can determine the meaning of the roots in the list below. If you need help, refer to a dictionary.

Meanings of roots:
a. bio — *connected with life and living things*
b. -graph — *picture; something written or drawn*
c. patho — *suffering, disease*
d. astro — *relating to the stars or outer space*
e. auto — *of or by oneself; independently*
f. cyclo — *circular*
g. dyn — *power or force*
h. poly — *many*
i. geo — *relating to the Earth*

> **Workbook Practice:** Vocabulary 2 Exercises A–B
> (WB pp. 45–46)

Process Writing (WB pp. 46-47)

The expository paragraph is used to explain or analyze an idea. The Workbook contains an explanation, exercises, and a checklist.

Unit Reflection (SB p. 75)

It would be helpful to divide the newsletter into categories so students can be more focused in identifying the developments in science and technology in those specific areas. Some categories might include: computer technology, communication technology, transportation technology, gene manipulation, disease prevention/cure, medicine, etc.

> **Helpful Internet Resources**

Key word search: Star Trek, cloning

Two useful sites directly related to the themes in this unit are:

http://home.wxs.nl/~cavdwaal/startrek/a-z/a-z.html
The Ultimate *Star Trek* Collection: contains almost everything you could possibly want to know about *Star Trek* and its spin-offs.

http://www.acs.ucalgary.ca/~browder/cloning.html
The Brave New World of Mammation Cloning: contains information and links to many different aspects of the Dolly cloning issue.

UNIT 6

It Stands to Reason

OVERVIEW

Theme: Human Intelligence

Topics:
- brain teasers and other puzzles SB pp. 76–78
- intelligence and intelligence testing (Reading 1) SB pp. 79–82
- speeches by famous political figures (Listening 1) SB pp. 85–87
- solving a murder mystery (Reading 2) SB pp. 88–90
- the problem-solving process SB p. 93

Vocabulary:
Student Book
analogy
analysis
argument
conclusions
deduce
ignorance
ingenuity
logic
potential
rational
reasoning
riddle
spatial
wisdom

Phrasal verbs:
account for
bring about
figure out
find out
focus on
work towards

Workbook
knowledge
opinion
physical
puzzle

Expressions of Cause and Effect:
because of
causes
forced to
impose
lead to
result from
result in
source

Grammar:
If Statements (Conditionals) (SB pp. 83–84)
Modals of Deduction, Expectation, and Probability (SB pp. 91–92)
Grammar Expansion — *If* Statements with Modals (WB pp. 52–54)

Process Writing:
Cause and Effect Paragraphs (WB pp. 55–57)

ONE STEP AHEAD

This unit may be challenging for some students because of the subject matter. Teaching notes therefore include suggestions for varying or simplifying some activities, and for helping students work through activities step-by-step. Let your students know that in many cases the attempt and reasoning process are more important than finding the right answer.

Getting Started

Have students work in pairs or small teams to complete the domino activity on pages 76 and 77 of the Student Book. Instruct them to cover the answers at the bottom of page 77 so they aren't tempted to look at them. Explain the instructions and model the first match. Discuss why the bottom of domino A matches the top of domino I. When taking up the answers, have students explain why their matches work. Then continue with the discussion questions at the top of page 76.

Vocabulary (SB p. 78)

Aims/Skills
- use themed vocabulary in context
- use words in various grammatical forms

Answer Key

Below are a number of words associated with the subject of intelligence. Fill in the blanks using the appropriate words.

1. Her *reasoning* in this case is faulty. She clearly did not understand all the facts.
2. The comparison of the human brain to a vast computer is a common *analogy*.
3. Despite her high IQ, the woman never realized her full *potential*.
4. "What can we *deduce* from the facts?" asked the detective.
5. The effective problem-solver goes beyond logic to solve problems. She uses *ingenuity*.
6. His *ignorance* of the facts of the case prevented him from solving it.
7. Einstein said, "*Wisdom* is more important than knowledge."

8. The danger of publishing scientific studies in mainstream newspapers is that people may draw false *conclusions*.

9. Use *logic* to solve this brain teaser.

10. A thorough *analysis* of the clues led the detective to the killer.

11. How to determine the suspect's innocence remains a *riddle*.

12. His speech was weakened by his unconvincing *argument*.

13. He made a *rational* decision based on the facts.

14. This map reading activity is designed to develop your *spatial* reasoning.

 One Step Beyond (SB p. 78)

Try this test of your word knowledge. The answer to each of the questions below is one of the 14 words in the bull's eye target. As you hit each answer, you may cross it off, since no word in the target is used more than once. When all the questions have been answered, the three unused words can be arranged to form a popular English proverb.

Which word:

1. has five syllables? *ingenuity*

2. uses an *s* in British spelling, but a *z* in North American spelling? *analyze*

3. without its last letter makes a word that is the opposite of *digital*? *analogy*

4. is a verb that in its noun form adds *-tion*? *deduce*

5. is an adjective that relates to the position of objects and the distances between them? *spatial*

6. rhymes with a word that is a musical instrument popular in country music? *riddle*

7. can mean the ending of a story? *conclusion*

8. without its third syllable means *purpose*? *reasoning*

9. is a noun, but adds the suffix *-ative* in its adjective form? *argument*

10. contains the following smaller words: *is, sow, do,* and *mow*? *wisdom*

11. can also be associated with energy in physics? *potential*

Proverb: *Ignorance is bliss.*

Workbook Practice: Vocabulary 1 Exercises A–B (WB pp. 48–49)

Aims/Skills

• complete an IQ quiz
• take notes from a reading
• draw inferences from a reading
• read a chart
• read for main ideas

ONE STEP AHEAD

Are You A Genius?
This IQ quiz was taken from *Reader's Digest* magazine. It may be quite challenging and take your students between 30 minutes to an hour to complete. While some students will enjoy the challenge, others may find it intimidating. Here are some suggestions to reduce your students' stress:

(1) Try assigning this pre-reading activity for homework and tell students not to worry about completing it, but just to answer what questions they can. Let them know that they will not be graded on this quiz and that you will not ask them to share their scores. It is the process that's important, not completing the task or getting all of the right answers.

(2) Alternately, have students work in small teams and let them spend half an hour in class to answer what they can and to think about the process.

Note-Taking (SB p. 80)

Review good note-taking strategies with students, especially how much detail to include in notes. Later in the "Main Ideas" section on page 82, students are asked to share their notes and work together to ensure that they have covered the main ideas. They can also use their notes to write the summary suggested in the Writing section (page 82).

 Comprehension Check (SB p. 82)

Read each statement below and decide whether the reading supports the statement (S), refutes the statement (R), or neither supports nor refutes the statement (N).

1. **S** *(lines 38–42)* Men generally do better than women on IQ tests.

2. **R** *(lines 33–36, 47–49)* An IQ test can predict how successful someone will be as a business leader.

3. **N** *(the reading suggests that the tests may be culturally and socially biased)* Minorities generally receive lower scores on IQ tests because they are disadvantaged in learning.

4. **R** *(lines 63–68)* Teachers are the most objective assessors of a person's intelligence.

5. **N** *(the reading doesn't address this point)* People who have low IQ scores usually have exceptional abilities in music or math.

6. **S** (*chart on page 81*) According to commonly accepted categories of intelligence, as many people are below average intelligence as are above average intelligence.

 One Step Beyond (SB p. 82)

1. What are the two opposing definitions of intelligence discussed in this reading?
One definition defines intelligence as a single entity (the basic mental abilities of a person) that can be measured without regard to what has been learned. (lines 17–19)
The second definition views humans as having multiple intelligences such as spatial, musical, personal, and athletic intelligences that can be influenced by culture. In the second definition intelligence is "the ability to solve problems, or to create products, that are valued within one or more cultural settings." (lines 80–90)

2. The reading states that traditional IQ tests may be biased towards the white male. What implications might this have for our society?
Possible answers:
White males may be favoured to get jobs and to get into universities and other institutions or positions where IQ is measured to predict work or academic performance. Educational and work opportunities for minority groups may be limited. The bias may also cause white males to view themselves as intellectually superior to people of minority, and cause people of minority to view themselves as intellectually inferior. Minorities may be prevented from making significant contributions because of limited opportunities, and they may be at a disadvantage when it comes to achieving financial and social success.

Culture Note

Intelligence and ways of thinking may be defined differently in different cultures, as noted by Dr. Howard Gardner. One culture may define intelligence as being skilled at solving verbal, quantitative, and analytical problems. Another culture may define it as knowing how to treat people politely in different situations, or respecting the traditions of elders. Consequently, applying the same definition of intelligence and the same measuring instruments to all cultures may not be appropriate. Similarly, ways of thinking vary from culture to culture. One culture may value a linear, sequential way of thinking, whereas another culture may value a more circular or organic approach to thinking. Invite discussion with your students.

Writing (SB p. 82)

Aim/Skill
• write a summary
Refer students to the notes they took from the reading.

Speaking (SB p. 82)

Aims/Skills
• present an argument
• support an argument
• state an opinion

Students will be able to use the knowledge gained from the IQ quiz and the reading in this debate.

Language Note

Various terms labelled as "politically correct" are coming into increasing use in English. "Politically correct" language avoids terms that may be offensive to particular groups or that may be seen as derogatory (although some terms are controversial as they can be seen as going too far in trying to avoid offence). Examples include the following.

No longer used	*Politically correct term*
mentally retarded	mentally/developmentally challenged
handicapped	person with a disability or physically challenged
deaf	hearing impaired
blind	visually impaired
housewife	homemaker
negro (used only in specific historical contexts)	Black or African Canadian/American

Students may have heard or be aware of other terms.

**G**rammar Focus 1 (SB pp. 83–84)

Exercise A (SB p. 83)

> **ONE STEP AHEAD**
> Refer students to the reading "Intelligence: The Human Miracle" if they have difficulty completing the sentences.

 Answer Key
Complete the sentences.

Possible answers:

1. *If your IQ is over 120*, you are in the superior intelligence category.

2. If you are in the low average intelligence category, *your IQ falls between 80 and 90.*

3. If a student was failing in France at the turn of the century, *he or she was expelled from school.*

4. *If you don't read Howard Gardner's book Frames of Mind, you will have missed an interesting book about human intelligence.*
5. *If we believe that we are intelligent, we are more likely to act intelligently.*

 ## Exercise B (SB p. 84)

There are ten sentence parts below. Some express causes and some results. Rebuild the sentences by matching causes with results and insert *if* at the appropriate point.

Note: Clauses may be in the reversed order.

1. *We wouldn't be motivated to set our standards high if*
5. *we knew our IQ was low.*

2. *If IQ tests predicted success in life,*
6. *they would be used more readily.*

3. *He wouldn't have become one of the greatest science fiction writers of our time if*
7. *Asimov's professor had been accurate in saying Asimov couldn't write.*

4. *If women and minorities didn't consistently score lower on IQ tests,*
10. *perhaps we wouldn't question the social and cultural biases of the tests.*

8. *If we judged people's value to society based on their IQ,*
9. *the efforts of many great people would go unnoticed.*

> **Workbook Practice:** Grammar Focus 1 Exercises A–D (WB pp. 49–50)

Expansion

Grammar Game
Play this game with the whole class to practise making sentences with "if" statements. First, make up cards with the verbs below.

hear	take care of	ask	see	know
look for	call	find	tell	hold
laugh at	notice	obey	question	resist
answer	write	send	time	warn
yell for	bet	bring	catch	choose
draw	meet	pay	teach	radio
remember	recognize	go with	fly with	drive with
face	show	beg	share with	eat with
think about	threaten	tickle	travel with	translate for
reason with	carry	date	speak to	accept
advise	argue with	check	believe	calm
identify	chase	complain to	dance with	defeat
discourage	entertain	embarrass	forget	force
greet	humour	kiss	introduce	recommend
report	remind	reward	select	support
understand	convince	watch	read to	welcome

Next, divide the class into two teams (A and B) and have them line up in rows. Write this sentence on the blackboard: *If I had listened to her, I wouldn't be in jail now.* Tell students they will each have a chance to choose a card with a verb on it. They will have to change the verb "listen to" in the "if" clause to the verb on their card, then change the result clause to any appropriate result. They can change the time/tense in the result clause, but not in the "if" clause. The content of a result clause cannot be repeated in subsequent turns.

EXAMPLE: with the verb phrase "eat with" the sentence may change in this way
From: If I had listened to her, I wouldn't be in jail now.
To: If I had eaten with her, I wouldn't be hungry now.
Or: If I had eaten with her, I wouldn't have accepted your lunch invitation.

Model the activity with a few verbs before beginning the game. The first student on Team A picks up a card and reads out the verb. Anyone on Team A can respond. If the response is appropriate and grammatically correct (to be decided by Team B), Team A gets a point. If Team A's response is inappropriate or grammatically incorrect, Team B gets a chance to respond. If Team B's response is appropriate and correct, it gets a point. Now the player on Team B follows the same procedure. The Team A and B players then go to the end of the line and the two players next in line choose cards. The game ends when each student has chosen a verb card, after a set time limit, or after a specific score is achieved.

The difficulty level of the game can be increased by imposing a time/tense in the result clause or by adding pronoun or noun cards to replace the object in the "if" clause as well.

 ## Listening 1 (SB pp. 85–87)

See Tapescript 6.a

Aims/Skills
- listen for key messages in a speech
- listen for details
- analyze a speech's impact based on images, language, and tone

Before You Listen (SB p. 86)

In question 3 ("Think of speeches you have heard that have left a lasting impression on you. Discuss, in detail, what makes a good speech."), encourage students to consider the delivery of a speech as well as the speech itself.

Comprehension Check (SB p. 86)

1. What feelings are you left with after listening to this speech? What adjectives would you use to describe the speech?
   Answers may vary.

2. What is the central message of this speech? That is, what is Dr. King asking the people to do? Why is he asking them to do this?
   The central message is the call on people to protest peacefully for what is right (that is, for justice, the end of oppression, and the end of segregation and humiliation).

 ## Focused Listening (SB p. 87)

Listen to the speech again in segments. First read the questions below for each segment, then listen for the answers.

a) **First Segment** Dr. King creates a sense of unity in his audience by discussing two things they all have in common. What are those two things?
   They are American citizens and they believe in democracy.

b) **Second Segment** The title of the speech is "There comes a time when people get tired." What are the people tired of?
   They are tired of being mistreated, segregated, humiliated, and oppressed.

c) **Third Segment** Dr. King asks his people to act. What does he ask them to do?
   He asks the people to protest.

d) **Fourth Segment** In this segment, Dr. King compares the protests of organizations such as the Ku Klux Klan with the protests of blacks. Complete the following chart.

	White Citizens' Councils/Ku Klux Klan	*Black Community of Dr. King*
The group's goal	*fighting for continuation of injustice*	*fighting for the birth of justice*
The group's methods	*lead to violence and lawlessness*	*guided by law and order*
	coercion	*persuasion*
		guided by love and their Christian faith

e) **Fifth Segment** Dr. King is trying to convince his audience that what he is asking them to do is "right." What comparisons does he make to convince the listeners of this?
   He compares their protest for justice with the principles of the Supreme Court, the Constitution of the United States of America, God, and Jesus.

f) **Sixth Segment** In this final segment, Dr. King asks his people to behave in a certain way throughout their struggle. What two contrasting behaviours does he encourage?
   He encourages behaving courageously, yet with dignity and love.

One Step Beyond (SB p. 87)

 Answer Key

Read the transcript of this speech on page 158. The language of formal speeches is quite different from that of everyday conversation. Not only are the words more formal, but the phrases are often very poetic or literary. Using language this way adds to the impact a speech can make on its audience. Martin Luther King, Jr. uses a number of these poetic phrases to create strong images in the listener's mind.

Read the sentences or phrases below and discuss what images they create. Then discuss what they mean and re-write them in simpler, less formal English.

1. "We are here also because of our deep-seated belief that democracy transformed from thin paper to thick action is the greatest form of government on Earth."
   Image: paper versus action = theory versus reality
   Meaning: democracy is not just a word written on a piece of paper, it is a right to act
   Possible re-write: We believe that government that turns the theory of democracy into actions is the best form of government.

2. "We are . . . tired of being kicked about by the brutal feet of oppression."
   Image: oppression = being kicked about by brutal feet; the kicking of any inferior creature (dogs and other animals were kicked. Black slaves were also treated this way.)
   Meaning: we are tired of being treated as inferiors through oppression
   Possible re-write: We are tired of being oppressed.

3. ". . . people get tired of being pushed out of the glimmering sunlight of last July and left standing amid the piercing chill of an Alpine November."
   Image: sunlight = good, cold = bad (July 4th is also Independence Day in America, when the Americans won their independence from Britain.)
   Meaning: we are denied the privileges of white people and get left behind
   Possible re-write: People get tired of being denied the same rights and privileges as white people, and always being left with less.

4. "Let your conscience be your guide."
   Image: conscience = inner voice that tells you what is right
   Meaning: follow that inner voice and you will do right
   Possible re-write: Be guided by your knowledge of what is good.

5. "If we fail to do this, our protest will end up as a meaningless drama on the stage of history."
   Image: drama = event, the stage of history = historical importance
   Meaning: if we don't behave in a peaceful, loving way, our protest will have no historical impact
   Possible re-write: If we don't act peacefully, our protest will be meaningless.

6. "Its memory will be shrouded with the ugly garments of shame."
   Image: shroud = the cloth used to cover a dead body for burial (garment = formal word for clothing)
   Meaning: the shameful actions will cover the good actions
   Possible re-write: It will be remembered as a shameful event.

7. "There lived a great people — a black people — who injected new meaning and dignity into the veins of civilization."
   Image: injection = a needle that puts something into you; veins = the tubes in your body that pump your blood to the heart; civilization = comparison to a living body or heart
   Meaning: black people will have put new meaning and life into the heart or core of civilization
   Possible re-write: Black people were a great people. They brought new meaning and dignity to civilization.

Writing (SB p. 87)

Aims/Skills
- write a biography
- explain images in writing

Expansion

A. Famous Quotations
Have students research and select a famous quotation that intrigues them and present the quotation in class, explaining its significance. Alternately, have them write and illustrate the quotation in a meaningful way and display the quotations in the room. Books on famous quotes are available in the library and on the Internet (see Helpful Internet Resources at the end of this unit). Students may also wish to write a meaningful statement of their own, modelled after some famous quotations.

B. Project Option – Famous Historical Figures Around the World
Rather than writing a biography of a famous historical figure, have students complete a project on famous historical figures from around the world. Students could present their projects orally to the class, or use poster board and other methods to display their historical figures around the classroom.

Speaking (SB p. 88)

Aims/Skills
- write a speech
- deliver a speech
- use images and persuasive arguments

In small teams, have students develop criteria to evaluate speeches delivered by their classmates. Students could design a form that they will complete for each speech given; these forms should be given to the presenter (with or without the teacher having skimmed them first). They should provide useful peer feedback to the presenter rather than give a grade.

Reading 2 (SB pp. 88–90)

Aims/Skills
- make logical deductions from a reading
- read for details
- read for clues
- read for facts
- use pictorial clues to understand meaning

Here are some suggestions for guiding your students through this reading.

A. Have students describe the picture of the murder scene in detail before reading (See "Before You Read" activity). You could give them two minutes to look at the picture, then have them close their books and quiz them on the following details.

1. On which side of the room is the bed — left or right? *right*
2. What is the time on the clock? *8 o'clock*
3. Is the window in the room covered with curtains or blinds? *blinds*
4. Are the curtains or blinds completely drawn? *no*
5. What is sitting on the mantel? *a glass flask*
6. Is the victim male or female? *male*
7. Is the clock hanging or standing? *hanging*
8. What did you notice lying on the window sill? *flies*
9. Is it day or night? *day*
10. Is the victim's face facing left or right? *right*
11. How many pillows can we see on the bed? *two*

The aim is to get students to see the details as important.

B. Discuss the vocabulary in the glossary on page 90 before students read the text.

C. Have students work with a partner or in small teams to complete the Comprehension Check Part A. Continue with parts B, C, D, and so on, stopping after each activity to discuss answers. The key to solving the mystery is in question 5 b). Encourage students to take notes and chart their information if they wish. This often helps in solving problems.

Comprehension Check (SB p. 90)

A. Get the facts.

1. Before solving the murder, you must be sure of the facts in the case. Complete the chart below:

Victim's name: *Ellington Breese (line 3)*

Victim's occupation: *founder and president of Breese Chemical Works (lines 3–4)*

Place, date, and time of the murder: *in the bedroom of his home near Gravesend (lines 4, 5, 8), June 5, 1925 (line 1), between 11:30 p.m. June 4 and 5:30 a.m. June 5 (calculated from lines 57–59)*

Person who found the body: *his servant (lines 12–13)*

Where and when the body was found: *in his bed at 8:00 a.m. (lines 12–13)*

How the victim died: *inhaling poison gas (lines 5, 18–21)*

Murder weapon: *poison gas (lines 5, 18–21)*

B. Now that you have the facts, consider your suspects.

2. Who are the suspects in this case? *Breese Walters, Ellington's nephew, and Adam Boardman, Ellington's confidential secretary (lines 38–40)*

3. What possible motives might each have for killing Ellington Breese? *Money from Ellington's will. Half his estate was divided equally between his nephew (Breese Walters) and his secretary (Adam Boardman), and the other half was bequeathed to charity. (lines 47–53)*

4. Does each suspect have an alibi? What is it? *Both suspects have a partial alibi. Adam Boardman had been with Ellington Breese, who was in bed with a flu, until about 11:30 p.m. He left the house at about 11:45 p.m. as confirmed by Mrs. Grew, Ellington's nurse. He could have killed Ellington Breese during the time he was with him. (lines 67–83)*
Breese Walters had been in Manchester all day. He got back to London in time for supper at his club, and went to Ellington's house at one o'clock in the morning. Mrs. Grew, Ellington's nurse, spoke to Breese Walters and confirms his arrival time. Walters told her he was going straight to bed. Mrs. Grew was awake until 2:30 a.m. Breese Walters could have killed Ellington Breese after 2:30 a.m. (lines 84–101)

C. The next step is to take a closer look at possible clues.

5. a) In point-form, describe the crime scene in detail. *Answers will vary.*
   b) Are there any clues at the crime scene that might be significant in solving this crime? If so, highlight them.
   Possible answers:
   - *Mr. Breese was in bed — suggests there was no struggle*
   - *A glass flask, the kind used in chemistry, was found with the stopper missing — suggests it was murder and that it was a poisonous chemical*
   - *There were dead flies on the windowsill. Why were they there?*

D. Now make some deductions based on the clues.

6. According to the police, what do you need to determine to discover which suspect committed the murder?
   If the murder happened before 11:30 p.m., Adam Boardman was the killer. If it happened after midnight, it was Breese Walters.

7. What clues can help you to determine this? (HINT: Consider the crime scene.)
   The significant clue is the flies on the windowsill. Everything in the room died instantly upon release of the poisonous gas. Therefore, the flies were by the window when the poison was released. Why would the flies have been by the window?

E. One Step Beyond — Finally, solve the crime.

8. Who killed Ellington Breese?
   Breese Walters

9. How did you deduce this?
   The murder must have taken place after dawn.
   Consequently, Breese Walters must have been the killer.
   We know that Ellington died after dawn for the following reasons.
   Fact: Everything in the room died instantly upon the release of the poisonous gas. (confirmed by experts in the chemical lab)
   Fact: The flies were on the windowsill, with the blinds partially drawn. (witnessed by the servant who found the body and police)
   Fact: Flies gravitate to light.
   Deduction: At night the room would have been dark. As it was getting light outside, a bit of light would have shone through the window and the flies would have gravitated to the window. If the gas was released when the flies were by the window, it must have been lighter outside than inside. Consequently, Ellington Breese was killed in the early morning hours rather than before 11:30 p.m.

Grammar Focus 2 (SB pp. 91–92)

ONE STEP AHEAD

You may wish to spend a little time discussing this question: What is the difference in meaning between "can't have" and "couldn't have?" The difference is in a suggested nuance. Both imply impossibility in the past based on deduction. But "can't have" suggests this conclusion was drawn in the present, whereas "couldn't have" suggests this conclusion was drawn in the past.

can't have = "I realize now that it was impossible then"

couldn't have = "I realized in the past that it was impossible then"

Exercise A (SB p. 91)

Rewrite the statements below using a modal to show the indicated degree of certainty.

1. The victim has four brothers. (95% certain)
   The victim must have four brothers.

2. The coroner didn't determine the exact time of death. (impossibility)
   The coroner couldn't have determined the exact time of death.

3. The murderer was not a family member. (50% based on deduction)
   The murderer might not have been a family member.

4. She didn't see him walking into the library. (impossibility)
   She couldn't have seen him walking into the library.

5. The maid saw the murderer. (75% certain)
   The maid could have seen the murderer.

Exercise B (SB p. 92)

Read the facts. What can you conclude or expect? Use modals in your answers.

Possible answers:

1. A letter from Belgium takes about five days to arrive in Canada. Mr. Van Riet sent a letter to his granddaughter about seven days ago.
   Conclusion: Mr. Van Riet's granddaughter must have / should have received the letter by now.

2. Nicholas and Christopher have been practising their piano duet for two months in preparation for the music festival today.
   Conclusion: They must play the duet well.

3. Mrs. Humphreys was told that Pia and Iris live in Zurich.
   When the girls arrive in Canada on a school exchange and stay with Mrs. Humphreys, she is surprised to hear them speaking German. She expected them to speak French.
   Conclusion: Mrs. Humphreys must not have known that German is spoken in Zurich.

4. Jennifer lives in New Brunswick.
   She is accused of stealing her neighbour's rubber hose.
   The hose was stolen last Saturday.
   Jennifer was in Montreal last weekend.
   Conclusion: Jennifer couldn't have stolen the hose.

5. An airplane crashes on the border between Canada and the United States.
   The survivors are buried in Canada.
   Conclusion: The survivors can't be buried in Canada because survivors aren't dead.

6. A man married his widow's sister.
   The man couldn't have married his widow's sister because if he had a widow, he would be dead.

Workbook Practice and Expansion: Grammar Focus 2 Exercise A (WB p. 52)
Grammar Expansion ("If" Statements with Modals) Exercise B, Exercise C (with reading "Becoming Better at Problem-Solving"), Exercises D and E (WB pp. 52–54)

Vocabulary 2 (SB pp. 92–93)

Aims/Skills
- identify phrasal verbs
- reconstruct sentences in appropriate word order
- guess or deduce meaning from context

Answer Key

1. The human mind is capable of making sense out of what appears to be senseless. The words in the following sentences have been arranged in alphabetical order. Each sentence contains a phrasal verb. Put the words in the correct order, identify the phrasal verb, and guess its meaning. [HINT: Look for words that form logical phrases first, then put the phrases in order.]

   a) a abilities. focus intellectual IQ measuring on person's tests
   IQ tests focus on measuring a person's intellectual abilities.

   b) couldn't figure how logic out puzzle. solve teacher The the to
   The teacher couldn't figure out how to solve the logic puzzle.

   c) able account for his not on performance poor student test. The the to was
   The student was not able to account for his poor performance on the test.

   d) a education education equitable is ministry more system. The towards working
   The education ministry is working towards a more equitable education system.

   e) a about bring Dr. free hard King Luther Martin of prejudice. society to worked
   Dr. Martin Luther King worked hard to bring about a society free of prejudice.

   f) and any between find graduate if infant intelligence. out psychology relationship student stimulation The to there wanted was
   The graduate psychology student wanted to find out if there was any relationship between infant stimulation and intelligence.

2. Write a synonym for each of the phrasal verbs.
   Note: Look for synonyms and/or synonymous expressions. Some of the phrasal verbs have more than one meaning. Focus on the meaning as used in exercise 1 above.
   Possible answers:
   focus on = *pay attention to*
   figure out = *solve*
   account for = *explain*
   work towards = *try to achieve*
   bring about = *cause something to happen*
   find out = *determine, discover*

3. Write a sentence using each of the phrasal verbs above.
   Answers will vary.

Expansion

Word Quiz (Reproducible 6.1)
Have students work in small teams to complete the Word Quiz (Reproducible 6.1). Give them 20 minutes to complete the quiz. The team with the most correct answers wins (count unfinished questions as incorrect).

 Answer Key

1. a) *wisdom* — all other words have 3 syllables
   b) *logic* — all other words are adjectives
   c) *spatial* — all other words are ways of thinking
   d) *analysis* — all other words begin with "r"

2. a) *physical* — ignorance and knowledge are opposites
   b) *conclusion* — rational is a type of argument
   (noun collocations)
   a rational argument / a logical conclusion

3. a) *deduce*
   b) *analyze / analyse*
   c) *reason*
   d) *argue*
   e) *conclude*

4. a) *about* face   phrasal verb: *bring about*
   b) *on* track   phrasal verb: *focus on*
   c) *out* and about   phrasal verb: *figure out / find out*

If you think your students will find this activity too difficult, give them a list of the words (answers) in random order and have them choose from the list.

Speaking (SB p. 93)

Aims/Skills
- follow the steps in a flow chart
- restate a problem
- analyze a problem's causes or effects
- brainstorm ideas
- suggest solutions
- express consequences
- express opinions

Have students work in small teams. You can expand on this activity by having students submit written work throughout the problem-solving process. For example, have students submit an analysis of the problem, the criteria for the solution, the solution (with reasons), and how the solution will be implemented and evaluated. This could take the form of a group or individual written report. Alternately, students could present their analysis and recommendations orally to the class.

Process Writing (WB pp. 55–57)

The Workbook covers writing cause and effect paragraphs. It includes exercises that develop the thought processes involved in identifying causes and effects and in supporting opinions with statistics, anecdotes, definitions, and reasoning. An editing exercise and useful Cause and Effect Paragraph checklist are also included.

Unit Reflection (SB p. 93)

"It stands to reason" is an intelligence-related idiomatic expression. Have students list as many other intelligence-related idioms or proverbs as they can. Examples include:

use your noodle
rhyme or reason
pick your brains
think tank
think before you leap
brainstorm
common sense
for argument's sake
see it in your mind's eye
read your mind
fly in the face of reason
off the top of your head
jump to a conclusion

Helpful Internet Resources

There are several interesting sites related to speeches, famous quotations, and intelligence.

Key word search: speeches, quotations, idioms, intelligence, puzzles

http://www.pacificnet.net/~sperling/cookie.pl.cgi
ESL Quote Page: a collection of random quotes and proverbs from around the world

http://www.starlingtech.com/quotes/
The Quotations Page: a rich site of quotations with an easy search tool

http://speeches.com/index.shtml
A site for everything you need to make a speech. Links to thousands of other speeches on the Web

http://access5.digex.net/~nuance/keystep1.html
Key Steps to an Effective Presentation: interesting article by Stephen Eggleston

http://www.tagsys.com/Ads/strategic/tencommpres.html
Ten Commandments of Presentations: a very interesting site with easy-to-follow steps to effective presentations. Click on previous articles for other tips on effective oral communication.

http://www.Tests_Surveys_Polls/Quizzes_ and _Tests/Interactive_Quizzes_and_Tests/IQ_Tests
A site with links to IQ tests, brainteasers, and puzzles

UNIT 7
All the Rage

OVERVIEW

Theme: Popular Culture

Topics:
- North American popular culture trends in the 20th century (Reading 1) SB pp. 94–99
- popular books/films (*Live and Let Die* by Ian Fleming — James Bond) (Listening 1) SB pp. 104–106
- popular TV programs (*The Simpsons*) (Reading 2) SB pp. 106–109
- pop culture heroes/popular music ("Superman's Song" by Crash Test Dummies) (Listening 2) SB p. 110; Princess Diana (essay WB p. 64)

Vocabulary:

Student Book

condemn	pretentious
cope	role model
craze	trauma
dysfunctional	trend
fad	trivia
folly	
gimmick	
hype	
icon	
idol	
mania	
obnoxious	
omnipresent	
opportunist	
outlet	

Grammar:

To + Base Verbals (SB pp. 101–104)

To + Base Verbals in the Perfect Tense (WB pp. 61–62)

Process Writing:

Five-Paragraph Essay Format (WB pp. 62–67)

Getting Started (Reproducible 7.1)

Individually, give students 10 minutes to complete a short survey (use Reproducible 7.1). Students do not put their names on the surveys. Then have students gather in teams of about six and in random order, distribute the completed surveys to the teams. Each team should tally the results on the surveys and report these to the class. How many people gave the same answers? As a class, list the most popular answers to the questions. Now generate a discussion of why so many students chose the same answers. What is it that makes something popular? How do you know what's hot? Students may discuss advertising, television, word of mouth, mass appeal, etc. All of these points are relevant. Then direct students to the opening activities on pages 94–95 of the Student Book.

Unit Opening Pages (SB pp. 94–95)

 ***Answer Key***

1. Motoring — "A Rich Man's Toy" (1900s–1910s) *Photo: p. 95 bottom left*
2. The Mah-Jong Craze (1920s) *Photo: p. 94 bottom left*
3. Gangster Movie Madness (1930s) *Photo: p. 95 bottom right*
4. Swooning over Sinatra (1940s) *Photo p. 94 bottom right*
5. The Car Cramming Craze (1950s) *Photo: p. 95 top left*
6. The Funky Look (1960s) *Photo: p. 95 top right*
7. Disco Fever — John Travolta (1970s) *Photo p. 94 top right*
8. Nintendo™ Fever (1980s) *Photo: p. 95 centre left*
9. *The X-Files* Craze (1990s) *Photo: p. 95 centre right*

Reading 1 (SB pp. 96–99)

(SB pp. 96–99)

Aims/Skills

- read for specific information
- read to select appropriate introduction and conclusion
- understand how vocabulary affects tone
- read for main ideas

ONE STEP AHEAD

If you are having your students work through the Process Writing program in the Workbook, refer them to pages 62–63 first to read about the basic components of an essay, focusing on the introductory and concluding paragraphs. Alternately, refer students to the Introductory Paragraph Checklist on page 75 (Unit 8) and the Conclusion Paragraph Checklist on page 83 (Unit 9) of the Workbook. Students can use these checklists as the criteria by which to judge which introduction and conclusion work best.

Reading (SB pp. 96–99)

You will read an essay about popular culture fads in the 20th century. An essay is made up of three parts: (1) an introductory paragraph, (2) several developmental paragraphs (the body), and (3) a concluding paragraph. Each part has a particular function. The writer of the following essay, "This Craz(e)y Century", wrote two introductions and two conclusions, then couldn't decide which introduction and conclusion worked best. Read the body of the essay first, then choose which introduction and which conclusion (on pages 98 and 99) you think fits best. Be prepared to give your reasons.

*The most suitable introduction for this reading is **Introduction 1**. Introduction 2 does not fit the body of this reading. Its focus is discussing the difference between fads and trends (see last sentence), yet that is not what is discussed in the reading. Introduction 1, on the other hand, focuses on looking at the history of North American fads of the 20th century and how these fads reflect the social, economic, and political issues of the times (see the middle of the paragraph, "Parading through the fads and mania that have won our affections..."). This is an appropriate thesis statement for the reading.*

*The most appropriate conclusion is **Conclusion 2**. Conclusion 1 introduces a new idea (predicting fads and designing products and services that might become fads — see 3rd last line of the paragraph, "Understanding the psyche of the times ..."), one that is not addressed in the reading. Conclusion 2, on the other hand, summarizes and refers to the introductory paragraph and the body, and leaves the reader with a concluding thought, as referred to in the Concluding Paragraph Checklist on page 83 of the Workbook and on page 63.*

Comprehension Check (SB p. 99)

1. What important development marked the change from a society where people worked most of the time to one where people enjoyed more leisure time? *the introduction of the automobile (lines 14–15)*

2. Why did many people resent cars at first? *Cars were seen as a rich man's toy and many of the rich flaunted their cars. Drivers were also reckless. (lines 16–25)*

3. What was Sinatra's appeal? *Some psychologists said his fans were frustrated with love, with many men away at war. Others said his fans had "an urge to feed the hungry," as he was very thin. (lines 48–52)*

4. What is the meaning of "anti-establishment" in the fourth paragraph? *against the established values — at that time the confining values of conservatism (lines 87–90)*

5. Why was cable and video technology so successful in the 1980s? *because of the then-developing trend known as "cocooning," a habit of staying at home to protect against the bad in the world outside (lines 106–111)*

6. What was the impact of video games on the children's entertainment market in the late 1980s? *video games were so popular that they hurt the sales of traditional toys (lines 103–105)*

One Step Beyond (SB p. 99)

1. What is the significance of the (e) in the title "This Craz(e)y Century?" *It's a play on the word "craze," which is a synonym for mania.*

2. Because fads are interests or behaviours that are very popular for a short time, they are associated with strong emotions and high energy. List some of the words and expressions the writer uses to create a "feeling" of energy and emotion. *Answers include: aroused (16), terrorized (20), reckless (21), flaunted (22), exploded (35), fervour (36), hottest (39), hit (39), frenzied (42), squealed (43), swooned (43), thrilled (45), lure (49), frustrated (50), rugged (54), fist-fighting (54), immensely (59), ardent (61), fever (63), ruckus (63), fire (68), outlandish (75), bizzare (84), revolutionary (85), shattered (92), instant (106)*

Language Note

Language is also influenced by popular culture. Words become fads too, i.e., they are very popular for a time and then fall out of favour. For example, *kiddo* (used to address someone in an informal, endearing way) and *swell* (nice, good, great) were popular words of the 1920s; *groovy* (interesting, good) and *far out* (fabulous, great) were popular phrases of the 60s. None of these terms is used often today. Have students brainstorm words that are currently trendy and may fall out of use. Possible words include *dis* (insult) and *cool* (great, good).

Writing (SB p. 99)

Aims/Skills
- write a review
- write a five-paragraph essay

> **ONE STEP AHEAD**
>
> Don't do the criteria checklist if you had students refer to the Process Writing in the Workbook as they completed the Reading exercises above. If you haven't already done so, you may wish to refer your students to the Process Writing section in the Workbook (pp. 62–67) now.

Vocabulary 1 (SB p. 100)

Aims/Skills
- identify words by sounds using picture clues
- match words with their meanings
- use words in sentences
- group words into categories

🔑 Answer Key

1. Below are some picture and letter clues to the pronunciation of words often used in the context of popular culture. Work with a partner to discover the words.

EXAMPLE: – n + d

fan (– n) = fa (+ d) = fad

a) m + – c + ia = *mania*

b) two words:  +

= *role model*

c) + = *idol*

d)  + con = *icon*

e) tr +  = *trend*

f)  – ft + – l = *gimmick*

g)  – p + v + 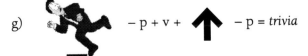 – p = *trivia*

h)  + – p + z = *craze*

highway

i) + p = *hype*

2. Now match the words you deciphered with their meanings below and then write a sentence for each word.

EXAMPLE: f a d

> (informal) something that is very popular for a short period of time

In the late 1980s Teenage Mutant NinjaTurtles™ were a fad. Today they're not even sold any more.

1) a trick or device used to attract attention *f) gimmick*

2) an extreme or abnormally high enthusiasm for a person, thing, or group, e.g., In the 1960s, crowds surrounded the Beatles wherever they went. People screamed and fainted. It was Beatle_____. *a) mania*

3) a person who is admired and looked up to as an example *b) role model*

4) a person who is greatly loved, admired, or respected and almost worshipped like a god *c) idol*

5) to make something sound very important or exciting, exaggerating its good qualities *i) hype*

6) an observable development or change in a situation *e) trend*

7) a very famous person or thing that represents a set of beliefs or a way of life *d) icon*

8) an enthusiastic but often brief interest in something shared by many people, e.g. The car _____ began with the development of the first Model T Ford. *h) craze*

3. Circle the word that doesn't belong in each group below and give a reason for your choice.

a) mania craze fad (gimmick) — *all others are synonyms*

b) icon (hype) idol role model — *all others are people who are admired*

> **Workbook Practice:** Vocabulary 1 Exercises A–C (WB p. 58)

Culture Note

Refer your students to the Trivia Boxes found throughout this unit. North Americans are fascinated by trivia, as evidenced in the popularity of games such as Trivial Pursuit™ and Jeopardy®, and numerous fan page web sites, which abound with trivia.

Trivia Pursuit

Ask students if their native culture shares the North American fascination with trivia. Have them identify pop culture icons (shows, entertainers, etc.) for which there might be fan pages (web sites) containing trivia, or for which they would like to know some trivia. Have them do an Internet search and share some of their "trivia" findings.

Speaking (SB p. 101)

Aims/Skills
- role-play a commercial
- discuss current trends
- brainstorm ideas

Project Option

This speaking activity could be expanded into a larger project.

Phase 1

Have students begin by looking in magazines, newspapers, and flyers, by watching television commercials, and by listening to radio advertisements to identify current trends and habits. The Internet is a good resource for determining current trends (see Helpful Internet Resources at the end of this unit page 63). Students can submit a written report of current trends including photos, illustrations, and sources.

Phase 2

Have students work in teams in class to brainstorm ideas for designing products. Students can submit sketched designs and a rationale for selecting this product which outlines how it reflects current trends. Students can also draw up a marketing plan that (1) identifies the target market with a profile of demographic and psychographic information, and (2) identifies effective ways to market the product, including the selection of appropriate media, promotion plans, etc.

Phase 3

Now students can present their project orally in class and role-play their television commercial. Alternatively, students can videotape their commercial and show the video in class.

Grammar Focus (SB pp. 101–104)

 ## Exercise A (SB p. 101)

Identify the nine *to + base* verbals in the paragraph below.

Feeling stressed is a fact of life for most people and while this may appear to be a problem of our modern times, stress has been around for longer than we realize. Many people are surprised to learn that only 150 years ago the normal work week was 70 hours — very stressful. While it is difficult to avoid stress altogether, it is possible to reduce or manage stress. There are several things we can do to manage the stress caused by our daily obligations. First and foremost, we need to balance the routines of work, family, and school with the enjoyment of our leisure time. Exercise is very effective in relieving stress. However, experts also advise us to participate in fun, sometimes nonsensical activities such as dancing, going to the movies, or simply watching television to relieve stress. This may be why so many people have eagerly embraced such silly fads as car cramming, goldfish swallowing, and collecting pet rocks. Many people participate in the latest craze simply to reduce some of the pressures of daily life.

Note: In the sentence "While it is difficult to avoid stress altogether, it is possible to reduce or manage stress" the verb *manage* is also an infinitive in the sense that the "to" before the verb *reduce* also applies to *manage*. The clause could read, "it is possible to reduce or to manage stress."

 ## Exercise B (SB p. 103)

Fill in the blanks.

Possible answers:

1. It was nice *to hear/to listen to* that song again.
2. It's a *mistake* to think that popular culture isn't important.
3. They went to the video store *to rent/to get/to buy* the latest James Bond film.
4. The idea was to persuade teens *to buy* the product.
5. The band *plans/wants* to release a new album by the end of this year.
6. The children begged *their parents* to buy the latest Nintendo™ system.
7. It's *interesting* to study the fads that were popular in the early 1900s.
8. The company made a *decision* to market the new toy to parents directly instead of to children.

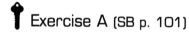 ## Exercise C (SB p. 103)

Write sentences using *to + base* verbals for the sets of key words below. You may use any forms of the key words and add words to your sentence, but do not change the order of the key words.

Possible answers:

1. company / advertising / appeal / teenagers
   The company designs its advertising to appeal to teenagers.
2. teachers / games / educate / children
   Many teachers use games to educate children.
3. parents / television / babysit / children
   Some parents allow the television to babysit their children.
4. teens / like / go / clubs
   Most teens like to go to clubs.
5. difficult / predict / trends
   It's difficult to predict trends.

6. books / discover / history
Read books to discover history.

7. fashion advertisers / models / sell / clothes
Fashion advertisers use models to sell their clothes.

8. not be / old / enjoy / classical music
You're not too old to enjoy classical music.

9. library / sign out / bestseller
Go to your library to sign out the latest bestseller.

10. not easy / learn / play / mah-jong
It's not easy to learn to play mah-jong.

🔑 Grammar In Use (SB pp. 103–104)

Possible answers:

1. What would each client be afraid to do?
Jocelyn would be afraid to take the private helicopter tour. He might be afraid to play tennis (running).
Tanja would be afraid to swim in the pool or at the beach, to take the helicopter tour, and perhaps even to go boating at the marina.
Ilse would be afraid to play golf and tennis, and to go boating.
Stefan would be afraid to go to The Rad, the live entertainment club, and to play golf (grass). He would also be afraid to go to the airport for a private helicopter tour, and the marina, if it were noisy.

2. What activities might each client plan to do?
Jocelyn might plan to golf, to swim at the pool or beach, to dine at the four-star restaurant, and to go boating.
Tanja might plan to play golf and tennis, to dine at the restaurant, and to go to the club.
Ilse might plan to swim in the pool or at the beach (provided there are no boats at the beach), to dine at the restaurant, to go to the club, or to take the private helicopter tour.
Stefan might plan to play tennis and dine at the restaurant (provided it's quiet).

3. What facilities would each client visit? For what purpose would the client visit that facility?
Jocelyn would visit the golf course to play golf, the tennis courts to play tennis, the pool or beach to swim, the four-star restaurant to dine, and the marina to go boating.
Tanja would visit the golf course to golf, the tennis courts to play tennis, the restaurant to dine and the club to hear a live band and dance.
Ilse would visit the pool or beach to swim, the restaurant to dine, the club to hear a band and dance, and the private airport to take a tour.
Stefan would visit the tennis courts to play tennis and the four-star restaurant to dine.

5. What would each client refuse to do?
Jocelyn would refuse to fly and play tennis.
Tanja would refuse to swim, to fly, and to go boating.
Ilse would refuse to play golf and tennis and to go boating.
Stefan would refuse to go to The Rad, to play golf, to fly, and to go boating.

6. Where would all clients agree to go?
All clients would agree to go to the four-star restaurant to dine.

Workbook Practice and Expansion: Grammar Focus
Exercises A–D (WB pp. 58–60)
Grammar Expansion (*to + base* verbals in the perfect tense)
Exercises A–C (WB pp. 61–62)

Expansion

Grammar Game

Play this game in teams of about six (or with the whole class). Make three sets of cards: (1) one set with each **letter** of the alphabet, (2) one set with the **verbs** listed under Grammar Focus on page 159 of the Student Book, and (3) one set with the **adjectives** listed in 2 e) on page 103 of the Student Book. Make all three sets for each team, then mix the cards so each team gets one pile.

To get students started, follow the instructions below, but use only the alphabet card set. When students get the hang of the game, introduce the verb cards. Finally, introduce the adjective cards. Alternatively, you can play the game over several days: Day 1 with the alphabet cards only, Day 2 with the verb cards only, and Day 3 with the adjective cards only. On Day 4 you can play with all sets of cards.

Process

Write this sentence on the board: *"On the weekend, I like to get up early."*

Tell students that they will make sentences. Each team member takes turns turning over the top card of the pile. If the student picks up a **letter** card, he or she must keep the same main verb, but change the infinitive verb to one that begins with that letter. For example, if a student picks up the letter card "c," the sentence might change like this.
Original: On the weekend, I like to get up early.
New: On the weekend, I like to chat with my friends on the phone.

If the student picks up a **verb** card, he or she has to replace the verb "like" with the new verb. For example, with the verb card "pretend," the sentence might change like this.
Original: On the weekend, I like to get up early.
New: On the weekend, I pretend to be a prince.

If a student picks up an **adjective** card, he or she must replace the verb with the adjective/adjective clause. For example, with the adjective card "important," the sentence might change like this.
Original: On the weekend, I like to get up early.
New: On the weekend, it's important to do homework.

You can simplify the adjective changes by writing the adjectives as clauses such as "It's important" or "I'm glad," etc.

The game continues until all the cards have been picked up or after a set time limit. If you play with more than one set of cards, have students discard their cards face up in separate piles (all the verb cards in one pile, and so on.) This way students can see what verb, letter, and so on they need to work with. If students choose a verb or adjective card, they don't have to use an infinitive that begins with the letter on the up-turned letter card. They can use any verb.

*L*istening 1 (SB pp. 104–106)

See Tapescript 7.a

Aims/Skills
- listen for main ideas
- listen for details
- listen for supporting facts
- anticipate what comes next from listening

 Comprehension Check (SB p. 105)

1. Where does the story begin? *at the international airport at Idlewild*

2. Which main characters are introduced in this excerpt? *Bond, Halloran, Captain Dexter, the African American woman, the passenger in the back of the sedan*

3. Summarize what happens. *Answers will vary. Key points to be included: Bond arrives at the airport and is met by Halloran who stamps his passport and gives him an envelope with money for his mission. They take a cab to the hotel to meet Captain Dexter. Bond notices the speeding black sedan with the African American woman driving it and the mysterious man in the back seat.*

 Focused Listening (SB pp. 105–106)

Read the questions below and then listen to the excerpt again to find the correct answers.

Note: Answers are circled.

1. Where does Halloran lead Bond once he approaches the secret agent?
   a) into a room marked PRIVATE
   b) towards a door marked US Health Service
   c) towards a black Buick ⟵
   d) beyond the Health Service building towards the Customs office

2. In the limousine Bond turns to Halloran and says, "Well, that's certainly one of the reddest carpets I've ever seen." What does he mean?
   a) it was unusual to have a red carpet in the limousine
   b) he hadn't expected to be treated so well ⟵
   c) he was referring to Communist spies at the airport who were dressed in red
   d) he saw a large billboard advertising of his hotel with a red carpet at the door

3. Where is Bond?
   a) Washington
   b) New York ⟵
   c) Los Angeles
   d) Moscow

4. What did Bond see across the street from the hotel as he was saying goodbye to Halloran?
   a) Captain Dexter
   b) his hotel
   c) a black sedan Chevrolet ⟵
   d) a chauffeur opening the limousine door for a negress

5. What does Captain Dexter ask Bond to do when he enters the hotel?
   a) to go straight to the check-in counter
   b) to keep his hat on ⟵
   c) to go straight to the elevator to take his luggage

6. In what room or on what floor of the St. Regis hotel would Bond stay?
   a) the first floor
   b) room 2003
   c) the top floor ⟵
   d) the 24th floor

7. What was unusual about what Bond saw?
   a) an accident almost occurred
   b) the limousine was from Harlem
   c) the chauffeur was a negress ⟵
   d) a giant was sitting in the back seat of the limousine

 One Step Beyond (SB p. 106)

In teams or with a partner, answer these questions.

1. The title of this chapter is "The Red Carpet." Why do you think the author gave it this title? Give the chapter another appropriate title. *Answers will vary.*

2. Bond is treated royally. What facts in the recording support this statement?
   Supporting facts: private escort, Halloran; limousine waiting for him; quick exit from airport; offered cigarettes and money; taken to hotel room; second escort, Captain Dexter; Halloran offers Bond anything he wants

3. Read the excerpt below. Then answer the questions.
   Bond turned to say goodbye to Halloran and thank him. For a moment Halloran had his back to him as he said something about Bond's luggage to the commissionaire. Bond looked past him across 55th Street. His eyes narrowed. A black sedan, a Chevrolet, was pulling sharply out into the thick traffic, right in front of a Checker cab that braked hard, its driver banging his fist down on the horn and holding it there. The sedan kept going, just caught the tail of the green light, and disappeared north up Fifth Avenue.
   It was a smart, decisive bit of driving, but what startled Bond was that it had been a negress [African American woman] at the wheel, and through the rear window he had caught a glimpse of the single passenger — a huge face which had turned slowly towards him and looked directly back at him, Bond was sure of it, as the car accelerated towards the Avenue.

a) Which sentences in this excerpt create a sense of suspense?

His eyes narrowed. A black sedan, a Chevrolet, was pulling sharply out into the thick traffic, right in front of the Checker cab that braked hard, its driver banging his fist down on the horn and holding it there. It was a smart, decisive bit of driving, but what startled Bond was that it had been a negress [African American woman] at the wheel, and through the rear window he had caught a glimpse of the single passenger — a huge face which had turned slowly towards him and looked directly back at him, Bond was sure of it, as the car accelerated towards the Avenue.

b) What verbs, adjectives, and adverbs does the author use to heighten the suspense?
Possible answers:
verbs: narrowed, banging (his fist), caught, disappeared, startled, accelerated
adjectives: thick (traffic), huge (face), smart, decisive, single
adverbs: sharply, slowly, directly, hard

4. What is your impression of Halloran? If you had to cast an actor in this role, how would he look and why? *Answers will vary.*

5. What role do you think the man, whom Bond sees in the car, will have in the story?
He will likely be Bond's rival, because he is introduced in the story in a suspenseful way. Bond speculates he is "Mr. Big."

Writing (SB p. 106)

Aims/Skills
- anticipate what happens next in a story
- write a description
- write maintaining tone, style, and context

Note: An audio recording of *Live and Let Die* may be available from your public library. If you can access it, let your students hear the second part of the excerpt, or have them listen to or read the whole novel.

Reading 2 (SB pp. 106–109)

Aims/Skills
- read for main ideas
- read for specific information
- read for supporting evidence
- make inferences from reading
- apply messages from reading to other situations

🔑 Comprehension Check (SB p. 109)

1. Why have some school principals condemned the show?
They see Bart Simpson as a poor role model. (lines 17–21)

2. How does the writer describe Homer Simpson?
". . . a boor of the Fred Flintstone variety, . . ." (lines 27–28)

3. How does the writer describe Marge Simpson?
". . . a scratchy-voiced, well-intentioned yet ineffectual mother who sports a towering teased-up hairdo." (lines 28–30)

4. What advice did Marge give Lisa in one episode when Lisa was feeling alienated from her peers? What was the result of this advice?
Marge says, "it's not what you feel inside that counts, it's how you look on the outside. That's what my mother taught me. Just push those feelings down deep inside and smile. And boys will like you, you will be invited to parties and happiness will follow." (lines 44–50) This advice results in other children taking advantage of Lisa's need for approval.

5. How did Groening show the folly of taking religious doctrines literally in one episode?
In one episode, the children are at Sunday school learning about heaven and hell, when one child asks if his pet will go to heaven. He is told that heaven is only for people, whereupon Bart asks whether an amputated leg would wait in heaven for its owner, or if a robot with a human brain would go to heaven. (lines 60–76) This demonstrates how silly it can be to take religious images literally.

🔑 One Step Beyond (SB p. 109)

1. The writer claims that the Simpsons are a typical North American family. What evidence does she give to support this? Do you agree or disagree?
Supporting ideas: She supports this claim by describing the negative personality traits (shortcomings) of each character, especially the parents. (lines 21–30) She points out that the show deals with problems real families face in their lives. (lines 35–41) She argues that the family and society are presented as dysfunctional, not ideal. The parents aren't perfect, they're human. They have their own problems and don't always have all the answers to their kids' problems. They sometimes give bad advice and the kids behave in negative ways. The writer provides examples of episodes where dysfunctional behaviour is shown. (lines 42–78)

2. How is *The Simpsons* television show cathartic?
By laughing with Bart at adult authority figures we can rid ourselves of some of our frustrations with them. We also laugh at Bart and all the rude kids like him that we have

come across and been ourselves. Laughing at the shortcomings and abuses of the characters allows us to laugh at our own shortcomings, our dysfunctional families, and our society. (lines 98–108)

3. How can families use *The Simpsons* television show to deal with some of the difficulties of family life? *Answers will vary.*

Vocabulary 2 (SB p. 109)

Aims/Skills
- match words with definitions
- complete a crossword
- use words in context

Answer Key

The mah-jong mania of the mid-1920s came to an end with the start of a new craze — crossword puzzles. Complete the crossword puzzle to the right, which includes words from the reading "Recognizing Ourselves in the Simpsons." Then design your own crossword, making up sentences for each of the words.

Down
1. annoying and offensive *obnoxious*
2. strongly exaggerated importance *pretentious*
3. way to release energy or emotions *outlet*
4. not working the way it should *dysfunctional*
5. to deal with successfully *cope*
6. shock *trauma*

Across
1. a person who takes advantage of every chance for personal success without regard for how his or her behaviour may affect others *opportunist*
2. being everywhere at the same time *omnipresent*
3. to disapprove of or criticize strongly, usually for moral reasons *condemn*
4. foolishness *folly*

Workbook Practice: Vocabulary 2 Exercises A–C (WB pp. 60–61)

Expansion

Mystery Word Game (Reproducible 6.2)

Refer to the word cards on Reproducible 6.2. The goal is to explain the meaning of the mystery word at the top of the card in a set time without using the forbidden words. Play the game in small even-numbered groups. Divide the groups into two teams. Copy enough sets of word cards for each group and shuffle them. Teams take turns explaining and guessing the mystery words.

One player from Team A picks up a word card and shows it to the other team, but not his or her own teammate. The player then tries to get his or her teammate to guess the word by explaining its meaning without using the forbidden words on the card. The opposing team members listen to ensure the forbidden words are not used. The player may speak single words or sentences, but may not use gestures or any form of the mystery or forbidden words. The player also may not say "t sounds like" to rhyme a word. If a forbidden word has been said, the player continues immediately with a new word card. If the teammate guesses the word, the team gets a point and the same player continues with a new word card. A turn ends after one minute (the opposing team keeps time). The team records how many words were guessed in that minute.

Now Team B repeats the procedure. The next time Team A plays, one of the teammates who guessed in the team's previous round gets the play. The game ends after all the cards have been played or after a set time limit.

Model one of the words for the whole class before beginning.

EXAMPLE Mystery word: fever
         Forbidden words: Saturday
                            disco
                            sick
                            temperature

Possible clues: This is something that children sometimes get when they aren't feeling well and then their parents give them an aspirin to bring this down.

Writing (SB p. 109)

Aims/Skills
- write a television episode narrative
- write a comparison essay
- write an analysis essay
- use themed vocabulary

If you have not already covered the Process Writing sections in the Workbook, refer students to the writing sections that deal with narrative paragraphs (WB pp. 16–18), comparison/contrast paragraphs (WB pp. 37–38), and expository paragraphs (WB pp. 46–47) if they need help.

Listening 2 (SB p. 110)

See Tapescript 7.b

Aims/Skills
- listen to song lyrics
- listen for refrain in a song
- listen for main ideas
- listen for symbols and images in a song

 ## Focused Listening (SB p. 110)

Listen to "Superman's Song" by the popular Canadian band Crash Test Dummies from their *The Ghosts That Haunt Me* CD. Then answer the questions below.

1. The vocalist compares Superman to what other famous fictitious character? *Tarzan*

2. What comparisons does the singer make between them?
   Superman: hero, does what is good, has special powers, admirable, real gentleman, had a straight job (he didn't use his strength to take advantage), carried on despite his struggles (deceased family on Krypton)
   Tarzan: not a hero, just jumps around in the jungle, can't speak, not admirable, not a ladies' man, dumb as an ape, did nothing
   The singer compares Tarzan to an ape, whereas Superman is a human hero.

3. A song's chorus, because it is repeated, contains the main message of a song. What is the main message of this song?
   Superman is not motivated by money, but by goodness. He spent his time saving the world. The singer sometimes despairs that the world might never see another man like him.

 ## One Step Beyond (SB p. 110)

Possible answers:

1. What might the jungle and the city symbolize in this song? *the uncivilized world and the civilized world*

2. Superman has permeated North American popular culture since 1938, appearing in comics, films and on radio, TV, and Broadway. Why do you think he has remained so popular throughout the decades?
   Answers will vary.

3. Popular culture has traditionally been viewed as light-hearted, nonsensical, and unimportant. Does this song support or refute this idea? How?
   The song refutes this view. It suggests that Superman as a pop culture superhero represents important heroic qualities. The song focuses on his heroic actions and his noble motivations.

Speaking (SB p. 110)

Aims/Skills
- describe physical and character traits
- discuss heroic qualities
- narrate a story
- express biographical information

Process Writing (WB pp. 62–67)

This section covers the basic elements of a standard five-paragraph essay. Exercises on narrowing topics, writing simple thesis statements, and preparing essay outlines are included, as is an Essay Outline Checklist.

Unit Reflection (SB p. 110)

As an alternative, ask students to work in teams to create a poster that reflects pop culture around the world. It should reflect a new, global pop culture that is created by combining images of pop culture idols from around the globe. Ask them to create a "global" slogan to title their poster.

Helpful Internet Resources

Accessing entertainment news and fan clubs is easy on the Internet.

Key word search: entertainment, crosswords, games, trivia

http://www.aol.com/webchannels/entertainment.html
America Online Entertainment: you can access any entertainment news and activities from here

http://www.tvguide.com
TV Guide online magazine: check out this site for anything on TV. Has some interesting articles on entertainers and television entertainment.

http://www.gamecenter.com/
Game Center: this site has on-line video games you can play, tryout, and download

http://ww.primate.wisc.edu/people/hamel/cp.html
A page maintained by Ray Hamel, Special Collections Librarian, with a host of links to crosswords puzzles

http://www.primate.wisc.edu/people/hamel/trivia/html
The Trivia Page — Another of Ray Hamel's great sites. This one links you to various trivia sites from television to sports.

UNIT 8
It's How You Play the Game

OVERVIEW

Theme: Sports and Recreation

Topics:
- sports (e.g., baseball, hockey, tennis) and their role in North American society (Reading 1) SB pp. 112–115
- sportscasts (intonation and pitch) SB p. 115
- sports idioms SB p. 116
- being a hockey parent (Listening 2) SB p. 117–118
- history of Olympics (Reading 2) SB pp. 120–123
- origins of various sports (Listening 2) SB p. 125

Vocabulary:
Student Book
Idioms:
ballpark figure
clear sailing
to be neck and neck
to beat someone to the punch
to bounce a few ideas off someone
to go the distance
to go downhill
to play hardball
to tackle
to wrestle with the hard facts

Onomatopoeic words:
booted
dribbled
groaned
pop
roar
slammed
slap

slices
smashed
tap

Workbook
badminton
badminton racquet
baseball
baseball bats
baseball gloves
birdies
net
shin pads
soccer
soccer ball
soccer shoes
softball

Intensifiers:
a bit
a little
a touch
awfully
considerably

extremely
kind of
much
pretty
quite
rather
really
reasonably
slightly
somewhat
sort of
substantially
very

Grammar:
Base + ing Verbals
(SB pp. 118–120)
Gerunds vs. Infinitives
(SB pp. 123–124)

Process Writing:
Introductory Paragraphs
(WB pp. 74–75)

Getting Started (Reproducible 8.1)

Copy Reproducible 8.1 and cut up one set of pictures for each team of three to four students. Have each team identify the sports and divide the pictures into two categories. Let the teams determine how and why they make the division. Some possible category divisions include: individual vs. team sports, costly vs. inexpensive, indoor vs. outdoor sports, etc.

Reading 1 (SB pp. 112–115)

Aims/Skills
- read for comprehension
- summarize content

ONE STEP AHEAD
Note that some of the answers to the following questions are not directly stated in the passages. They need to be deduced from context.

Jigsaw Reading (SB pp. 112-114)

Individually, read your assigned passage and then discuss the following questions with your team.

1. How do sports help build a sense of community?
2. The passage describes a certain degree of sports fanaticism. Give examples.
3. What descriptive words, phrases, and comparisons does the writer use to make the reader understand the importance of the game?

Answer Key

Extract 1

1. People come together because of their common love of the game. Ray hopes that his daughter will understand his devotion.

2. Ray changed his lawn into a baseball field.

3. (lines 10–11) "My heart sounds like someone flicking a balloon with his index finger."
(lines 32–34) "I've tended it like I would my own baby. It has been powdered and lotioned and loved. It is ready."
(lines 36–39) "I experience a tingling like the tiniest of electric wires touching the back of my neck, sending warm sensations through me."

Extract 2

1. People come together to feel close and share something in common — a sense of community. People of all ages and backgrounds come together for a common love of the game. They share a community of spirit — the spirit that binds.

2. On a snowbound night many people of different ages and backgrounds attend the games. Crowds are loud and passionate. Kids get up at five to practice. Their whole life is dreaming of the big leagues.

3. That was his life, (opening poem line 4)
(lines 3–6) People have a need to come together . . . to feel close, to share something in common.
(lines 20–21) . . .people will be back — louder, more passionate, and in even greater numbers.
(lines 22–23) To this community, hockey is part of a shared imagination
(lines 31–32) . . . there you find a community of the spirit, a feeling that binds.

Extract 3

1. Tennis is a good family activity and is also inexpensive to play, so it doesn't exclude anyone in the community.

2. Youngsters are flocking to tennis courts. The young couple loved tennis so much they took their infant son with them and hung his chair on the fence. When he was older the boy became a ball boy and then learned to play himself.

3. (lines 10–11) . . . great majority of youngsters flocking to tennis courts today . . .
(lines 25–29) . . . ball boy, a position he initially filled with enthusiasm if not grace. He was thrilled by his contribution to the proceeding, and as time went on, he became highly competent in the performance of his duties.
(lines 32–33) There are few sports more ideally suited to children . . .
(lines 34–35) Also, tennis is a non-violent, non-contact sport, which is an important consideration for parents . . .
(lines 43–46) . . . it is a predominantly individual sport. Team sports do provide plenty of opportunity for a child to learn leadership and cooperation with others but their basic structure can also lead a child to develop a tendency to pass the buck, to blame others for a poor showing . . .

Expansion

Survey

Have students design a survey to determine the viewing habits of sports fans. They could find out which sports people like to watch on TV and which they prefer to watch in person; the amount of time per week spent watching sports; which sports are most popular; typical sponsors of the sports; popularity of male vs. female sports; age of viewers, etc. Students should survey at least 10 people and then pool their results with their team. Each team can make graphs or bar charts to present their results visually. Team results can be compared and discussed.

Speaking (SB pp. 115–116)

Aims/Skills

• identify and practise intonation patterns
• identify stressed words

Pronunciation Practice

See Tapescript 8.a

1. Listen to the following sentences. Underline the stressed words and draw arrows to show the intonation patterns.

Note: It is not really important that your students identify the exact intonation; however it is important that they are able to hear the rise or fall of the voice.

EXAMPLE: Strike three. You're out.

(a) He shoots. He scores!

b) Going, going, gone — it's a home run.

c) The horses are neck and neck. Silver Streak has just taken the lead by a nose.

d) Shots up. What a rejection by Jones!

e) We have just witnessed the fastest 100 metres ever.

f) Schneider lines it up and lasers it at the goalie.

g) Goal — a great finish on that shot.

h) Another ace! Sampress has his big gun going today.

i) A great dig, but an even bigger spike!

j) Smith punches it into the end zone. Touchdown!

3. Try to identify the sports represented in each sentence.
   a) *hockey*
   b) *baseball*
   c) *horse racing*
   d) *basketball*
   e) *100 metre dash (track and field)*
   f) *hockey*
   g) *soccer*
   h) *tennis*
   i) *volleyball*
   j) *football*

Vocabulary 1 (SB pp. 116–117)

Aims/Skills
• identify and understand sports idioms

Answer Key

1. Sports are an important part of our culture. As a result, we have many expressions and idioms which are based on sports references. Fill in the blanks below with the unscrambled words and complete the crossword puzzle.

Across

1. I wasn't sure if I could go *the **distance*** (edcaitsn) and finish my degree part-time after I started my family, but I managed to finally graduate.

2. The union is notorious for *playing **hardball*** (dlhralba) when it comes to wage negotiations; consequently, it usually gets a good deal for its members because it doesn't back down easily.

3. Since my grandmother fell and broke her hip last winter, her general health has been going steadily *down**hill*** (lilh).

4. Because of government financial cutbacks, post-secondary institutions have had to (twerlse) ***wrestle** with the hard facts* and cut both programs and staff.

5. The candidates for the leader's position are *neck and neck* (knec). At this point nobody can really say who the winner will be.

Down

1. I know you can't give me an exact quote, but can you at least give me a *ballpark **figure*** (egfuir) as to how much you think it will cost?

2. Even though it is a big job, Katalina has agreed *to **tackle*** (eltkca) the labelling and organization of all the photos I've taken over the last ten years because she loves a challenge.

3. If you have a minute, I'd like to ***bounce*** (bcunoe) *a few ideas* off you. I really value your opinion.

4. We've overcome all the major obstacles that we faced. From here on it's *clear **sailing*** (iilsgna).

5. Mohamed *beat me to the **punch*** (hpucn) and asked Yasmine to the dance before I could.

2. Working in teams of four or five, discuss the idioms in the crossword puzzle. Which sports do you think they originated from?

Possible answers:

Across
1. *marathon running*
2. *baseball*
3. *skiing*
4. *wrestling*
5. *horse racing*

Down
1. *baseball*
2. *football*
3. *basketball*
4. *sailing*
5. *boxing*

3. For five minutes, brainstorm as many sports idioms as possible. Compare your results with those of other teams and give your team a point for each idiom your team found that no other team has.

Possible answers:
blowing hot air
by a nose
on the line
out in left field
hit something on the nose
take a dive
take it on the chin

Expansion

Idiom Pictures
Have students choose a sports idiom and draw a picture to illustrate it. Post the pictures and let all students look at them for five minutes to see who can identify the most idiomatic expressions.

Workbook Practice and Expansion: Vocabulary 1
Exercises A–B (WB p. 68)
Vocabulary Expansion (identifying sports equipment)
Exercises C–D (WB pp. 68–69)

See Tapescript 8.b

Aims/Skills
• take a survey
• listen for details

 Before You Listen (SB p. 117)

Complete the following chart by surveying your classmates for the appropriate information.

Possible answers:

Individual or Team Sport	Equipment Required	Approximate Cost of Equipment	Support Needed from Parents
Soccer	soccer shoes, shin pads, socks, shorts, shirt	$100+	take to games, coach
Baseball	glove, baseball shoes, bat, uniform, ball, batting helmet	$150+	take to games, coach
Tennis	racket, running shoes, shorts, t-shirt, tennis balls	$150+	take to court
Hockey	skates, helmet, jersey, pants, pads, socks, gloves, stick, puck	$500+	take to games, raise funds, coach
Swimming	swim suit, goggles	$50+	take to pool

 Focused Listening (SB p. 117)

Now listen for the answers to these questions.

1. What are two commitments that parents must make to have their children involved in hockey?
get kids to practices and games; fundraising activities

2. What are three benefits of participating in hockey as a youth?
learn importance of being a team player; meet kids from neighbouring schools and establish friendships they will have in high school; keep active and out of trouble

3. What two benefits do parents receive from having their children on a sports team?
kids understand their parents' commitment to the family; parents meet great people and establish lasting friendships

Culture Note

The statistics concerning the physical fitness of children in North America are becoming increasingly alarming as more and more children spend countless hours in front of the TV or playing video games rather than getting involved in physical activities. Research shows that the rate of obesity amongst the young is a direct result of this behaviour.

Aims/Skills
• write an expository paragraph

The aim of the paragraph is to explain one's opinion about violence in sports. Students need to make a clear statement as to their opinion and provide suffficient details or anecdotes to support that opinion.

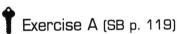 Exercise A (SB p. 119)

1. Identify the *base + ing* verbals in the following passage. Where applicable, indicate the nouns the verbals are describing.
Note: Have students circle the verbals and underline the nouns.

(Playing) sports is an important part of growing up. On the weekends, (playing) fields throughout the community are full of people of all ages participating in (interesting) sports. (Hoping) to be star athletes, many youths dedicate themselves to long hours of practice. However, few can really expect to reach international stardom.

(Being) at the top of a sport requires a lot of hard work, talent, and dedication. When training, athletes build their endurance by (practising) their sports for long, (exhausting) hours. They do not mind (dedicating) their lives to their professions because they enjoy (pushing) their performances to the peak of their abilities. Before major competitions, athletes avoid (taking part) in any activities that might distract them, (hoping) not to risk (losing) their competitive edge. At important competitions, you can often see athletes (giving) the best performances of their careers because they are totally "psyched" for the competition. As a result, they tend to be very single-minded and refuse to let anything stand in the way of (achieving) their goals. They have chosen to dedicate themselves wholeheartedly to their sports, which for them are (thrilling.)

Note: "participating" in the second sentence and "training" in the second sentence of the second paragraph may confuse some students, but they are part of reduced clauses and are not verbals.

2. In the passage, find examples of each type of *base + ing* verbal outlined in the grammar explanation.

1. *Base + ing* Verbals Naming an Action

   a) in the subject position
      (Playing) *sports is an important part of growing up.*
      (Being) *at the top of a sport requires a lot of hard work, talent, and dedication.*

   b) in the object or complement position after certain verbs
      They do not mind (dedicating) *their lives to their professions because they enjoy* (pushing) *their performances to the peak of their abilities.*
      Before major competitions, athletes avoid (taking part) *in any activities that might distract them, hoping not to risk* (losing) *their competitive edge.*

   c) after a preposition
      When training, athletes build their endurance by (practising) *their sports for long, exhausting hours.*
      As a result, they tend to be very single-minded and refuse to let anything stand in the way of (achieving) *their goals.*

2. *Base + ing* Verbals Describing a Noun

   a) as an insert
      (Hoping) *to be star athletes, many youths dedicate themselves to long hours of practice.*
      Before major competitions, athletes avoid taking part in any activities that might distract them, (hoping) *not to risk losing their competitive edge.*

   b) as a post-modifier in a noun phrase
      At important competitions, you can often see athletes (giving) *the best performances of their careers because they are totally "psyched" for the competition.*

   c) as an adjective in the complement position after *be* or other linking verbs
      They have chosen to dedicate themselves wholeheartedly to their sports, which for them are (thrilling.)

   d) as a pre-modifier in a noun phrase
      i) verbal describes what noun does — noun responsible for action
         (interesting) *sports*
         (exhausting) *hours*
      ii) verbal describes noun — noun not responsible for action
         (playing) *fields*

Exercise B (SB pp. 119–120)

Build sentences from the following phrases using an appropriate verbal.

EXAMPLE: *practise:* six hours a day / common / professional figure skaters.
   Practising six hours a day is common amongst professional figure skaters.

1. *watch:* Sports fans / enjoy / fast-paced basketball game.
   Sports fans enjoy watching a fast-paced basketball game.

2. *score:* Kyle / won / most valuable player award / most goals in the tournament.
   Kyle won the most valuable player award for scoring the most goals in the tournament.

3. *try:* Elvis / practise / quadruple every day / perfect the landing.
   Trying to perfect the landing, Elvis practises the quadruple every day.

4. *climb:* many children / enjoy / playground equipment / park.
   Many children enjoy climbing playground equipment in the park.

5. *thrill:* was / participate / Olympic team.
   It was a thrilling experience to participate on the Olympic team.

6. *run:* athletes / have / custom-made / shoes.
   Many athletes have custom-made running shoes.

Grammar in Use (SB p. 120)

Based on the passage (on p. 120), answer the following questions. Note how often verbals are used in the answers.

1. What are some physical activities that the writer enjoyed as a child?
   The writer enjoyed playing soccer, basketball, and tennis.

2. What activities does the writer enjoy now?
   Now the writer mostly enjoys playing tennis, but plans on spending lots of time teaching his daughter to play soccer and baseball.

3. What does the writer consider dangerous? What does the writer think he risks if he takes part in these sports?

The writer considers playing hockey and boxing dangerous. He thinks he risks losing his front teeth playing hockey.

4. What does the writer consider important? What is he determined to do to keep fit during the next year? *The writer considers participating in sports to keep fit important. He is determined to keep playing tennis and to spend lots of time chasing his daughter around the park and teaching her to play soccer and baseball.*

Workbook Practice: Grammar Focus 1 Exercises A–I (WB pp. 69–72)

 **Reading 2 (SB pp. 120–123)**

Aim/Skill
• scan for information

ONE STEP AHEAD

Olympic Facts

Here are some interesting background facts about the Olympics:

• the Olympics in 1916 were cancelled due to World War I
• the Olympics in 1940 and 1944 were cancelled due to World War II
• Olympic events for women made their first appearance in 1912
• winter sports were introduced into the Olympics in 1924 at Charmoix, France
• the winter games are now held in even-numbered years, in which summer games are not contested
• throughout most of modern history, the Olympics have been open only to amateurs; however, in recent years the governing bodies of many sports have opened competition to professionals as well
• Canadians first participated in 1900; the first real national team of 84 members was sent to London in 1908
• the Olympic rings were conceived by Baron Pierre de Coubertin. The joining of the rings symbolizes the conjunction of continents during the athletic games and represents the ideal of peace on the whole planet. The colours were chosen because at least one of the colours is found in the flag of every nation.
• the Olympic flame was introduced in 1934. The torch lighting, starting at an ancient Olympic site and ending at the site hosting the games, demonstrates the link between the ancient and modern games. The flame symbolizes the purity of the Olympic philosophy and the need to work towards the unity of humankind.

 Scanning (SB p. 120)

Quickly scan the article for the following facts.

a) the name of the cook who won the first race in 776 BC *Coroebus (line 9)*
b) the prize that Coroebus won *crown of laurel leaves (lines 26–27)*
c) the origin of the word *Olympics comes from the Greek word olympiad, which stands for a period of time spanning four years (lines 38–40)*
d) the name of the person responsible for the end of the ancient Olympics *Emperor Theodosius I (line 76)*
e) the number of athletes who took part in the first modern Olympics *311 (line 97)*
f) the year figure skating became part of the Olympics *1908 (lines 107–108)*

For Discussion (SB p. 123)

Working in teams of four or five, describe five significant changes that have taken place since the modern Olympics began.

Possible answers:
1. *number of athletes and countries participating have increased*
2. *number of events has increased*
3. *variety and quality of events have grown*
4. *records have been broken and re-broken*
5. *Olympic winter games became a separate competition*

Expansion

Project Option
Have students research the origin and development of an Olympic event. They can write a short research paper citing at least two sources or present their findings orally to the class.

 **Writing (SB p. 123)**

Aims/Skills
• identify similarities and differences
• practise point-by-point or block style comparisons and contrasts

You may wish to review the section on writing a comparison/contrast paragraph in Unit 4 of the Workbook pp. 37–38 and the essay format on pp. 62–67.

Grammar Focus 2 (SB pp. 123–124)

Exercise A (SB p. 123)

Using your knowledge of how *base + ing* and infinitive verbals are used, complete the following sentences with the appropriate form of the verb in brackets.

1. *Collecting* (collect) hockey cards is a popular hobby for young kids.
2. Kyle promised *to get up* (get up) without a fuss for hockey practice at 5 a.m.
3. The tennis pro intends *to earn* (earn) millions for endorsing Nike™ shoes.
4. My sister enjoys *playing* (play) basketball with my friends.
5. Everyone expects Carlos *to win* (win) the tournament.
6. Athletes cannot risk *injuring* (injure) themselves before major meets.
7. It's important *to practise* (practice) consistently if you want to improve your game.
8. Have you finished *preparing* (prepare) the field for the game yet?
9. What about *batting* (bat) left-handed?
10. Tennis is considered *to be* (be) a game of skill.

Exercise B (SB p. 124)

Working in teams of two or three, discuss how the following pairs of sentences differ in meaning. Note which event is first and which is second.

1. a) Did you remember (1) to order pizzas (2) for the team party?
   b) Do you remember (2) ordering pizzas (1) for the team party?
   In sentence 1, the pizzas may not have been ordered. In sentence 2, the pizzas are there and someone is questioning who ordered them.

2. a) I forgot (1) to wash (2) my soccer uniform.
   b) I forgot (2) washing (1) my soccer uniform.
   In sentence 1, the uniform is dirty. In sentence 2, the uniform is clean. In sentence 1, the person forgot to wash the uniform. In sentence 2, the person forgot that he or she had already washed the uniform.

3. a) Raphael stopped (2) kicking (1) the ball.
   b) Raphael stopped (1) to kick (2) the ball.
   In sentence 1, Raphael is no longer kicking the ball. In sentence 2, Raphael stopped whatever he was doing to kick the ball.

4. a) We regret (1) to inform (2) you that you did not make the team.
   b) We regret (2) informing (1) you that you did not make the team.
   In sentence 1, they are in the process of telling the person he or she didn't make the team. In sentence 2, they already told the person but now regret it.

Workbook Practice: Grammar Focus 2 Exercises A–E (WB pp. 73–74)

Vocabulary 2 (SB pp. 124–125)

1. Answers are in Student Book page 158.
2. Onomatopoeic words are words that sound like what they mean. Listen to the following words and number them in order as you hear them. Do you think the words sound like what they mean?

   slices (5)   groaned (9)
   dribbled (3)   smashed (4)
   slap (6)   roar (7)
   slammed (2)   booted (1)
   pop (10)   tap (8)

3. Complete the following sentences using words from the list above.
   a) Michael Jordan *dribbled* the basketball down the court and then *slammed* it in the hoop.
   b) Tiger Woods rarely *slices* the ball — he usually gets so close to the hole that he only needs to *tap* it in with a single stroke.
   c) The fans *groaned* when the soccer player *booted* the ball in his own net.
   d) On his last at bat, Roger hit a *pop* fly which the backcatcher easily caught. This time he *smashed* the ball way out into left field.
   e) To the *roar* of the crowds, John took a *slap* shot from the corner and got the winning goal.

Workbook Practice and Expansion: Vocabulary 2 Expansion (verb expansion, adverbs of intensity) Exercises A–E (WB pp. 72–73)

Listening 2 (SB p. 125)

See Tapescript 8.d

Aims/Skills
- listen for details
- fill in a chart

ONE STEP AHEAD

The following is some background information you may find helpful.

Archery

- bow and arrow were invented at least 50 000 years ago, perhaps even 100 000 years ago — by the time history was recorded, distribution of the bow was widespread
- archery was an important military and hunting skill
- officially became part of the Olympics in 1972
- Canadian Archery Association was formed in 1927

Wrestling

- early universal sport
- two types are contested at Olympics: Greco-Roman and Freestyle
- classified by weight; wrestlers earn points for certain manoeuvers; highest accumulated total points wins if no fall
- first Canadian amateur wrestling championships were held at Toronto's Argonaut Rowing Club in 1901
- Canadian Amateur Wrestling Association was formed in 1969; amateur wrestling was considered fastest growing sport in the country

Track and Field

- track consists of the running events; field consists of the throwing and vaulting events
- more countries compete at the Olympics in track and field than in any other sport
- ancient Greeks were preoccupied with the contest and did not keep track of records; now athletes strive to break each other's records or achieve their personal best
- origins of Canadian Track and Field: Native peoples' running and throwing competitions; colonial athletics of officers and civil servants; the Caledonian games of Scottish immigrants; tests of strength at rural "bees" and farms

Weightlifting

- Olympic sport since first modern games in 1896
- International Weightlifting Federation is one of the largest federations in the world
- consists of two events — the snatch and the clean jerk — and includes 10 bodyweight categories

Recent changes have allowed professional hockey players to participate in the Olympics. Surveys have indicated that of the Canadian households watching the Olympics, 75% of the men watch the hockey games while the majority of the women watch the figure skating competitions. Figure skating has soared to an all-time high in popularity. Canada has had many world champions and Olympic medallists in the sport including Karen Magnussen, Brian Orser, Kurt Browning, and Elvis Stojko. The sport was brought into an unfortunate limelight through the Tonya Harding / Nancy Kerrigan incident in 1994 when Nancy Kerrigan was attacked by a person hired by Harding's ex-husband in an attempt to eliminate her from the competition. Kerrigan recovered from her knee injury and received the silver medal at the Olympics.

 Focused Listening (SB p. 125)

You will hear a number of short passages about the possible origins of various sports. As you listen, complete the following chart.

ONE STEP AHEAD

There is no space in the chart for archery. When students put these headings in their books, have them insert Archery between Lacrosse and Basketball.

	Origin	Date of Origin	Interesting Point
Bowling	German tribes	300 AD	priests devised the game to get tribe members to put down dangerous clubs; sometimes called kegeling
Wrestling and Boxing	Khafaje	5000 years ago	part of ancient religious rites; styles have changed little
Soccer	China	207 BC	activities were similar to today's soccer drills
Lacrosse	North America		before arrival of European explorers natives played with an average 70 people per side; has been called a national sport
Archery	Egypt	3000 years ago	bowmen may have been imported mercenaries
Basketball	Canada / USA	1891	devised to get youth off street; peach baskets were first used as baskets
Golf	Scotland	ancient time	shepherds hit pebbles into holes with their sticks out of boredom

Note: James Naismith, a Canadian, was working at the YMCA in Springfield, Massachusetts at the time he invented basketball. The first official game was played on January 20, 1902.

One Step Beyond (SB p. 125)

As an alternative to this activity, you could have students use common items found around the home to invent a new game. Each team should teach its game to the other teams. The class could select the best "new" game.

The Workbook provides exercises on introductory paragraphs including identifying good introductory paragraphs, identifying the key elements of the paragraph, writing thesis statements, and an Introductory Paragraph Checklist.

Unit Reflection (SB p. 125)

Many individual sports are games of skill, so technique is important. Similarly, in team sports, the success of the team as a whole is dependent on each player playing his or her position well. Therefore, how the players play in both individual and team sports is more important than whether they win or lose.

This expression ("it's how you play the game") can apply to any aspect of our lives where process is more important than outcome.

Helpful Internet Resources

Key word search: name of sport, Olympics

http://CNNSI.com
A source of journalistic sports writing from Sports Illustrated

http://olympics.tufts.edu
A source providing information on the ancient and modern Olympics, including a visual tour of ancient Olympia

http://sports.yahoo.com
A source that provides countless links to up-to-date sporting news

http://www.aasla.com/Olympic Information Centre/Olympic Primer/Olympic Primer_.htm
A complete reference on the Olympic Games

UNIT 9
Food For Thought

OVERVIEW

Theme: The Politics of Food

Topics:
- influences food manufacturers have on shopping patterns (Reading 1) SB pp. 128–131
- eating disorders (Listening 1) SB pp. 132–133
- world hunger (Reading 2) SB pp. 136–139
- poverty and hunger in industrialized nations (Listening 2) SB p. 140

Vocabulary:

Student Book
atmosphere
dictate
diversification
enticement
impulse
interloper
onslaught
perishable
tread
unique

Suffixes: -ly -ist -al -ion -er -less -ness -ity

Workbook
benefits
counterproductive
declares
dosage
emerged
govern
nutrition
prevailing
secretion
substance
wiser

Grammar:
Base + d/t/n Verbals (SB pp. 134–136)

Process Writing:
Main Body Paragraphs / Concluding Paragraphs (WB pp. 81–83)

Getting Started

Write the following list on the board:

1. Convenience
2. Taste
3. Portrayal of food in commercials
4. Nutritional content
5. Medical reasons (e.g., allergies)
6. Ability to prepare quickly
7. Cost
8. Accessibility in supermarket
9. Number of calories
10. Ready to heat and eat

Have students identify the top five influences on their eating habits from the list. Tally the top choices for the class. Discuss the choices that were not in the top five. Ask students why they did not rate the other points as highly. Were there any points that they felt had absolutely no influence?

Unit Opening Pages (SB pp. 126–127)

Working in teams of three or four, have students look at the photos and discuss what they think the main topics of the unit might be. Compare the answers of the different teams to find out if they came up with common topics. Note: Any topic not covered could be a starting point for a project later in the unit.

Reading 1 (SB pp. 128–131)

Aims/Skills
- scan for information
- summarize

> **ONE STEP AHEAD**
>
> The purpose of the Shopper's Quiz on page 128 is to introduce students to the idea that big business has a tremendous influence on how we shop. Getting all the right answers is not as important.

Scanning for Information (SB p. 131)

List the facts supporting the idea that consumer buying habits are manipulated by the food industry.

Possible answers:

- *it's difficult to find a variety of fresh foods — the answer lies in the powerful control of our food supply by giant companies that decide what will be marketed and what you and I will eat solely on the basis of profitability (lines 29–32)*
- *there is much more money to be made from the sale of highly processed, mass-produced, standardized food than from fresh foods (lines 35–37)*
- *the big chain stores and the major food wholesalers have special trade arrangements, and interlopers are not welcome (lines 45–47)*
- *numerous "competing" products are made by the very same company, and . . . a few giant corporations control the entire market. (lines 56–57)*
- *Corporate control of the food we eat ... robs the consumer of a real variety of choices, reduces quality, and fixes prices through the elimination of meaningful competition (lines 59–62)*
- *Supermarket planners have mapped out the traffic patterns shoppers will follow as they walk around the store (lines 108–110)*

 Summarizing (SB p. 131)

The ability to summarize an article or text is an important skill. When summarizing, the goal is to explain briefly the main points of the reading in your own words. Therefore, the summary should be about one-quarter the length of the original text at most.

Below are a number of sentences that can be used to summarize the main ideas of the article you have just read. They are not in the order that the ideas appear in the article, but a summary does not have to reflect the exact order of ideas — just the ideas in general. Also, some sentences below do not relate to the content in the article.

Using only appropriate sentences from those provided below, write a brief summary of the article. You may need to add sentence connectors or short transition sentences to make your summary coherent.

Note: Connectors and transitions are underlined.
Possible answer:

(c) Big business controls every aspect of our shopping experience from the availability of products to their placement on the shelf. (g) Supermarkets carry a high percentage of processed or frozen foods because they are less perishable than fresh foods and therefore more profitable. As a result, (d) farmers have little direct access to supermarkets, [and] they are forced to grow what large corporations will buy. However, (a) only a very small portion of the price we pay for a product in the supermarket goes to the farmer who

produced the food. Most goes to the intermediaries such as processors, packagers, truckers, etc. (f) In addition, the development of new, highly processed, profitable products is mostly controlled by a few large corporations. This control is further evidenced by (h) marketers who place most popular foods at eye level in highly frequented aisles.

Expansion

Field Study
Have students go to their local supermarkets and note the placement of products. Based on the knowledge that designers position popular brands at eye level and impulse items near cash registers, have students identify the most popular items (brand and kind) for the following categories: cereal, soup, coffee, pickles, laundry soap, shampoo, spaghetti sauce, cheese, facial tissues, and salad dressing. Also ask students to answer the following questions:

1. Where is the dairy case located in relation to the front door?
2. Where is the fresh bread located in relation to the front door?
3. Are there any candy-free checkouts?
4. What other items are available near the checkouts?

Have students compare their findings in teams of three or four. Did they identify the same popular items? Are there similarities in the supermarket designs? Why are essentials such as milk, bread, and eggs generally located so far from the front door?

 Vocabulary 1 (SB p.131)

Aims/Skills
- match words from reading with definitions
- identify parts of speech
- form nouns, verbs, and adjectives

 Answer Key

1. Find words in the reading "The Big Business of Food" to complete the definitions below.

   a) An *interloper* is someone who becomes involved in a situation without being asked or wanted.
   b) To *tread* carefully is to proceed or behave cautiously.
   c) The *atmosphere* is the general mood created in a place.
   d) Something that is *perishable* decays or rots quickly.
   e) An *impulse* is a sudden strong desire to act, usually without thinking about the results.
   f) A *unique* experience is unusual or special in some way.

g) An *onslaught* is a powerful, continuous presentation of something (almost an assault).

h) An *enticement* is something pleasant or attractive used to attract or tempt a person.

i) To *dictate* is to command or control someone or something.

j) *Diversification* is the variation of things.

2. Look at the words as they appear in the context of the reading. Identify whether they are used as nouns, verbs, or adjectives and write them in the appropriate columns below. *See chart below. Answers are in bold italics.*

3. For the ten words that you have studied in this exercise, write out the noun, verb, adjective, and adverb forms where appropriate and use each in a sentence. *See chart below. Answers are in italics.*

Nouns	Verbs	Adjectives
1. *interloper (47)*		
2. tread	***tread (103)***	
3. *atmosphere (7)*		atmospheric
4. perishables	perish	***perishable (38)*** / perished / perishing
5. impulse		***impulse (104, 114)*** / impulsive
6. uniqueness		***unique (28)***
7. *onslaught (34)*		
8. *enticement (119)*	entice	enticing
9. dictate / dictator / dictatorship	***dictate (63)***	dictatorial / dictated / dictating
10. ***diversification (77)*** / diversity	diversify	diversified / diversifying

Workbook Practice and Expansion: Vocabulary 1 Exercises A–B and Expansion Exercise C (newspaper article on nutrition) and Exercises D–E ("old wives' tales") (WB pp. 76–78)

Expansion

Making Inferences (Workbook Reading)
Have students reread the newspaper article in the Workbook on pages 76–77 and answer the following questions:
Note: Answers given below in italics need to be inferred.

1. Why have the nutritionists, dieticians, and researchers attended the conference?
They want to learn more about the latest research on food and nutrition.

2. Why are people more likely to believe reports about the health benefits of foods when they come from a scientist rather than when they are written on a product label?
People believe scientists are more objective and base their reports on sound studies. Product labels are influenced by marketing concerns and are not consistently regulated.

3. What is the prevailing diet recommendation?
a diet low in fat and high in carbohydrates

4. How might diet affect diabetes?
A high-fibre diet can condition the body to produce more insulin and thus reduce reliance on drugs.

5. By what percentage would the average Canadian have to increase his or her intake of dietary fibre for it to be effective?
by almost 100% (from 10–15 grams to 25 grams a day)

Writing (SB p. 132)

Aims/Skills
- express an opinion
- write an editorial

ONE STEP AHEAD
Bring in examples of newspaper editorials for students. Explain that editorials express an individual's viewpoint and are not necessarily based on objective facts. They can often be quite radical or controversial.

Expansion

How Healthy Do You Eat? (Reproducible 9.1)
Give students a copy of Reproducible 9.1. Have them chart their eating habits for one day. They can then compare their eating habits to the guidelines below from Canada's Food Guide to Healthy Eating.

Expansion

Food Guide to Healthy Eating

Because different people need different amounts of food, the Food Guide suggests the following number of servings:

Grain Products: 5–12 servings per day

Vegetables and Fruit: 5–10 servings per day

Milk Products: 2–4 servings per day

Meat and Alternatives: 2–3 servings per day

Other Foods: Foods and beverages not part of the above food groups — to be used in moderation

The number of servings you need every day from the four food groups and other foods depends on your age, body size, activity level, whether you are male or female, and if you are pregnant or breast-feeding. The triangles on Reproducible 9.1 represent the absolute minimum number of daily servings recommended.

The Food Guide to Healthy Eating makes the following overall recommendations:

1. Enjoy a *variety* of foods.
2. Emphasize cereals, breads, other grain products, vegetables, and fruit.
3. Choose lower-fat dairy products, leaner meats, and foods prepared with little or no fat.
4. Achieve and maintain a healthy body weight by enjoying regular physical activity and healthy eating.
5. Limit salt, alcohol, and caffeine.

Eating is one of the best things life has to offer. Food helps you celebrate with your family and friends. It nourishes your body. It gives you energy to get through each day. The right balance of food and activity helps you stay at a healthy body weight.

Culture Note

Many people may think that Canada's national foods are the hamburger and hot dog. While North American families tend to eat a lot of fast food, many are also very international in their eating habits. Because Canada is such a multicultural society, Canadians have access to many ethnic dishes both in restaurants and at friends' homes. They may cook or eat Chinese one night and Italian another, for example. In larger cities like Toronto, there are large ethnic neighbourhoods where people can experience the culture and food of the ethnic group.

North Americans tend to eat a very fast breakfast of cereal, toast, waffles, juice, etc. Lunch is often soup and a salad or sandwich. The largest meal of the day is dinner (or supper) which is generally eaten between 5 and 7 p.m. Because both parents work in many families, convenience or quick cooking foods are generally consumed during the week with a traditional "home cooked" meal like roast beef and potatoes on Sundays.

Speaking (SB p. 132)

Aims/Skills

- conduct a survey
- identify and discuss conclusions
- chart or graph survey results

Students should ask their partners the survey questions. They could change the statements into a questions.

Listening 1 (SB pp. 132–133)

See Tapescript 9.a

Aims/Skills

- form definitions from context
- take notes
- listen for specific information

ONE STEP AHEAD

You may find the following background information helpful when discussing the topic of eating disorders with students.

Anorexia Nervosa

Anorexia is characterized by a significant weight loss resulting from excessive dieting. Anorexics consider themselves to be fat, no matter what their actual weight is. An estimated 10 to 20% of sufferers eventually die from complications related to anorexia.

Bulimia Nervosa

Bulimia is characterized by a cycle of binge eating followed by purging to try and rid the body of unwanted calories. A binge is different for all individuals. Purging methods usually involve vomiting and laxative abuse. Other forms of purging can involve excessive exercise, fasting, use of diuretics, diet pills, and enemas.

Compulsive Overeating

Compulsive overeating is characterized by uncontrollable eating and consequent weight gain. Compulsive overeaters use food as a way to cope with stress, emotional conflicts, and daily problems. The food can block out feelings and emotions. Compulsive overeaters usually feel out of control and are aware their eating patterns are abnormal.

 Before You Listen (SB pp. 132–133)

Answers to questions 1 and 2 are open to discussion.

3. The following words, which you will hear in the lecture, are often found in association with food. Discuss their meaning. If you are not familiar with any of the words, look them up in a dictionary.

   sustenance — *food and drink needed to keep one alive and healthy* satiate — *to completely satisfy oneself with food*

cope — *to deal with a difficult situation*

purge — *to make free of; to rid of*

metabolic rate — *the rate a body processes food to produce energy*

binge — *an activity like eating done in an excessive way*

compulsive — *very strong, irresistible desire*

addiction — *a compulsion to do something harmful or to do something incessantly*

gorge — *to fill oneself completely with food; to eat a lot in a greedy way*

obese — *extremely and unhealthily overweight*

Focused Listening (SB p. 133)

As you listen, write point-form notes in response to the following questions.

1. What are three roles that food can play in people's lives?
   (1) *sustenance*
   (2) *pleasure*
   (3) *to cope*

2. Why are diets an unsuccessful way to lose weight?
   lowering calorie intake lowers the metabolic rate leading to easier weight gain

3. What are two similarities between compulsive eating and alcoholism? *both are chronic and progressive addictions*

4. Describe three feelings that compulsive eaters have about food. *pleasure; overwhelming feelings of guilt, remorse, and self-hate; resentful and angry*

5. List at least four traits of the compulsive eater.
   • *they feel worthless and powerless*
   • *they have a strong need to control their world*
   • *they have difficulty expressing feelings, especially anger*
   • *they have confused feelings about their sexuality*
   • *they have difficulty in intimate relationships*
   • *they have a distorted body image*
   • *they are perfectionistic*

6. In the past, what were two things that women did to their bodies in order to be socially acceptable? *wore whalebone corsets; bound girls' feet*

For Discussion (SB p. 133)

ONE STEP AHEAD
The following information may be helpful in your discussions.

Programs for Eating Disorders
Individual Therapy: a one-to-one relationship with a therapist; once trust is established, individuals are able to talk about their feelings and focus on what is needed to change the behaviour

Group Therapy: sharing with others who understand your problem, which reduces the feeling of isolation

Family Therapy: involves the people who are living with or are very close to the person with the eating disorder (parents, siblings, spouses, even grandparents); usually an eating disorder indicates that there are problems within the family (e.g., martial problems, substance abuse, physical or sexual abuse, lack of communication, difficulty in expressing feelings)

Support Groups: not usually run by a professional; leaders are often people who have experienced an eating disorder themselves and groups can meet anywhere from daily to once a month. Support groups can be helpful to people with eating disorders because they realize that they are not alone and that recovery is possible. The members also help and support each other during difficult periods.

Medical Treatment: an individual's health should be monitored by a physician who is aware of the eating disorder. Many physical complications can result from eating disorders. If left untreated, they can lead to serious health problems or death.

Nutritional Counselling: many people with eating disorders have no idea what "normal eating" really is and a qualified nutritionist will be able to help them develop a healthy eating pattern

Medications: in some cases medication has been useful in treating eating disorders

Hospitalization: if the person's weight is extremely low or if they are bingeing/purging several times a day, hospitalization may be necessary

Language Note

Food plays a vital part in our daily lives. We have several idiomatic expressions that originate from food. The following are just a few:

to be a couch potato — to be lazy

to be chicken — to be afraid to do something

to quit cold turkey — quit immediately, without ever touching the thing again

to be as cool as a cucumber — to be very calm

to bring home the bacon — to earn money for essentials like rent, food, clothes, etc.

to be a piece of cake — to be very easy to do

to walk on eggshells — to be extremely careful in what you say or do

to be a lemon — to be bad or defective (often used with automobiles)

to go nuts/bananas — to go crazy or act very strangely

to have your cake and eat it too — to have the best of a situation

Grammar Focus (SB pp. 134–136)

Exercise A (SB p. 134)

Refer back to the reading "The Big Business of Food." Identify all of the *base + -d/t/n* verbals in the first two paragraphs. You should find six verbals.

1. *limited*
2. *temperature-controlled*
3. *fluorescent-lit*
4. *piped-(music)*
5. *canned*
6. *frozen*

Exercise B (SB p. 134)

Fill in the blanks with an appropriate verbal formed from the following verbs:

reduce, can, process, plan, control, burn.

EXAMPLE: *freeze*
Many North Americans purchase *frozen* turkeys to cook for Thanksgiving dinner.

1. There must be at least 50 varieties of *canned* soup available.
2. We eat a lot more *processed* food than our parents did at our age.
3. Tightly *controlled* markets discourage farmers from growing some crops.
4. Fat-*reduced* products have become very popular.
5. The bakery cannot sell *burned / burnt* baked goods.
6. Carefully *planned* shopping routes entice consumers to buy more than they originally planned.

Exercise C (SB p. 134)

Create sentences from the following words placing the verbal in an appropriate place.

EXAMPLE: *wrap:* fruit / decorative cellophane / most / expensive
The fruit *wrapped* in decorative cellophane is the most expensive.

1. *stack:* cereal / floor / on sale
   The stacked boxes of cereal on the floor are on sale.
2. *locate:* superstores / across North America / popular / shop
   Superstores located across North America are popular shopping destinations.
3. *sell:* corn / dozen / costs $4
   Corn sold by the dozen costs $4.
4. *bottle:* water / French Alps / popular beverage
   Bottled water from the French Alps is a popular beverage.
5. *market:* diet pills / primarily for women / multi-million dollar industry
   Diet pills, marketed primarily for women, are a multi-million dollar industry.

Exercise D (SB p. 135)

Fill in the blanks with the appropriate form of the word in brackets.

1. *(shock)* A *shocked* Maria couldn't believe what she had seen.
2. *(frustrate)* It is *frustrating* for Juan that he cannot lose any weight.
3. *(bore)* It's a *boring* experience to eat the same thing for breakfast every day.
4. *(surprise)* I was *surprised* to learn that so many people do not like their bodies.
5. *(interest)* An *interested* Ali listened intently to the advertisement.

Exercise E (SB p. 135)

Combine the following sentences to form a new sentence containing a verbal.

1. Henry was enticed by the smell of fresh baking. He bought two dozen cookies.
   Enticed by the smell of fresh baking, Henry bought two dozen cookies.
2. Stores are designed by marketing experts. The stores are well-planned.
   Well-planned stores are designed by marketing experts. / Designed by marketing experts, the stores are well-planned.
3. Felicity worries about her appearance. She goes on many crash diets.
   Worried about her appearance, Felicity goes on many crash diets.
4. Children are enticed by the shelves of candy. They beg their parents for treats.
   Enticed by the shelves of candy, children beg their parents for treats.
5. Diet pills are often taken incorrectly. Diet pills can lead to serious health problems.
   Taken incorrectly, diet pills can lead to serious health problems.

Exercise F (SB pp. 135–136)

Identify the verbals in the following sentences and determine which pattern they fit.

1. (Proven) through many studies, the similarities between eating disorders and alcoholism are indisputable. *(descriptor of the subject)*
2. Coffee, (grown) on plantations in Colombia, is a favourite North American after-dinner beverage. *(post-modifier in a noun phrase)*
3. (Convinced) that thinness equals acceptance, countless women diet to achieve their elusive ideal weight. *(descriptor of the subject)*

4. Many women are (frustrated) by their inability to lose weight and keep it off. *(adjective in the complement)*

5. Lisette was (interested) in the latest health food studies. *(adjective in the complement)*

6. Fitness equipment (designed) to sculpt the perfect body is expensive. *(post-modifier in a noun phrase)*

7. The (burnt) brownie was still alluring for Geneva, who craved something sweet to eat. *(pre-modifier in a noun phrase)*

8. Though (loved) by millions, Karen Carpenter starved herself to death. *(descriptor of the subject)*

9. A (bored) Nigel often eats junk food for something to do. *(pre-modifier in a noun phrase)* **Note: In this case some students might suggest that although Nigel is bored by the lack of something to do, he could in fact be considered responsible for having nothing to do. However, it would completely change the meaning if "boring" were to be substituted.**

10. Richard Simmons, (known) as an exercise guru, was once extremely overweight and out of shape. *(post-modifier in a noun phrase)*

🔑 Grammar In Use (SB p. 136)

Gina has suffered from low self-esteem all her life. It started when she was in grade seven and some of her classmates began to tease her because she was a little overweight. Even though she was a pretty, fun-loving, intelligent girl, all she could focus on was her weight. She began to withdraw and kept to herself. Her personality changed dramatically and she no longer participated in extracurricular school activities. She started making herself throw up after every meal. Her parents worried about her. They took her to a counsellor. The counsellor helped Gina understand that everyone has different body types and that Gina's was fine the way it was. The counsellor explained that young girls were under tremendous pressure from media to emulate an impossible perfect figure. Gina learned to accept herself and value what a truly special person she was. Since Gina learned that valuable lesson in her early teens, she has volunteered countless hours helping other young girls realize that, no matter what shape or size they may be, they are special and fine just the way they are.

Write at least eight sentences using *base + d/t/n verbals* based on the information in the paragraph.

Possible answers:

1. *Gina, teased by her classmates in grade seven, has suffered from low self-esteem all her life.*

2. *A teased Gina suffered from low self esteem.*

3. *Withdrawn and suffering from low self esteem, Gina began to isolate herself.*

4. *Focused on her weight, Gina began to withdraw and kept to herself.*

5. *Due to Gina's changed behaviour, she no longer participated in extracurricular school activities.*

6. *Worried about her, Gina's parents took her to a counsellor.*

7. *Encouraged by the media, young girls like Gina try to emulate an impossibly thin figure.*

8. *Gina's eating disorder was a learned behaviour.*

> **Workbook Practice and Expansion:** Grammar Focus Exercises A–F (expansion with article "Foods That Harm, Foods That Heal") (WB pp. 78–80)

Expansion

Workbook Reading

1. Have students make a point-by-point comparison chart identifying the current differences between American and Canadian labelling practices outlined in the article.

2. Have students visit a supermarket and examine the labels of at least five products identified as "calorie-reduced" and five products identified as "low-fat." For these specific products, what do the labels actually mean?

Reading 2 (SB pp. 136–139)

Aims/Skills
- scan for information
- infer meaning from context

🔑 Comprehension Check (SB p. 139)

1. Which continents are home to most of the world's hungry? *Africa, Asia, Latin America*

2. Why aren't the media interested in the chronic hunger of the underfed who toil to grow and harvest the world's food? *It doesn't have enough drama.*

3. What factor has proven to be one of the leading contributors to famine throughout human history? *war*

4. How many children die each year from preventable causes? *14 million*

5. Why are farmers going broke when there is such a shortage of food? *North American and European surpluses depress the prices.*

6. What are some possible solutions to world hunger? *reduce poverty, educate the young, make ending hunger a top priority, organize the powers, dedicate more money*

7. What are some obstacles to significantly decreasing world hunger? *lack of political will, powerful want to keep their privileged status*

Project Option (Reproducible 9.2)

Have students work in teams of four or five. Provide each team with a copy of the project outlined on Reproducible 9.2. You may wish to discuss some sample initiatives to steer teams in the right direction.

 riting (p. 139)

Aims/Skills
- write a summary
- write an expository essay

 Answer Key

1. Write a brief summary of the reading. Your summary should consist of no more than one sentence per paragraph, but preferably less.

Possible summary:

People in the rural areas of countries responsible for the majority of the world's grain and rice harvest are starving. Unlike famines and hunger crises sparked by war, chronic hunger attracts little media attention. Despite the fact that many people in the world are starving, North American farmers are being driven out of farming because of depressed prices caused by surpluses. Hunger must be solved from the grassroots level. The starving are generally powerless and their fates are controlled by the privileged few who seek to maintain the gap between the rich and poor. The solution will only come from a concerted effort from the public and politicians.

S peaking (SB p. 139)

Aims/Skills
- discuss issues collaboratively
- prepare a report outline
- present a report

Rather than have each team do a report, you may want to have each team be responsible for one aspect such as population / environment. Teams could just present brief summaries to the class on their individual aspect and invite a discussion as to the plausability of their recommendations.

V ocabulary 2 (SB p. 139)

Aims/Skills
- identify word parts
- identify the meaning of suffixes

 Answer Key

Scan through the reading "The World Hunger Crisis" carefully to find at least two words with the following suffixes. Complete the chart below by identifying the root and the meaning of the suffix.

Note: There are more words in the reading with these suffixes.

Suffix	Words	Root	Meaning of Suffix
-ly	terribly directly indirectly relatively carefully collectively effectively subtly commonly	terrible direct direct relate care collect effect subtle common	— in the stated way
-ist	specialist nutritionist economist sociologist anthropologist	special nutri eco socio anthrop	— forms adjectives and nouns — describes a set of beliefs or way of behaving
-al	agricultural conventional political national	culture convene politic nation	— connected with
-ion	malnutrition production profession solution situation action decision organization	nutri produce profess solve situate act decide organize	— shows action or condition — forms a noun
-er	farmers teenagers maker greater	farm teenage make great	— people who are connected or involved with — forms the comparative
-less	relentless powerless	relent power	— without
-ness	illness powerlessness	ill power	— quality or condition
-ity	fatality ability vitality majority	fatal able vital major	— state or quality

Workbook Practice: Vocabulary 2 Exercises A–C
(WB p. 80)

Listening 2 (SB p. 140)

See Tapescript 9.b

Aims/Skills
• recognize language functions
• listen for verbal gambits

 Before You Listen / Focused Listening
(SB p. 140)

Note: Answers for both the Before You Listen and Focused Listening sections are given in the list below.

During an interview, the interviewer and interviewee have specific responsibilities to carry out if the interview is to be a success. The following is a list of some of those responsibilities. Working in pairs, determine which are the responsibilities of the interviewer, which are the responsibilities of the interviewee, and which are the responsibilities of both.

As you listen, jot down specific key phrases the interviewer uses which reflect his responsibilities.

- puts the guest at ease (interviewer)
  "Welcome to the show Dr. Manders."

- expresses himself or herself clearly (both)
  Interviewer: " . . . we hear on the news that the prices of grains are plummeting due to surplus supplies"
  Dr. Manders: ". . . there is no one simple solution to world hunger . . ."

- uses specific language (both)
  Interviewer: ". . . Canada has an income gap between the rich and the poor that is nearly twice that of other industrial countries. . . ."
  Dr. Manders: "Commitment is the key."

- keeps control of the interview (interviewer)
  Interviewer: "How many people suffer from worldwide hunger? Millions?"

- supports ideas with examples, illustrations, and anecdotes (interviewee)
  Dr. Manders: "Solutions include grassroots movements, effective government policies, and the implementation of knowledge already available."
  There's a proverb which states: "Give a man a fish and you feed him for a day. Teach him how to fish and you feed him for life."

- changes the topic (interviewer)
  Interviewer: "Why have we seen so little progress?"

- clarifies (both)
  Interviewer: "You are referring to Third World countries . . ."
  Dr. Manders: "In fact, powerful regimes in Third World countries . . ."

- uses clear and concise phrases (both)
  Interviewer: "Today we are talking about poverty and hunger."
  Dr. Manders: "Commitment is the key."

- answers the questions (interviewee)
  Dr. Manders: ". . . over one billion people suffer from a chronic lack of food."

- summarizes (both)
  Interviewer: "What can we do about the hunger problem in Canada and worldwide?"
  Dr. Manders: "Commitment is the key."

- keeps the conversation on track (interviewer)
  Interviewer: "We don't have powerful regimes in Canada."

- is unbiased (interviewer)
  Interviewer asks questions or provides information but does not present his own views.

Speaking (SB p. 140)

Aims/Skills
- practise interview skills
- demonstrate understanding of interviewer's and interviewee's roles

Students should try to use some of the strategies from the Listening activity when writing their dialogues.

Process Writing (WB pp. 81–83)

The Workbook covers Body and Concluding Paragraphs with exercises on determining the topics of body paragraphs, writing topic sentences based on the thesis statement, using transitional sentences, and writing concluding paragraphs. Checklists for Body and Concluding paragraphs are also provided.

Unit Reflection (SB p. 140)

Have students examine the posters from the National Eating Disorder Information Centre on pages 127 and 133. What are the elements that make these posters effective? Consider the following: strong visual that makes a clear statement immediately, short clear title, catchy phrases or slogans to get point across, etc.

Helpful Internet Resources

Key word search: eating disorders, health guide, hunger, poverty

http://aceis.agr.ca/newintre.html
Agriculture and Agri-Food Canada Electronic Information Service with links to agriculture, research and technology, publications, environment, education, inspection, acts and regulations, etc.

http://www.hc-sc.gc.ca/
The Canadian Health Network: about health Canada, health information, speeches, publications, travellers information

http://www.stud.unit.no/studorg/ikstrh/ed/
Links to eating disorders resources on the Internet

http://www.brown.edu/Departments/World_Hunger_Program/
Hungerweb: Research, fieldwork, advocacy and policy, education and training. Free exchange of ideas and information regarding causes of, and solutions to, hunger

UNIT 10
The Circle of Life

OVERVIEW

Theme: Life Stages

Topics:
- nursery rhymes and children's stories
  SB pp. 142–144
- poetry about parent/child relationships (Listening 1)
  SB pp. 144–145
- human development (Reading 1)
  SB pp. 146–148
- life stages (Listening 2)
  SB pp. 152–153
- reminiscing (Reading 2)
  SB pp. 154–156

Vocabulary:

Student Book
apprentice
contemporary
develop
evolve
flaming
flourishing
global
mature
resolve
revolution
serene
span
strive
theory
tryout
turbulent

Workbook
Preposition collocations:

evolve into   evolve from . . . to   evolve over   evolve for
revolve around
span across   span over   span from . . . to
strive for   strive to

Grammar: Tense Review (SB pp. 149–152)
Shifting Tenses (WB pp. 86–89)

Process Writing: Narrative/Descriptive Essays (WB pp. 89–91)

Getting Started (Reproducible 10.1)

If you have access to Milton Bradley's *The Game of Life* board game, play it with your students. Have them discuss if they liked the game, specifically what they liked and didn't like about it, and if they think it is a good game for children. Then refer them to the opening of Unit 10 on page 141.

Alternatively, have your students complete the quiz (Reproducible 10.1) on page 117.

Discuss any statements whose answers surprised students. Ask students about some other myths about aging with which they're familiar, focusing first on myths about their own age group. Probe for attitudes about the "negativity" often associated with growing old. Then refer them to the opening of Unit 10 on page 141. The "Thought of the Day" on this page does not paint old age as negative.

Answer Key to Quiz (Reproducible 10.1)

1. T
2. T
3. F   a Swedish study showed that cohabitors are more likely to get divorced, but the evidence does not show a causal relationship
4. F   the decline is gradual
5. F   with recent developments in reproductive technology, a post-menopausal woman may become pregnant
6. T
7. T
8. F   although some couples find it difficult to "let go," most parents find a sense of new-found freedom after the last child leaves home
9. T   at this age women are often freed from their traditional feminine, passive social roles
10. F   most elderly people continue to live in their own homes and communities

Aims/Skills
• use rhyming to match parts of a verse
• use meaning to connect speech
• practise speaking with the rhythm of English
• note sound-symbol correspondence of vowel sounds
• identify meaning in children's tales

> ### ONE STEP AHEAD
> Before students begin the activity on pages 142–143, read the contents of A to L aloud to model the rhyming and rhythm. You may also need to review some unfamiliar vocabulary. In each answer, discuss why the match is correct and how the order was determined.

 ### Answer Key

1. Below are six common nursery rhymes that have been separated into two parts. Match the rhymes in the boxes with their corresponding parts in the circle. Use rhyming and meaning to guide you. Then decide whether the box or the circle begins the rhyme.

A. Hey diddle, diddle
The cat and the fiddle,
The cow jumped over the moon;
L. The little dog laughed
To see such sport,
And the dish ran away with the spoon.

B. Humpty Dumpty sat on a wall,
Humpty Dumpty had a great fall;
G. All the King's horses and all the King's men
Couldn't put Humpty together again.

F. Little Boy Blue,
Come blow your horn,
The sheep's in the meadow,
The cow's in the corn.
H. Where is the boy
Who looks after the sheep?
He's under a haystack
Fast asleep.

I. Jack and Jill
Went up the hill,
To fetch a pail of water;
Jack fell down,
E. And broke his crown,
And Jill came tumbling after.

J. The man in the moon looked
out of the moon,
Looked out of the moon and said,
D. "'Tis time for all children
on the Earth
To think about getting to bed!"

K. Little Miss Muffet
Sat on a tuffet,
Eating her curds and whey;
C. There came a big spider,
Who sat down beside her
And frightened Miss Muffet away.

3. Find all the words in the nursery rhymes that rhyme with the words below. Note that words do not have to be spelled the same to rhyme, e.g., bl*ue* and kn*ew*.
   a) tune: *moon, spoon*
   b) brown: *crown, down*
   c) crawl: *wall, fall, all*
   d) grey: *whey, away*
   e) dead: *bed, said*

4. In small teams, write as many other rhyming words as you can for the words above within a set time limit. Share your words with other teams. Give your team one point for each word you have that no other team has.
   Possible answers:
   a) tune: *boom, broom, dune, fume, goon, groom, June, loon, noon, room, soon, swoon, womb, zoom*
   b) brown: *clown, frown, gown, town, bound, found, hound, mound, noun, pound, round, sound, wound*
   c) crawl: *brawl, shawl, doll, fall, hall, mall, pall, tall, wall*
   d) grey: *bay, clay, day, fray, gay, hay, jay, lay, may, nay, pay, play, pray, ray, say, stray, stay, sway, sleigh, tray, way, yeah*

5. What letter combinations give you the vowel sounds below? Brainstorm as many words as possible with these sounds to find the letter combinations.
   a) uw (spoon) — oo (soon), u (flu), ew (blew), ue (true), wo (two), o (to)
   b) aw (brown) — ou (sound), ow (cow)
   c) ey (grey) — ey (freight), ay (day), eigh (sleigh)
   d) a (crawl) — a (all), aw (law), o (frog), au (applaud)
   e) ɛ (dead) — e (bed), ea (head), ai (said)

6. Say these words. What vowel sound does each underlined letter combination make?
   a) sleigh ey
   b) bought aw
   c) leopard ɛ
   d) shoe uw
   e) filet ey (French pronunciation)

Language Note

Many food and cooking terms in English are borrowed from the French. Examples include *filet, sauté, hors d'oeuvres, canapés, entrées,* and *buffet.*

Culture Note

Children's stories both reflect culture and influence it. In North America, for example, *Mother Goose Nursery Rhymes*, *Winnie the Pooh* stories, and Disney characters have infiltrated even adult culture. You may see references to, or parodies of, these stories and characters. In some cases, they have even become part of the language. For example, if something is too easy or has little substance (a negative connotation), we can say it is *mickey mouse* (e.g., *This is a mickey mouse course; What a mickey mouse speech.*) Ask students if children's stories and characters have similar impacts in their native culture. Which stories or characters are they?

Writing (SB p. 144)

Aims/Skills
• write a narrative
• create a children's story

The more children's stories students hear or read, the better they will be able to write one. Encourage students to read children's books/stories from the library or the Internet (see Helpful Internet Resources at the end of this unit on page 95).

Listening 1 (SB pp. 144–145)

See Tapescript 10.a

Aims/Skills
• listen for details
• listen for underlying meaning
• interpret poetic language

 ## Focused Listening (SB pp. 144–145)

Some poetry is valued as representing universal, timeless truths. This poem, by the early twentieth-century poet Kahlil Gibran, is an example of such poetry. Listen to the poem and fill in the missing words.

Your children are not your children,
They are the sons and daughters of Life's *longing* for itself.
They *come* through you but not from you.
And though they are with you yet they *belong* not to you.
You may *give* them your love but not your thoughts,
For they have their own thoughts.
You may *house* their bodies, but not their souls,
For their souls *dwell* in the house of tomorrow, which you cannot visit, even in your dreams.
You may *strive* to be like them, but seek not to make them like you,
For life *goes* not backward nor tarries with yesterday.
You are the bows from which your children as living arrows are *sent* forth.

 ## For Discussion (SB p. 145)

Possible answers:

1. In your own words, tell what this poet is saying.
   He is advising parents that they do not own their children, they are children of life. He says parents must not try to mould their children in their own image. Children belong to the world of the future, unknown to parents, and not the parents' past world.

2. What feelings do you associate with this poem?
   Answers will vary.

3. Who is the target audience for this poem? *Parents*

4. What does the poet mean when he says "They came through you but not from you?"
   Parents (mothers) bear their children, but the children's source is life itself, not the parents.

5. The writer refers to some common mistakes parents make in raising their children. What are some of these mistakes?
   Parents think they own their children and try to control them. Parents try to make their children have the same thoughts and values as they have. They try to make their children like them.
   What do you think could be done to make parents realize some of their errors? *Answers will vary.*

 ## One Step Beyond (SB p. 145)

1. You will notice that the lines in this poem do not rhyme. This is an example of a prose poem. Nonetheless, the poem clearly sounds like poetry when read. What elements of language do you hear and see in this poem that make it poetry and not just "good advice?"

   The lines are very rhythmic. The vocabulary and many of the phrases are formal and poetic: life's longing for itself (the continuation of the life cycle); house their bodies (take care of them/raise them in your home); for (because); their souls dwell in the house of tomorrow (they belong to the future); strive (try); seek not (don't try); tarries with yesterday (stay longer than expected; are sent forth (go ahead).

   The poem is full of images (pictures): house; bows and arrows.

   The poem also contains symbols (images that represent something else): body and soul (physical and the spiritual); house (world); dreams (imagination); bows (parents); arrows (children).

   *The sentence structure is long and formal with word order different from spoken language: you may (imperative form); though they . . . yet . . . (generally we don't use **though** and **yet** in the same sentence); they belong not to you (they don't belong to you); they come not from you (they don't come from you); seek not to make them like you (don't try to make them like you); life goes not backward (life doesn't go backward).*

Poetry (Reproducible 10.2)

Take the poem "Your Children Are Not Your Children" and omit some of the parts. Then ask students to complete the poem using their own words and ideas. Have students share their work with their classmates. Use the sample provided on Reproducible 10.2 or design your own.

Writing (SB p. 146)

Aim/Skill

• write a prose poem

You may wish to have students work with a partner or in small teams to develop the contents of a prose poem and then write it individually. Team/partner discussions should begin with a main message and a "feel" for the poem (e.g., reflective, humorous, light, severe, sad). Students could then exchange their poems in their teams or with their partners for review and observe how the same content and ideas can be expressed differently in a poem. Give them guided questions to discuss during their peer review session. These could include:

1. What do you like best about this poem?
2. Is the vocabulary in the poem poetic (and creative)? Give examples.
3. Does the poem contain images, symbols, and similies? Give examples.
4. How does reading this poem make you "feel?"
5. Read the poem aloud. Does it have a rhythm?
6. Does the poem reflect the content/main message your team discussed?

Reading 1 (SB pp. 146–148)

Aims/Skills

• read a graph
• anticipate contents of a reading
• read for details
• sequence information
• apply what is read to other contexts

Before You Read (SB p. 146)

ONE STEP AHEAD

You may wish to ask students the following specific questions about the graph.

a) What is the average life expectancy of a woman in the 1990s? *81 to 84 years*

b) What was the average life expectancy of a woman in the 1950s? *71 years*

c) What is the difference in the life expectancy of a man in the 1990s compared to the 1950s? *From 65.5 years in the 1950s to 74–81 years in the 1990s = difference of 8.5 to 15.5 years*

d) What ages are associated with adolescence in the 1990s? *12 to 30 years*

e) At what stage of life is a 50-year-old in the 1990s? *midlife passage and marriage and family building*

f) What years are considered middle age in the 1990s? *60 to 75 years*

g) What years were considered middle age in the 1950s? *45 to 60*

h) What stage of life is experienced around age 50 that in the 1950s was experienced around age 40? *midlife passage*

i) Two numbers are given for projected longevity for men and women in the 1990s. What does the lower number mean? *projected longevity for those under 65*

What does the higher number mean? *projected longevity for those already 65 or older*

j) In your own words, summarize the main idea of the graph. *People entered the six life stages about ten years later in the 1990s as compared to the 1950s. They also spent a greater number of years in adolescence in the 1990s than in the 1950s. Finally, the life expectancy of people in the 1990s was about ten years longer than in the 1950s.*

k) Can you speculate on some of the reasons for the shifts illustrated in the graph? *Answers will vary.*

For Discussion (SB p. 148)

With a partner or in teams, discuss these questions.

1. What happened in the 1950s that revolutionized the study of human development?
Erik Erikson, an American psychologist, explored the stages of human development beyond childhood (lines 5–8).

2. Discuss three ways in which Gail Sheehy's theory of adult development differs from Erikson's theory?
Erikson believed there were eight stages of human development (including three stages in adult life) and that the conflicts associated with each stage had to be resolved in order to move on to the next stage (lines 8–14). He also believed that life stages were associated with specific age ranges (lines 28–29). Sheehy theorizes that five generations occupy contemporary adulthood today. Also there has been a significant shift in the age ranges

associated with particular life stage, and the way in which people deal with the tasks of each life stage is changing (lines 29–36).

3. What factors will affect how stages of adulthood will be defined in the future?
The globalization of cultures and economies, and advances in technology and health care will influence how we define stages of adulthood in the future (lines 59–63).

Organization (SB p. 148)

The sentences below are all from paragraphs in the article you have just read. They are not in the proper order. Without looking at the text, put the sentences into a logical order and rewrite the paragraph.

Answer: c, e, b, a, f, d

c) *The way we look at human development has changed dramatically over the last 100 years.*

e) *Until the 1950s the study of human development was mainly concerned with identifying and defining the developmental stages of childhood.*

b) *In the 1950s however, Erik Erikson, an American psychologist, revolutionized the way we thought about human development by exploring stages of the human life cycle beyond childhood.*

a) *According to Erikson, there were eight stages of human development, including three stages in adult life: Young Adulthood, Maturity, and Old Age.*

f) *The stages were regarded as steps on a ladder.*

d) *Each step, he claimed, was ridden with conflicts that had to be resolved before a person could move to a higher stage.*

One Step Beyond (SB p. 148)

1. According to the article, today's Generation Xers don't expect their careers to evolve in the same ways as their parents' careers. How do you expect the careers of this generation to differ given today's technological, business, and economic environment?
Possible answer: According to experts there is already a trend towards working on contract, working from home, consulting, and self-employment. Workers will not work for the same company for many years; as a result, they won't develop the sense of loyalty previous generations did. Today's workers are more likely to invest privately towards their pension and rely less on company and government pension plans.

2. Sheehy suggests that the Endangered Generation will have to deal with the Pulling Up Roots stage, a time when we strive to become independent of our parents, differently from previous generations. Why is this, and how do you think this generation will deal with the tasks of this stage?
Possible answer for why?: Firstly, this stage is being experienced at a later time than previously, partly because young people stay in school longer, especially women, who don't get married as early. Secondly, the opportunities for

independence are not as great in today's employment market, especially for those who have not finished high school or college and university. It's not as easy to earn money. Thirdly, even when young people are ready to go to work and find work, they often have considerable student loans to pay back, making them less financially independent. Many young people live at home longer or move back home after having lived independently for several years. How?: Answers will vary.

Culture Note

People at various ages are valued differently in different societies. North America traditionally has been a youth culture. Advertising and the media in general focus on images of young people. This is changing somewhat now as more and more "baby boomers" become older. Products and services are being developed and marketed to this generation now in the 40–55 age range. Nonetheless, in North America children are encouraged to be participatory members of their families and school communities. They are encouraged to have opinions and speak out. Children's freedoms and rights to health, safety, and education are strongly protected under the law. The very old, on the other hand, often complain of a lack of respect by younger age groups. Have students discuss how each generation is viewed in their native culture and why they think this is so.

 Vocabulary 1 (SB pp. 148–149)

Aims/Skills

- guess meaning from context
- discover alternate meanings for words
- examine adjective/noun collocations
- learn various grammatical forms of words

 Answer Key

1. Guessing Meaning (SB p. 148)

Gail Sheehy has described various decades of adulthood as follows:
Tryout Twenties
Turbulent Thirties
Flourishing Forties
Flaming Fifties
Serene Sixties

a) Based on the meanings of the adjectives and your own experiences with people in these age groups, discuss what Sheehy means by each of these terms. Then, write the meaning of each adjective.
tryout: *experiment with new and different things to see how they work*
turbulent: *a state of confusion and disorder*
flourishing: *to grow successfully*
flaming: *forceful, energetic*
serene: *calm, peaceful*

b) Discuss other uses of the adjectives. What nouns might you describe using these adjectives? Write a sentence for each adjective.

tryout: *audition (especially in sports)*
Sylvia did not do well in the tryouts and was consequently not chosen for the team.
Note: Tryout is normally used as a noun, as in this example, or as a two-word verb "to try out."
turbulent: *strong and uneven movements (with air and water)*
Passengers on Flight 404 to Miami were advised to fasten their seat belts due to turbulent weather.
flourishing: *to wave something in your hand to draw attention to it*
Proud of having received an A on his term essay, Andrew walked into the class flourishing his paper for all to see.
Note: Flourishing is normally used as an adjective or verb, although in the sentence above it is used as an ing verbal in an adverbial phrase.

flaming: *angry and severe*
The sales manager anticipated that news of the lost advertising account would meet with a flaming response from his supervisor.

2. **Word Forms** (SB pp. 148–149)
Learning new vocabulary is more than knowing the meaning of a word. You must learn to use a word in different grammatical forms. Copy and complete the chart on the next page. For each word:
a) find another grammatical form of the word in the reading
b) write a definition for the word based on its meaning in the sentence
c) list other forms of the word and identify their grammatical use.
The first one has been done for you.

Word	Form in Reading	Meaning	Other Forms
1. global	globalization ". . . with the continued *globalization* of cultures and economies. . ."	the process of spreading across the world	globe (*n*) global (*adj*) globally (*adv*) globalize (*v*)
2. revolution	revolutionized (6)	completely changed	revolution (*n*) revolutionary (*adj*) revolve (*v*) revolutionize (*v*)
3. apprentice	apprenticeship (42)	period of time spent learning a trade or craft from an expert	apprentice (*n*) apprenticeship (*n*) apprentice (*v*)
4. develop	development (1) developmental (4)	process of growing to become something better	develop (*v*) development (*n*) developmental (*adj*) developmentally (*adv*) developing (*adj*) developed (*adj*) developer (*n*)
5. mature	maturity (11)	state of being completely grown	mature (*adj*) maturing (*adj*) maturity (*n*) maturation (*n*) mature (*v*) maturely (*adv*)
6. theory	theory (26) theorizes (30)	formal statement of rules that explain a fact or event	theory (*n*) theorem (*n*) theorize (*v*) theoretical (*adj*) theoretically (*adv*) theorist (*n*)

3. Formality Register (SB p. 149)

The article you read is an example of academic writing and has a formal tone. One way to achieve this tone is to use formal vocabulary. Find the words below (or forms of them) in the reading and write an informal equivalent for each one. Use a thesaurus if you need help.

a) strive *(line 38) try*
b) contemporary *(line 31) modern, today*
c) span *(line 30 spanning) ranging*
d) resolve *(line 13 resolved) solved*
e) evolve *(line 49) develop*

Workbook Practice and Expansion: Vocabulary 1 Exercises A–D (WB pp. 84–85)

Expansion

Guess the Word

Have students work in teams of three (or with one partner). Write the unit vocabulary words on cards or paper strips and copy one set for each team. One student chooses a card. The other team members take turns asking yes/no questions to guess what word the cardholder has.

EXAMPLE:
A: Is this word a synonym for modern? (contemporary)
Cardholder: No.
B: Is this a word you could use to describe a bumpy airplane ride?
Cardholder: Yes.
B: Is the word *turbulent*?
Cardholder: Yes.

Students may not ask about any letters in the word. They must ask about meaning or grammatical form. It may help to list the unit words on the blackboard.

Grammar Focus (SB pp. 149–152)

🔑 Exercise A (SB p. 150)

Read the following paragraphs and identify the main time perspective of each passage. Each paragraph will only have one main time perspective: P (Past), Pr (Present), F (Future), or NST (No Specific Time).

1. **P** Grandfather loved to tell stories of his childhood on the farm. He once told me of a time when he was seven. He had been playing with his friends when his brother dared him to ride one of the horses bareback. Confident in his own riding ability, he accepted the challenge. When he lost control of the horse, however, he rode right through his mother's laundry line.

2. **F** In the future there will be lots of work, but few jobs. Freelance and consulting work will be common work patterns for many people. Young people entering the workforce in 20 years will have to arm themselves with a different set of skills than those of their predecessors because they will be bidding for work instead of attending job interviews. They will not only have to have job-related skills, but will also have to be able to sell themselves, work independently, and be self-motivating. Luckily for me, I will already have retired by that time.

3. **NST** One of the most interesting areas of brain research proves that early stimulation of the infant and child brain has significant effects on later intellectual development. For example, researchers have found that children who learn to read and play musical instruments at a young age eventually do better in mathematics than children who do not receive music training. The sets of neurons in the brain that develop with music training are the same sets of neurons that are involved in calculating mathematical problems. Consequently, the neurons used when doing mathematics are better developed in children who have received early music training.

4. **Pr** Mother is washing the dishes again. I watch her from the dinner table, now cleared of dirty plates, grimy glasses, and left-over meatloaf. The steam from the hot, soapy water rises. As she rinses a glass, I see her hands, red and swollen. How many dishes have those hands washed? How many meals have they cooked, these hands that tell a life story? How many shirts have those hands ironed? How many dirty socks have those fingers turned right-side-out? How many soiled diapers have those hands changed? How many scraped knees have they cleansed and bandaged? How many tears have they wiped? With these thoughts still racing through my mind I get up slowly, grab a dish towel and help — because I am a good daughter.

5. **F** I'm going home next spring. As soon as I get there I'm going to call may best friend Tanja. By then we won't have seen each other for a whole year. Then we're going to go to all the spots where we used to hang out: the clubs, the shops, and our special swimming spot along the river. It'll be great.

🔑 Exercise B (SB p. 151)

Read the paragraphs on the previous page again and identify the verbs in each sentence. Using a chart like the one below, try to identify the specific tenses of all the verbs in each paragraph.

ONE STEP AHEAD
Students may identify verbs that are not main verbs in the sentence. The asterixed answers below refer to verbs used as parts of relative clauses or participles that are not considered main verbs.

Past Perspective		Present		No Specific Time		Future Perspective	
loved	simple past	is washing	present continuous	proves	simple present	will be (lots of work)	simple future
told	simple past	watch	simple present	has	"	will be (common work patterns)	simple future
had been playing	past perfect progressive	rises	"	have found	present perfect	will have to (arm)	simple future with modal "have to"
dared	simple past	rinses	"	do	simple present	will be bidding	future progressive
accepted	simple past	see	"	are	"		
lost	simple past	have washed	present perfect	are developed	"	**Note: attending is also part of the verb phrase in simple future, although the auxiliaries "will be" have not been repeated**	
rode	simple past	have cooked	"	*children who learn to read (relative clause — not a main verb)		will have to (have)	simple future with modal "have to"
*a time when he was (relative clause — not a main verb)		have ironed	"	*children who do not receive (relative clause — not a main verb)		will have to (be able to)	simple future with modal "have to"
		have turned	"	*sets of neurons that develop (relative clause — not a main verb)		**Note: sell, work, and be self-motivated are also parts of verb phrases in the future simple tense, although the auxiliary and modals "will have to be able to" have not been repeated**	
		have changed	"	*neurons that are involved (relative clause — not a main verb)		will have retired	future perfect
		have cleansed	"	*the neurons used when (reduced relative clause — not a main verb)		am going	present continuous
		have wiped	"	*children who have received (relative clause — not a main verb)		as soon as . . . get	simple present
		get up	simple present			am going to call	simple future (be going to + v)
		grab	"			won't have seen each other	future perfect (will)
		help	"			are going to go	simple future (be going to + v)
		am	"			will be	simple future (will)
		*now cleared of dirty dishes (participial phrase — not a main verb)				*spots where we used to	(relative clause — not a main verb)
		*With these thoughts racing through my mind (ing verbal as part of an adverbial clause — not a main verb)					

Exercise C (SB p. 152)

The sentences below are in different tenses. Identify the tense of the main verb and discuss why it is used. Then, decide where the sentence fits in the tense chart on the previous page.

1. Generation Xers enter the Pulling Up Roots Stage almost ten years later than the World War II Generation. *enter — simple present*

2. Erikson revolutionized the way we thought about human development. *revolutionized — simple past*

3. For centuries, philosophers have been trying to understand how people change over the course of their lives. *have been trying — present perfect progressive*

4. In the mid-seventies, psychologists at the University of California were studying how people's lives change during young and middle adulthood. *were studying — past progressive*

5. She had always considered herself a mature adult until the birth of her first child. *had considered — past perfect*

6. The definitions of life's stages will continue to be redefined in the future. *will continue — simple future (will)*

7. The way we look at human development has changed dramatically over the last 100 years. *has changed — present perfect*

8. People now in their thirties are complaining that they will be left to clean up the economic mess their parents' and grandparents' generations have created. *are complaining — present progressive*

9. By the year 2005 the number of people between the ages of 40 to 49 will have increased by about one million compared to 1995. *will have increased — future perfect*

10. In the future, advertisers will no longer be targeting the youth market. *will no longer be targeting — future progressive*

11. Until the 1950s psychologists had been concentrating their efforts on defining the stages of childhood. *had been concentrating — past perfect progressive*

12. These days, by the time many couples gets married, they will likely have been living together for at least one year. *will have been living — future perfect progressive*

Grammar In Use (SB p. 152)

ONE STEP AHEAD

If you feel your students will have difficulty anticipating eight questions, give them the following prepared questions. Alternatively, have them anticipate eight questions and prepare responses, but during the panel discussion ask the eight questions given here. Tell them these are the questions the students want addressed. It may be interesting for your students to see how closely their anticipated questions match those students actually have.

Panel for elementary school and high school graduates:

1. Describe your first day in high school/ at college/ at university.
2. What surprised you the most about high school/college/ university?
3. What was the most difficult adjustment you had to make?
4. Do you think it is a good idea to get involved in extra curricular activities in high school/college/university? Does getting involved interfere with studying?
5. How did you manage your work load in high school/ college/university?
6. What activities did you participate in that you felt helped you to adjust or relax?
7. What are tests and exams like in high school/college/ university?
8. What do you think are the three keys to success in high school/college/university?

Workbook Practice and Expansion: Grammar Focus Exercises A–C (WB pp. 85–86)
Grammar Expansion (Shifting Tenses) Exercises A–E (WB pp. 86–89)

Grammar Dictation

Dictate the following story to your class. Read it twice at normal speed. The first time have students listen for meaning and plot. The second time have students jot down key words or phrases that will help them reconstruct the story. They should not try to write the story as you read it. Have students work with partners and then in small teams to reconstruct the story. The goal is not to rewrite the story word for word, but rather to capture the main events. At the end show students the original story to see how closely they were able to reconstruct it. Also discuss the use of tenses in the story.

A Frightening Experience

Everyone has one or two stories they tell again and again. They are the kind of stories that are told many years into the future. Of course, when you look back you think they are funny, but there was nothing funny about this event when it happened.

It happened one night last spring. It was a Friday night and I was home alone. I'd been watching TV for most of the evening. At about midnight I turned off the TV, turned out the lights, and headed upstairs for bed.

While I was washing in the bathroom, I heard a noise. It sounded like glass breaking. I rushed out of the bathroom toward the noise. I was surprised to see my wife's favourite vase broken on the floor of my bedroom. My wife's great aunt had given it to her six months before and it had been sitting on the dresser near the window since then. My wife loves that vase and I knew she would be terribly upset. Suddenly the closet door moved. I grabbed a rifle which was hanging on the wall. I'd been hunting on safari the previous year and had brought it home as a souvenir. I opened the closet door and out leaped a big, ugly Tom cat. It must have climbed in the open window and knocked over the vase. I was so frightened that I fainted.

I'm sure I will tell this story a few more times, maybe even to my grandchildren. You see, there is a good lesson to be learned from this story: Never leave your windows open at night.

See Tapescript 10.b

Aims/Skills

• take notes from listening

• listen for viewpoints

• listen for language and tone

 Focused Listening (SB p. 153)

Now listen to the interviews and note each character's answers in point form

1. What do you enjoy doing in your spare time?
   8-year-old boy: reading, thinking about airplanes, playing with friends
   17-year-old girl: spending time with friends, going to fun places, going to dances
   40-year-old woman: gardening, reading, would like to travel (but can't)
   86-year-old man: working; it keeps him young

2. What kinds of things frighten you or worry you at this stage in your life?
   8-year-old boy: monsters and ghosts, being beaten up after school, getting in trouble for not doing school work
   17-year-old girl: death, grades, and making it (being successful)
   40-year-old woman: health (becoming a quadriplegic), losing the ability to take care of family
   86-year-old man: death; other than that, nothing

3. What's the best thing about being a person your age?
   8-year-old boy: being young, playing, running
   17-year-old girl: doing fun and crazy things without a reason, not having much responsibility
   40-year-old woman: having the confidence and experience to make choices that don't leave you with regrets
   86-year-old man: still being alive

4. What's the worst thing about being a person your age?
   8-year-old boy: getting bossed around by grown-ups
   17-year-old girl: pressure from parents, parents not letting you go out
   40-year-old woman: tremendous responsibility (responsible for children and aging parents)
   86-year-old man: nothing really

5. What is the most important thing or who are the most important people in your life at this time?
   8-year-old boy: mother, father, brother, aunt, uncle, grandparents (close family), and himself
   17-year-old girl: friends, school
   40-year-old woman: children and husband (spouse), would like to win the lottery to have more options
   86-year-old man: health; wife (spouse), has no children; there aren't many people left

6. What do you want to tell younger people about people your age?
   8-year-old boy: sometimes people scream at you when you didn't do it, but other times if you're really good you get a reward
   17-year-old girl: it's fun, but you have to be patient with your parents and concentrate on school
   40-year-old woman: getting older (grey hair, sagging a bit, going up a dress or shirt size) is not so bad, but you have to age gracefully
   86-year-old man: don't be rude to older people; they're not stupid. Treat them with respect.

7. What do you want to tell older people about people your age?
   8-year-old boy: people were better runners when they were children
   17-year-old girl: teens may annoy you and do stupid things, but they're just learning. They are trying, so be patient.
   40-year-old woman: Let us make our own choices, stop treating us like children
   86-year-old man: not asked

One Step Beyond (SB p. 153)

1. The dialogues you have just heard are actual transcripts from authentic interviews. Listen again to each interview and compare how each character uses language and tone of voice differently to communicate.
Possible answers:
8-year-old boy: uses simple words and structures ("neat airplanes")
17-year-old girl: uses simple words and structures (". . . family and stuff"), makes minor grammatical errors ("I want to do good in school" — do well in school), rising intonation after many statements
40-year-old woman: more complex sentence structure, more reflective, confident tone
86-year-old man: confident in answering

2. How have values and what is important changed from previous generations? Imagine that four people in the same age groups as the ones in this listening exercise had been asked these questions in the late 1930s. How would their answers be different from the ones you just heard? *Answers will vary. Note: You may wish to expand on your students' speculations by asking how values and what is important will change in the future. Imagine that four people in the same age groups as the ones in this listening exercise will be asked these questions in 2050. How will their answers be different from the ones you just heard?*

Expansion

Comparative Interviews
Have students interview various people in the same four age groups, asking the same questions. Then compare their answers to the ones of the characters in the listening exercise.

 **Writing (SB p. 154)**

Aims/Skills
- express hopes and plans in writing
- use future tenses in writing

 **Speaking (SB p. 154)**

Aims/Skills
- discuss symbols
- describe their generation
- use a variety of tenses to express ideas

If you wish to model the activity, make up an imaginary time capsule from a future period and bring it to class. Have students look at the items, illustrations, etc., and speculate on the generation that created the capsule, the estimated year in the future, and what the contents say about the lives of those people.

Expansion

Project Option
Have students research a period and place in history to discover what life was like for a given generation (for example, the life of an adolescent girl in ancient Egypt), then create a time capsule.

 Reading 2 (SB pp. 154–156)

Aims/Skills
- scan for information
- summarize a reading
- read for underlying message
- examine style
- examine how language and literary strategies contribute to tone

 Comprehension Check (SB p. 156)

Note: Ask students to "scan" not "skim" the paragraphs.

1. To find the answers to the questions below, **scan** the paragraphs indicated in the numbered boxes.
   a) In your own words, tell what two things make the box on the shelf special. (1)
   The box contains personal treasures. The box has been with the writer for a long time.
   b) What did each family member's lunch bag contain? (3)
   Each lunch bag contained a sandwich, apple, milk money, and sometimes a note or a treat.
   c) What food items were in the paper bag? (4)
   The bag contained two animal crackers and two chocolate kisses.
   d) What lie did the father tell his daughter? (6)
   The father said he forgot to bring the bag home. This was a lie. He had thrown the bag in the garbage.
   e) What did the father say to his daughter when he returned the bag? (11)
   He didn't say anything, but after dinner he asked her to tell him about the stuff in the sack.

f) How did the father know the daughter still trusted him? (13)
The daughter gave him the bag again a few days later. She gave it to him a few times over several months.

2. This story contains a lot of information that isn't necessary to understanding the "key" actions, but that helps create the "feeling" of the story. Identify the essential information that tells the actions in the story. Then summarize the story in one paragraph using the W5H question format as a guide: Who, What, Where, When, Why, and How.
Possible answers:
Essential Elements
— *Father finds a lunch-sized brown paper bag he has saved for fourteen years that contains some odds and ends from his daughter when she was young. This prompts him to tell the story of the bag.*
— *When his daughter became school-aged, she helped make the family lunches. Each family member took a bagged lunch.*
— *One time the daughter gave the father two paper bags for lunch. When he opened the second bag at lunchtime, he found that the bag contained little things that young girls collect such as hair ribbons, stones, pencil stubs, and so on.*
— *Father thought it was cute, but threw out the bag.*
— *When he came home that night, the daughter asked for the bag, saying she had forgotten to put a note in it. The note read: "I love you Daddy". The daughter explained that the things in the bag were important to her. She had thought he might like to see them. Now she wanted the bag back.*
— *When the dad explained that he didn't have the bag, she became upset, thinking maybe he had lost it. The dad, feeling terrible, lied and said he had forgotten the bag and would bring it home the next day.*
— *The same night he went back to the office and retrieved the bag from the waste paper basket.*
— *The next day he brought it home to her and asked her to explain each item in the bag.*
— *After that, once in a while the daughter would give the dad the bag to take along.*
— *Eventually she lost interest in the bag, but the dad kept it as a reminder of how much his young daughter loved and trusted him.*

Discussion (SB p. 156)

The real purpose of this story is not to tell what happened to the father. It is to send a broader message — to make a statement about being a parent. What phrase in the story reveals the "key" message the writer wants to leave us with?

Sometimes I think of all the times in this sweet life when I must have missed the affection I was being given. (lines 108–109)

One Step Beyond (SB p. 156)

1. The tone of this reading is very different from the tone of "A New Look At Human Development." Describe and compare the styles of the two readings. Then note what language and literary strategies contribute to the tone of each.
Possible answer:
"A Look At Human Development": academic writing; stimulates your intellect and shares knowledge; contains facts and charts; relies on expert sources to support its thesis; provides examples, but not unnecessary details (we don't become connected to the reading or the people in it, i.e., Erikson, and Sheehy); vocabulary is formal and sophisticated
"The Cardboard Box Is Marked 'The Good Stuff'": personal story; stimulates emotions and shares experience; contains anecdotes and personal thoughts; relies on a personal stirring of emotions to support its thesis; provides many details unnecessary to the plot, but necessary to giving a personal connection to the characters in the story (we can picture the family making lunches and we connect personally and emotionally with the father and to a lesser extent with the daughter); the vocabulary is simple, full of emotion, and as spoken in daily life (except for the poetic phrase "Such as I have, I give to thee.")

2. In paragraph 16 the writer uses the sentence: "Such as I have, give I to thee." What strikes you as unusual about this sentence and why has the writer used this element?
This poetic phrase is unusual because the rest of the reading contains very simple language as it is used in daily family life. The writer uses the phrase to draw attention to a key message in the reading, i.e., the daughter gave to him all that she had at that time in her life. The poetic language makes the message appear more serious, and elevates it to become universal truth.

Writing (SB p. 156)

Aim/Skill
• write a narrative essay

You may want to refer students to the process writing section in the Workbook (pp. 89–91) before completing the writing activity.

To help students focus, ask them to begin by writing a sentence or two about the broader message they want to address. Then they can think about an experience that illustrates that message. Alternatively, ask students to recall an event that left them with a very positive or negative feeling and analyze what message lay in that experience.

Process Writing (WB pp. 89–91)

The process writing program culminates with the writing of narrative/descriptive essays. Activities include sequencing main events, describing pictures using sensory imaging, and writing narrative and descriptive essays through illustrated stories, interviews, and personal anecdotes.

Unit Reflection (SB p. 156)

You could have students prepare a visual presentation of their circle of life. It might include personal photos, illustrations, or magazine photos, food labels, photocopies of book titles/excerpts, and so on. Encourage students to be creative.

Helpful Internet Resources

There are some good sites for this unit, but it is most helpful to preview them and design projects or tasks for students before sending them to the sites. This is especially important for the sites on human development.

Key word search: storytelling, children's stories, aging, youth, adolescence, teenagers

http://www.csrnet.org/csrnet/substitute/story.html
A great site of story resources and links on the Internet.

http://www.gl.umbc.edu/~vdotte1/index.html
On Aging: an interesting site designed for sociology students and others interested in the aging process. Site includes articles and relevant links.

www.yahoo.com/society_and_culture/cultures_and_Groups/Teenagers
For Teens: site for teens to browse with links to anything from teen magazines to social agency links

Reproducibles

1.1   Venn Diagram: Newspaper vs. Journal Articles

1.2   Designing a Disaster Shelter

1.3   Passive Sentence Game

2.1   Strip Story

2.2   Prefix Memory Game

3.1   A Travel Fair

4.1   Interpreting Body Language Game

4.2   Role Play — Cards

4.3   Role Play — Questions and Summary

4.4   Conversation Management

5.1   Inventors and Inventions

5.2   Creating Hybrids

6.1   Word Quiz

7.1   Survey: What's Hot and What's Cool

7.2   Mystery Word Game

8.1   Sports Categories Game

9.1   Healthy Eating

9.2   World Committee on Initiatives for Better Nutrition

10.1   The Seasons of Life

10.2   Composing a Prose Poem

Reproducible 1.1. Venn Diagram: Newspaper *vs.* Journal Articles

Complete the diagram below. Write those points relating to newspaper articles in the left circle, those relating to journal articles in the right circle, and those relating to both in the central overlapping part of the circles.

- most recent and important developments stated early in article, usually in the first paragraph
- are generally longer
- vocabulary is familiar
- do not necessarily give all the pertinent news/facts in the first paragraph
- information is presented clearly and precisely
- direct quotations add authority
- must use exact statistics
- use academic terms/vocabulary
- headline entices reader and relates to main thread of the story
- numbers/statistics can be rounded off or approximated if exact number is not a central issue
- use simple, straightforward writing style

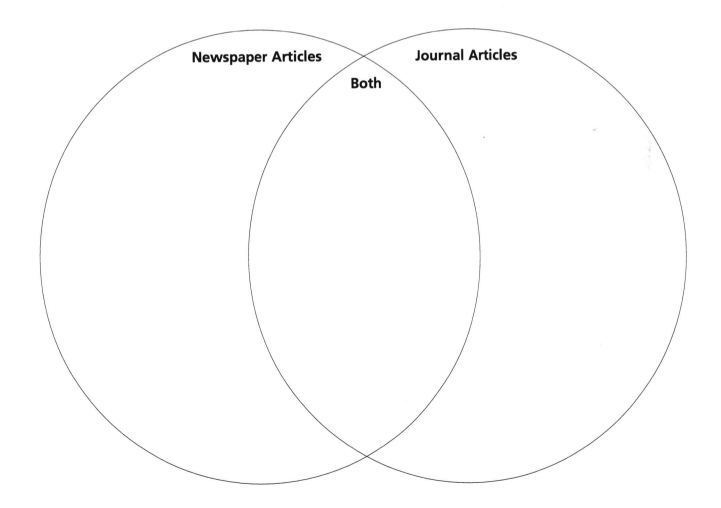

Reproducible 1.2. Designing a Disaster Shelter

Instructions:

1. In teams of three to four, design a disaster shelter.

2. Use at least three sources such as the Internet, texts, newspapers, magazines, and journal articles.

3. Write a report using the following headings:
   • Description of Natural Disaster
   • Warning Signs
   • Evacuation Plan
   • Shelter Features
   • Post-Disaster Plans
   • Sources (appropriately identified)

4. Present your plan to the class. Your presentation should be between 5–10 minutes and should include the following:
   a) an introduction of the presentation team
   b) a clear and concise explanation of the natural disaster you are preparing for, how potential victims will be warned, the steps they should take to get to the shelter, the features of the shelter, and what will happen after danger has passed
   c) visual and audio aids where appropriate to illustrate information
   d) a brief period for taking questions from classmates.
   Note: The information must be presented NOT READ.

Marking Scheme:

Written Report   **(10%)**

    Content/Structure (7%)
            Relevant and complete information
            Current sources and information
            Logical sequence
            Clear and concise writing
            Appropriate vocabulary
            Standard English sentence structure
            Appropriate use of connectors

    Mechanics   (3%)
            Standard English spelling
            Standard punctuation and capitalization
            Appropriate source documentation

Presentation   **(10%)**
            Effective introduction to presentation
            Information presented clearly and concisely
            Appropriate voice, pronunciation, and pace
            Information sequenced effectively
            Use of appropriate vocabulary
            Effective conclusion or summary
            Appropriate visuals and audio materials used
            Presented, not read
            Question period handled well
            Fluency in presentation

Reproducible 1.3. Passive Sentence Game

Reproducible 2.1. Strip Story

One evening last summer I had a bizarre experience.

I was walking my dog, Charlie, in a field across from where I live.

Charlie had been busily exploring the underbrush of bushes
as he ran around the field in his usual way.

Suddenly, he stopped, looked up to my left, and began
to whine in a strange manner.

I turned to look in that direction and was surprised to see
a floating figure in the distance.

The figure was as tall as a man and seemed to be holding something
in its hand — a leash perhaps. But the figure didn't appear human.

By now Charlie, who had been inching his way toward the figure,
was in front of it and his whining had stopped.

The figure leaned forward and seemed to be putting something
around Charlie's neck.

Suddenly I panicked and ran towards the place where
Charlie and the stranger were.

But by the time I got to them, there was nothing.
Both of them had disappeared.

I never saw Charlie or the figure again.

Reproducible 2.2. Prefix Memory Game

pre-	sub-	para-	super-
syn-	tele-	post-	de-
trans-	mono-	dis-	mal-
before	under or below	above or beyond	beyond or beside
same or common	far	after	alone
opposite of	across	negative of	bad

Reproducible 3.1. A Travel Fair

Instructions:

1. Put together a vacation package. Choose a destination and write to or call the local tourist office for information. You can also get information from airlines, travel agencies, or the Internet. Find the following information:

   - cost of airfare
   - hotel availability and descriptions
   - amenities available at hotel
   - facilities for the guests
   - recreational activities available
   - local tourist attractions
   - currency used
   - meal plan
   - choose a target age group

2. Use pictures, drawings, and written descriptions to advertise your vacation package in a booth at a travel show. You get a commission for each person who chooses your tourist destination package so it is important to SELL your site.

3. Establish a criteria checklist for what you consider to be the most important features of a great trip. Using the play money provided by the teacher, visit the other booths at the fair and go shopping for your best vacation buy.

Marking Scheme:

Your booth will be evaluated according to the following criteria.

Written Content/ Grammar	(6%) Information presented clearly and concisely Good use of descriptive language Correct use of adjective order
Visuals	(4%) Attractive visual appearance to booth Text and format easy to read Effective attention grabber Visuals relevant to task

Reproducible 4.1a. Interpreting Body Language Game

Body Movement

Put the palm of one or both of your hands flat against your cheek(s) and tighten your face muscles.

Body Movement

Stand holding your arms crossed over your chest with hands gripping the upper part of the opposite arm.

Body Movement

Stroke your chin, moving your head slightly up and down.

Body Movement

Shuffle across the room with your hands hanging limp at your sides and your head bent forward.

Body Movement

Stand straight with the tips of your fingers on your left hand pressed against those of your right hand in a steeple position.

Body Movement

Open your eyes and mouth wide and cover your mouth with the palm of your hand.

Body Movement

Pat someone on the arm or back and smile.

Body Movement

Widen your eyes and rub your hands in front of you in anticipation of a treat and smile.

Body Movement

Shrug your shoulders and hold your hands out, palms up, in front of you.

Body Movement

Lower your head slightly, close your eyes, pinch the bridge of your nose, and take a deep breath.

Body Movement

Raise your hand to head level and cross your fingers.

Body Movement

With your head slightly bent down and to the side, peek at the audience and then turn your eyes away while smiling and drawing in your bottom lip.

Message Card
Embarrassment

Message Card
Confidence

Message Card
Hoping for good luck

Message Card
Defensiveness

Message Card
Everything will be fine.

Message Card
A tough decision

Message Card
Dejection

Message Card
Thinking or evaluating

Message Card
What do you want from me?

Message Card
Shyness

Message Card
Expectation

Message Card
Astonishment

Reproducible 4.2. Role Play — Cards

Customer Role Card

Four days ago you transferred $24 000 from your bank account to your cousin's bank account in Santiago, Chile. The money was supposed to be picked up by your cousin, who was going to use it to close a real estate deal today. If your cousin doesn't pay the money today, the deal will fall through. Last night your cousin called you desperate that the money hadn't arrived at the bank yet. You became very worried, because you arranged the transfer and are now wondering where the money went. Today you go into your bank to solve this problem.

You want:
• to know where the money is
• to know what the bank is going to do to find your money
• the money to be received in Santiago today so that your real estate deal will not fall through

You have to communicate:
• that you are very frustrated
• that you are confused about how the money could get lost
• that you are furious the money is lost and that the bank isn't doing anything to help you
• that this is a very important business deal and it is urgent that the money reach Santiago

You cannot leave the bank until your problem is solved.

Bank Teller Role Card

In two weeks you are starting a new job at another bank. This job pays more money and you cannot wait to leave your current job. You are still nice to people, but you know you aren't going to be in the job for much longer and you don't really think it's your responsibility to deal with people's problems, especially if they can't be solved right away. You have no intention of going out of your way in this job. You've had a terrible morning and you just want to go home. A customer comes to the bank with a problem. The customer transferred some money into a foreign bank account a few days ago, but it never arrived. You check on the computer and discover that the money was transferred out from your branch. You don't know why the money isn't at the other branch and, to your knowledge, there is no way of finding out why the money isn't there. Your records indicate that everything is fine.

You think that:
• the customer is rude
• the customer is blaming you for the mistake
• the customer is overreacting
• you did everything according to procedure and the missing money is the customer's problem, not yours

You feel:
• embarrassed
• annoyed
• mistreated

You would like to tell this customer how you feel, but you must be professional because you want to leave your present job on good terms. As far as you are concerned, there is nothing you can do for this customer.

Reproducible 4.3. Role Play — Questions and Summary

Role Play 1

Questions:

1. What is the problem?
2. Whose responsibility is it to solve the problem?
3. How does the customer communicate his/her feelings? What does he/she feel?
4. How does the bank teller communicate his/her feelings? What is the teller thinking?
5. What should the customer do to get results?
6. What should the bank teller do in this situation?

Role Play 2

Comparison Chart:

	Customer 1	Customer 2
How does the customer describe the problem?		
	Bank Teller 1	*Bank Teller 2*
How does the teller react to the customer's problem?		
	Customer 1	*Customer 2*
How does the customer express emotions non-verbally?		
	Bank Teller 1	*Bank Teller 2*
How does the teller express emotions non-verbally?		
	Customer 1	*Customer 2*
What does the customer do to resolve the problem?		
	Bank Teller 1	*Bank Teller 2*
What does the teller do to resolve the problem?		

Reproducible 4.4. Conversation Management

Expert

Talk as if you know everything, but be vague. Contribute at least 5 major points to the discussion. Even if you don't know anything about the topic, make up information and pretend that you know everything. You want to find a solution to this problem. Your goal is to dominate the discussion and make sure the solution adopted by the group is your idea or appears to be your idea.

Disbeliever

You are the sceptic and the one who disagrees in the group. You don't believe what others say and you don't think the solutions put forth will work. Your job is to challenge what others say and disagree with them. Ask the other team members for evidence and justification of their ideas. Challenge at least 4 ideas put forth in the discussion. You don't think a solution is possible.

Diverger

You love to talk about everything except the topic at hand. You don't want to talk about this subject. Ask questions, interject, or do whatever you have to to get the team sidetracked. Get the discussion off track at least 4 times during the exercise.

Concerned Listener

You are very concerned about how people "feel" in the discussion. You want to make sure that the process is fair, that everyone has a turn to speak, and that no one gets offended. Invite silent members to participate, control those who are talking too much, and ask how people are feeling about the discussion. You are not that concerned about finding a solution to the problem. Your goal is to make sure the discussion process is fair and that everyone is happy.

Clarifier

You want to make sure that everyone understands the ideas being put forth. Clarify each major point in the discussion by restating it, summarizing, or asking questions that clarify. Your goal is to clarify at least 6 ideas in the discussion. You are not as concerned about finding a solution as you are about making sure everything is understood.

The Task Master

You want only one thing: to get a solution to this problem in the given time period. Your job is to make sure the discussion stays on track, that ideas are put forward, and that the team comes up with a solution. If there is no solution by the end of the activity, you haven't done your job.

The Problem

You are a group of high school teachers. Ana Follati, a senior high school student, is having problems. Until now, Ana was an excellent student. She got good grades, actively participated in school sports and other extra curricular activities, and was well-liked. In her early high school years she also volunteered to tutor students in an after-school program. This year one of her family members became very ill and this has affected her performance at school. At first teachers and classmates were sympathetic, covering for her lack of effort and making excuses for her tardiness and absences. Her classmates have been covering for her in team projects, taking on her workload so that she has time to spend with the sick family member. However, her poor performance has dragged on for several months and there is no sign of her situation changing in the near future. Through the help of her friends she has maintained acceptable grades, but her classmates and teachers are becoming annoyed at her lack of effort. She needs to continue with her studies and graduate from high school this year because her family is moving to another country next year; if she fails the year or drops out, she will not graduate. You know that Ana is an intelligent young woman and under normal circumstances would have no difficulty graduating from high school. Together find a solution to this problem.

Reproducible 5.1. Inventors and Inventions

1. A method of cleaning fabrics without immersing them in water.

   Invention: _____ Inventor: _____

2. A method of transmitting signals from one location to another through a series of different sounds.

   Invention: _____ Inventor: _____

3. A machine to join pieces of fabric together.

   Invention: _____ Inventor: _____

4. An instrument that transmits the human voice and allows people to communicate over a distance.

   Invention: _____ Inventor: _____

5. A form of energy that can be created from water and used to power appliances.

   Invention: _____ Inventor: _____

6. A simple, round, disk-like object that revolves and is used by all modes of transportation on roadways.

   Invention: _____ Inventor: _____

7. A compound that causes great explosions.

   Invention: _____ Inventor: _____

8. A material manufactured from trees and used for writing and drawing on.

   Invention: _____ Inventor: _____

9. A machine with skis used to move across snow.

   Invention: _____ Inventor: _____

10. A machine enabling people and goods to be transported in the sky.

    Invention: _____ Inventor: _____

Reproducible 5.2. Creating Hybrids

Reproducible 6.1 Word Quiz

Work in teams to solve these word puzzles.

1. Circle the word that doesn't belong in each group below. Be prepared to explain your answer. [Note: Consider the form of the words, meaning, number of syllables, etc.]

   a) conclusion   opinion   wisdom   argument
   b) rational   potential   analogous   logic
   c) reasoning   logical   deducing   spatial
   d) reasoning   riddle   analysis   rational

2. Make the analogy.

   a) ignorance is to wisdom as mental is to _____

   b) rational is to argument as logical is to _____

3. Identify the mystery word. The first one has been done for you.

Verb Form	Adjective Form	Noun Form	Mystery Word (verb)
a) 2 syllables	3 syllables / ends in "tive"	ends in "tion"	*deduce*
b) 3 syllables	5 syllables / ends in "al"	ends in "sis"	
c) 2 syllables	3 syllables / ends in "ing"	same as verb or adjective form	
d) 2 syllables	5 syllables / ends in "ative"	ends in "ment"	
e) 2 syllables	3 syllables / ends in "ing"	ends in "sion"	

4. Fill in the blank with a preposition that:
   - completes the idiomatic expression; and
   - when used after a certain verb makes a phrasal verb with the meaning in parentheses

Then identify the phrasal verb.

EXAMPLE:

for what it's worth   (phrasal verb: to explain) **account for**

   a) _____ face   (phrasal verb meaning "to cause to happen") _____
   b) _____ track   (phrasal verb meaning "to pay attention to") _____
   c) _____ and about   (phrasal verb meaning "to discover") _____

Reproducible 7.1 Survey: What's Hot and What's Cool

Take 10 minutes to jot down quickly your answers to these questions. Do not put your name on this paper.

1. Name a popular movie that is currently showing in the theatres.

   _____

2. Name a current hit song.

   _____

3. Name a current hit television show.

   _____

4. Name a band that is hot at the moment.

   _____

5. Name a famous fashion designer.

   _____

6. Name a current bestseller (fiction or non-fiction).

   _____

7. Name a popular female actor.

   _____

8. Name a popular male actor.

   _____

9. Name a popular toy.

   _____

10. Name a currently popular pastime.

   _____

Reproducible 7.2a. Mystery Word Game

Mystery word: OMNIPRESENT

Forbidden words: always
person
around
here

Mystery word: DYSFUNCTIONAL

Forbidden words: not
working
broken
family

Mystery word: OPPORTUNIST

Forbidden words: person
advantage
selfish
others

Mystery word: PRETENTIOUS

Forbidden words: importance
exaggerate
trait
strongly

Mystery word: COPE

Forbidden words: deal
situation
overcome
bad

Mystery word: CONDEMN

Forbidden words: disapprove
criticize
moral
dislike

Mystery word: TRAUMA

Forbidden words: shock
bad
event
believe

Mystery word: FOLLY

Forbidden words: silly
foolish
stupid
insane

Mystery word: OBNOXIOUS

Forbidden words: annoying
offensive
behaves
nerves

Mystery word: OUTLET

Forbidden words: mall
release
energy
emotions

Reproducible 7.2b. Mystery Word Game

Mystery word: FAD
Forbidden words: trend
mania
craze
popular

Mystery word: MANIA
Forbidden words: fad
craze
trend
popular

Mystery word: ROLE MODEL
Forbidden words: admire
copy
fashion
idol

Mystery word: IDOL
Forbidden words: admire
look
copy
role model

Mystery word: ICON
Forbidden words: idol
religion
represents
role model

Mystery word: TREND
Forbidden words: pattern
social
fad
mania

Mystery word: GIMMICK
Forbidden words: trick
attention
attract
popular

Mystery word: TRIVIA
Forbidden words: unimportant
little
details
tabloids

Mystery word: CRAZE
Forbidden words: mania
fad
popular
trend

Mystery word: HYPE
Forbidden words: important
exaggerate
qualities
advertise

Reproducible 8.1. Sports Categories Game

Reproducible 9.1. Healthy Eating

Note the following guidelines for servings in the main food groups outlined in Canada's Food Guide to Healthy Eating. Record your food intake for one day by pencilling in the triangles and boxes for each serving you consumed. For example, if you ate one bagel, fill in two triangles ▲ ▲ under Grain Products (1 bagel = 2 servings).

		Your Day's Intake
Grain Products	**5 to 12 servings required daily** 1 serving = 1 slice of bread; 3/4 cup of hot cereal; 30 g cold cereal 2 servings = 1 bagel, pita, or bun; 1 cup of pasta or rice	△ △ △ △ △ ☐ ☐ ☐ ☐ ☐ ☐ ☐
Vegetables and Fruit	**5 to 10 servings required daily** 1 serving = 1 medium-sized vegetable or fruit; 1/2 cup frozen or canned vegetables or fruit; 1 cup salad or 1/2 cup juice	△ △ △ △ △ ☐ ☐ ☐ ☐ ☐
Milk Products	**2 to 4 servings required daily** 1 serving = 1 cup milk; 50 g cheese; 3/4 cup yogurt	△ △ ☐ ☐
Meat and Alternatives	**2 to 3 servings required daily** 1 serving = 50–100 g meat, poultry, or fish; 1–2 eggs, 125–250 ml beans; 100 g tofu; 350 ml peanut butter	△ △ ☐
Other Foods	**no required servings; no more than 10 servings suggested** Examples include coffee, tea, candy, etc.	☐ ☐ ☐ ☐ ☐ ☐ ☐ ☐ ☐ ☐

Note: The triangles represent the minimum number of servings required in the range of daily serving requirements. The additional boxes represent the maximum number of servings required in the range of daily serving requirements.

Your teacher will give you more information on recommendations for healthy eating. Write a brief report explaining how closely your eating habits mirror the recommendations. This report is for your personal information. You will not be asked to share it with others.

Reproducible 9.2. World Committee on Initiatives for Better Nutrition

Background Information

Representatives from a number of countries have agreed on a World Declaration on Nutrition and a Global Plan of Action for Nutrition. The World Declaration maintains that "access to nutritionally adequate and safe food is a right of each individual." It also states that nutrition is necessary for the development of societies and is a key objective of progress in human development. Nutritional well-being, therefore, "must be at the centre of . . . socio-economic development plans and strategies." The Declaration challenges countries to set measurable goals and time frames for action on nutrition and food issues, with the overall goal of "nutritional well-being for all people in a peaceful, just, and environmentally safe world."

The Global Plan of Action sets out the following as *universal objectives*:

- making sure all people have access to sufficient supplies of safe foods for a nutritionally adequate diet
- achieving and maintaining health and nutritional well-being of all people
- ensuring that all development which contributes to improved nutrition and health is environmentally acceptable and able to be sustained
- eliminating famines and famine deaths

The Global Plan of Action also states the following *specific target objectives*:

- incorporating nutrition objectives, considerations, and components into development policies and programs
- improving household food security
- protecting consumers through improved food quality and safety
- preventing and managing infectious diseases
- promoting breastfeeding
- caring for the socio-economically deprived and the nutritionally vulnerable
- preventing and controlling specific micro-nutrient deficiencies (such as people developing blindness due to a lack of a simple vitamin in their diets)
- promoting appropriate diets and healthy lifestyles
- assessing, analyzing, and monitoring nutrition situations

The Task:

Your team is responsible for developing new initiatives and policies for a country which suffers from chronic hunger and turmoil (e.g., Ethiopia, Rwanda). Using the information above, develop *specific initiatives* to ensure access to nutritionally adequate and safe supplies of food. Present your plan to the class by role-playing a World Declaration on Nutrition Forum.

Reproducible 10.1. The Seasons of Life

How do your views of aging compare with some recent research done on the topic? Mark T (true) or F (false) beside each statement below. Then check the answers with your teacher and discuss the issues.

- ☐ 1. The early adult years for many people are spent trying to be successful in the career/work world.
- ☐ 2. In men, early adulthood is signalled by a shift from constraint to control. In women, on the other hand, this stage is marked by a shift from being cared for to caring for others.
- ☐ 3. Divorce is less likely with couples who live together before getting married.
- ☐ 4. Physical strength and ability decline significantly during middle adulthood.
- ☐ 5. Menopause ends a woman's child-bearing years.
- ☐ 6. At around age 40, people experience a psychological shift in how they view their age. Before then, they think about how many years have passed since they were born. After age 40, they think about how many years they have left.
- ☐ 7. Women experience mid-life crises earlier than men.
- ☐ 8. Most parents suffer from "empty nest syndrome" when their adult children leave home.
- ☐ 9. Women tend to be more assertive in their 50s than at earlier ages.
- ☐ 10. Most elderly people live in institutions, or with their children.

Critical thinking begs us to ask questions about claims, research results, and information at large. Discuss possible cultural, gender, or other biases in the information above.

SOURCE: Spencer A. Rathus and Jeffrey S. Nevid, *Adjustment And Growth: The Challenges of Life* (Orlando, Florida: Harcourt Brace College Publishers), 1995, pp. 3, 24, 425–453.

Reproducible 10.2. Composing a Prose Poem

Your Children Are Not Your Children

Your children are not your children,

They are the sons and daughters _____

They_____ but not _____

And though they are _____ yet they _____

You may give them your _____ but not your _____

For they have their own _____

You may _____ but not _____

For _____

You may strive to _____ but seek not to _____

For life _____ nor _____

You are _____ from which your children _____

UNIT QUIZZES

(WRITTEN & ORAL)

•

MID-TERM ASSESSMENT

FINAL TERM ASSESSMENT

UNIT 1 QUIZ
The Calm Before the Storm

Name: _____ Date: _____

A. Vocabulary (5 marks)
Complete the following sentences by filling in the blanks.

1. A _____ forced all cars to pull off the road because they couldn't see to drive.

2. People could feel the _____ long after the earthquake had occurred.

3. A menacing _____ touched down and destroyed the neighbourhood in mere seconds.

4. The village at the base of the volcano was quickly evacuated when _____ started to flow down.

5. An ongoing _____ in the prairies has caused crop failure.

B. Grammar (10 marks)
Write passive sentences using the following key words.

1. Native legend / seasons / control / winds

_____

2. mountains / form / touch of a buzzard's wings

_____

3. nature / not / control / humankind

_____

Rewrite the following sentences changing the active voice to passive voice.

4. Natural disasters have caused countless deaths.

_____

5. Soldiers rescued the victims from the rubble.

_____

C. Writing (optional) (12 marks)
Write a brief scientific report detailing the process of a volcanic eruption. Use the following cues, which are in order:

- molten rock forms at core of the earth
- magma rises due to expanding gases
- pressure creates fissures in the outer rock of the volcano
- water and gas expulsion accompanies lava expulsion
- lava forms long narrow rivers
- vapours, lightning, strong winds accompany eruption
- causes craters to form at top of newly formed volcano

UNIT 2 QUIZ
Strange But True

Name: _____ Date: _____

A. Vocabulary (10 marks)
Fill in the blanks with an appropriate word.

1. I don't just believe in ghosts, I've actually seen them. I once saw a _____, one of those very active ghosts, as it hurled objects across the room.

2. There's no doubt in my mind that _____ phenomena exist.

3. There is a legend about a village in the Caribbean that was _____ for more than one hundred years. Each year on the third full moon, all the women of the village suffered pitiful stomach pains while the men were struck with severe headaches.

4. I once attended a _____ where Susanna Moodie, the famous Canadian pioneer writer, was contacted.

5. I didn't see the ghost of Ms. Moodie, but she spoke to us through the _____.

6. Last year I had a _____ that my sister would be in a car accident. It wasn't a dream. It was just a strong sense. Sure enough, a week later, she was hit in a head-on collision.

7. Beatrice claims she has communicated in her mind with others at a distance through _____.

8. I believe that on a _____ level we are all in touch with the spiritual world.

9. Do you believe that people are _____ after death as animals or plants, or even other people?

10. I have an aunt with _____ powers. She can start a fire by just thinking about it.

B. Grammar (10 marks)
Report what each person says.

1. Brenda: Do you believe in the paranormal, Walter?

_____

2. Jim: The apparition of the leopard could have been an optical illusion.

_____

3. Alan: Bianca! Don't move.

_____

4. Karen: I've never had an encounter with the supernatural.

_____

5. Peter: My neighbour Kurt was clairvoyant.

_____

C. Writing (optional) (16 marks)
Your teacher will read you an account of the paranormal. Listen and then write a paragraph on a separate sheet of paper, retelling the story.

UNIT 3 QUIZ
The Road Less Travelled

Name: _____ Date: _____

A. Vocabulary (5 marks)
Complete the following sentences with appropriate adjectives or idioms.

1. He really _____. He waited too long to purchase his ticket and now the flight is full.

2. The hike that Liam and his friends did in New Zealand was so challenging and long that they were literally _____ when they reached the end. They couldn't have made it one more kilometre.

3. We aren't making any specific plans for the holidays. We'll just _____ .

4. I'm not sure if I'll make it to the top of the mountain but I'm going to _____ .

5. Early explorers had to be very _____ to explore uncharted countries.

B. Grammar (10 marks)
Write descriptive phrases by putting the following adjectives in an appropriate order.

1. waterfalls / cascading / Canadian / large

_____

2. ice / hand-carved / sculpture / magnificent

_____

3. colourful / gardens / exquisite / Japanese

_____

4. old / wood / mysterious / house

_____

5. destination / popular / tourist

_____

Combine the following sentences using relative clauses and appropriate punctuation.

6. The man went to Paris on business. The man lives next door.

_____

7. It's a cruise ship. The ship goes to Alaska.

_____

8. My father is spending the winter in Florida. He recently retired.

_____

9. The CN Tower is in Toronto. Toronto is the capital of Ontario.

_____

10. Tickets are still available for the train. It departs at 1 p.m.

_____

C. Writing (optional) (16 marks)
Select a picture from the book or one provided by your instructor and write a paragraph describing the scene.

UNIT 4 QUIZ
That's Not What I Meant

Name: _____ Date: _____

A. Vocabulary (10 marks)

Write a sentence that clearly shows the meaning of each word and expression below.

1. cue _____

2. vague _____

3. get the point of _____

4. beat around the bush _____

5. concise _____

B. Grammar (5 marks)

Join the ideas using appropriate words or expressions that show contrast. Use a different word or expression in each case.

1. Philip has a reputation for being an effective listener. In the meeting this morning he constantly interrupted what I was saying.

   _____

   _____

2. In Germany résumés are long and detailed. In North America résumés are brief and outline only major accomplishments, experience, and education.

   _____

   _____

3. She spoke clearly. She spoke quickly.

   _____

   _____

4. In communicating with others we spend most of our time listening. Many of us have poorly developed listening skills.

   _____

   _____

5. The test was not difficult. It was easy.

   _____

   _____

C. Writing (optional) (16 marks)

Write a paragraph comparing and contrasting cartoons and anecdotes.

UNIT 5 QUIZ
The Cutting Edge

Name: _____ Date: _____

A. Vocabulary (10 marks)
Fill in the blanks with an appropriate preposition.

1. Natalie wrote an article _____ cloning for the local newspaper.
2. John has a reputation _____ being a *Star Trek* enthusiast.
3. The writer has a degree _____ science.
4. Many people have come up with strong arguments _____ cloning because they feel it is tampering with nature.
5. The police will conduct an investigation _____ the car crash.
6. The debate _____ cloning will be held tomorrow.
7. This is an example _____ humankind trying to change nature.
8. After a thorough analysis _____ the evidence, the police developed a theory.
9. An examination _____ all the facts is necessary.
10. Research _____ the viability of cloning continues.

B. Grammar (5 marks)
Correct the following sentences.

1. Juan doesn't know what is cloning.

   _____

2. Kim wondered how much was the new computer.

   _____

3. Habib isn't sure if does Jean like science.

   _____

4. Martin is worried about the future holds.

   _____

5. It seems probable that cloning will try someone.

   _____

C. Writing (optional) (16 marks)
What concerns did your classmates raise about developments in science and technology during class discussions? Write a paragraph outlining the general concerns that people had. Give at least three specific examples from the class.

UNIT 6 QUIZ
It Stands To Reason

Name: _____ Date: _____

A. Vocabulary (15 marks)
Underline the inappropriate words in the following sentences and replace them with appropriate words.

1. The crash of stock markets in the Pacific Rim has worked towards serious declines in Canadian business profits.

2. In his speech, the minister drew an opinion between the treatment of ethnic minorities and the treatment of women.

3. It is difficult to figure out changes in attitudes without re-educating the public.

4. Despite having analyzed the problem's effects, the committee was not able to identify its spatial.

5. It was his argument rather than his reasoning abilities that made him a master at solving difficult business problems.

B. Grammar (10 marks)
Complete the sentences.
1. If the telephone hadn't been invented _____.
2. If you don't support your arguments in a debate _____.
3. The people will not vote the candidate into office if _____.
4. If he experienced anxiety when taking tests _____.
5. The government wouldn't have banned the product if _____.

C. Writing (optional) (16 marks)
Choose one of the following topics and write a paragraph about it.
1. The effects of denying a society freedom of speech
2. The causes of stress in teens

UNIT 7 QUIZ
All The Rage

Name: _____ Date: _____

A. Vocabulary (16 marks)
Fill in the blanks with an appropriate word.

1. Teenaged girls didn't just like or love Frank Sinatra, they worshipped him as an _____.

2. Many kids' TV shows today are just marketing _____ to sell toys.

3. He's a Beatles fanatic. He knows absolutely everything about them to the smallest detail. If you want to know any Beatle _____, ask him.

4. The film was _____ by some critics for its derogatory portrayal of aboriginals.

5. _____ families — families that don't operate effectively like the Simpsons — are more common than we may think.

6. Some people believe that blowing people up in video games is a harmless _____ for anger.

7. That fashion designer exaggerates the importance of his work. I think it was his instant fame that made him so _____.

8. After all the _____ about this film in the media, I was disappointed to find it so nonsensical.

B. Grammar (15 marks)
Some of the following sentences are correct and some are incorrect. Write C for Correct or I for Incorrect in the box beside each sentence. Then correct the incorrect sentences.

☐ 1. It takes a lot of hard work to become a great actor.

_____

☐ 2. They bought tickets to see the show.

_____

☐ 3. The important thing to remember is that you need balance your work or studies with your leisure time.

_____

☐ 4. The band left by the back door for avoid the crowds.

_____

☐ 5. Appreciating the humour in *The Simpsons*, you have to understand its intent.

_____

☐ 6. This television show is meant to entertain, not to educate.

_____

☐ 7. The purpose of any advertisement is to sell something.

_____

☐ 8. The rules of the game say that you may not to use gestures to explain your ideas.

_____

☐ 9. She appears not have to known about the awards ceremony.

_____

☐ 10. She was happy to see that he had bought himself the designer shirt.

_____

C. Writing (optional) (20 marks)
Write an OUTLINE for an essay on Fads.

UNIT 8 QUIZ
It's How You Play the Game

Name: _____ Date: _____

A. Vocabulary (10 marks)
Fill in the blanks with an appropriate idiomatic expression.

1. After his marriage ended, everything seemed _____. He lost his job, his car was stolen, and he became depressed.

2. Our competitor _____ by introducing its new soft drink on the market before we introduced ours.

3. "I know you can't give me an exact quote for the renovations, but just give me _____.

4. Now that he's found a new job that's secure, it's _____.

5. The management _____ by offering the job candidate $10 000 less than she had asked for. After tough negotiations, however, the candidate and company agreed on $1500 less than her original figure.

B. Grammar (10 marks)
Build sentences from the following phrases. Use the verb in italics as an *ing* verbal. (6 marks)

1. *skate:* ice dancers / enjoy / rhythmic music

_____

2. *kick:* my son / love / soccer ball / his dad

_____

3. *play:* the grass / cut short / field

_____

Complete the following sentences with an appropriate form of the verb in brackets. (4 marks)

4. _____ (compete) in the Olympics is every young athlete's dream.

5. Kim Lee intends _____ (join) a soccer team this summer.

6. How about _____ (try) a different sport?

7. They risk _____ (lose) their title at the competition.

C. Writing (optional) (12 marks)
Write a paragraph of at least five sentences about a sport that interests you. Why do you like the sport? Which aspect do you enjoy the most? What do you have to do in order to play?

UNIT 9 QUIZ
Food For Thought

Name: _____ Date: _____

A. Vocabulary (10 marks)
Use each word in a sentence that clearly shows its meaning.

1. perishable

_____

2. counterproductive

_____

3. dosage

_____

4. diversification

_____

5. nutrients

_____

B. Grammar (8 marks)
Complete the following sentences with a *base + d/t/n* verbal or *base + ing* verbal. Use a form of the following base verbs: *inform, suffer, design, concern, drive, follow, starve, mislead.*

1. _____ carefully, Canada's Food Guide to Healthy Eating could help improve the health of many North Americans.

2. An _____ consumer can make better nutritional choices when shopping.

3. _____ about her daughter's rapid weight loss, Leanne took her to see a doctor.

4. Currently, many labels are _____ because they don't follow any specific standards for terms such as "lite" or "low fat."

5. Half-_____ females suffering from anorexia look in the mirror and see themselves as fat.

6. Store aisles are _____ to encourage shoppers to spend more money.

7. Greg, _____ from compulsive overeating, ballooned to 100 kilos within months.

8. _____ by a desire to be thin, many college-age women have forced themselves to throw up after indulging in junk food.

C. Writing (optional) (12 marks)
Write a paragraph describing why you think world hunger coexists with a surplus of grains in industrialized nations.

UNIT 10 QUIZ
The Circle of Life

Name: _____ Date: _____

A. Vocabulary (15 marks)
Fill in the blanks with the correct form of a word from the list below.

apprenticeship	contemporary	aging	develop	mature
resolution	revolution	flourishing	senior	tryouts
serenity	strove	span	turbulence	flame
adolescent	globally	theory		

1. Erikson believed that people had to _____ the conflicts of one stage of human development before proceeding to the next.
2. The average life of a man in the 1950s _____ from birth to about age 65.
3. The musical tastes of young people of the 1930s differs dramatically from that of _____ youth.
4. That the earth was round, not flat, was a _____ idea in its time.
5. Many artists in past times _____ for years with masters before working on their own.
6. The boy's mental _____ lagged behind that of his peers, so that he was labelled "a slow learner."
7. Children _____ in an environment full of love, security, and physical and intellectual stimulation.
8. The mid-twenties to early thirties can be a _____ stage of life where men and women experience the ups and downs of leaving home, becoming independent, finding work, and getting married.
9. The gymnast was disappointed with her performance at the regional _____.
10. The mother's _____ reaction to the news that her teenage daughter had lied about spending the weekend with a girlfriend left no doubt that she was furious.
11. She described her grandmother as a _____ woman, always calm and peaceful.
12. Sheehy's theory that there is a shift in the age ranges traditionally associated with particular life stages may be a North American phenomenon, rather than a _____ one.
13. We must _____ to understand the driving concerns at different life stages in order to eliminate prejudice against both the young and the old.
14. His son _____ greatly while at university, having gone in as boy and come out a man.
15. _____ , older workers do not experience discrimination based on age, but the reality is quite different.

B. Grammar (10 marks)
Write the verb in parentheses in an appropriate tense.

When I _____ (**be**) a young child I _____ (**think**) the world _____ (**be**) flat. I _____
                    1   2   3   4
(**accept**) all popular ideas and thoughts. Now, in my teens, I _____ (**be**) rebellious. I _____(**reject**)
                                                                              5   6
all ideas — good or bad. In the future, I probably _____ (**accept**) some ideas yet _____ (**reject**)
                                                                    7   8
others. Hopefully, I _____ (**have**) the wisdom to make good choices. But by then I _____ (**have**)
                        9   10
many years experience to fall back on.

C. Writing (optional) (16 marks)
Imagine your life as an elderly person of 75 to 80 years. Write a paragraph describing what your life will be like — your home environment, your spare time activities, and the people who will surround you. Describe your personality when you are old. Begin with "When I am old . . ."

UNIT 1
Oral Evaluation

Part 1 (4–5 minutes)

Ask your partner what he or she considers to be the greatest human cause of destruction on our planet and what he or she as an individual can do about it.

Part 2 (1 minute each)

Student A: Look at the picture of the mountain climbers at the bottom of page 30 in your Student Book. Talk about what natural disaster could occur and what the climbers could do to survive.

Student B: Look at the picture of the starving children on page 137. Talk about what natural disaster could have caused their situation and what can be done to help them.

Part 3 (4–5 minutes)

Imagine that you and your partner have the opportunity to go back in history and explore an unknown part of the South American jungle. You can bring only three things with you from the modern era. Everything else you use must be from that era. Agree on an era, then look at the following items and determine which three you will bring with you.

UNIT 2
Oral Evaluation

Part 1 (4–5 minutes)

With a partner, discuss whether or not you believe in the paranormal and give evidence for your belief.

Part 2 (1 minute each)

Student A: Look at the picture of the seance on page 20 in your Student Book. Imagine you are one of the people there. Describe what happens.

Student B: Look at the picture of the Zodiac Wheel on page 28 in your Student Book. Choose the symbol of the animal whose characteristics most closely match those of your own personality. Describe how this animal's characteristics are like your own.

Part 3 (4–5 minutes)

You and your partner will tell a story. One person will begin the story, the other person will finish it. Your teacher will tell you when to switch. Look at the objects below and tell a story that includes the four objects.

UNIT 3
Oral Evaluation

Part 1 (4–5 minutes)

Ask your partner about his or her favourite tourist destination. Find out what the best and worst features and experiences were.

Part 2 (1 minute each)

Student A: Look at the picture of the volcano on page 3 of your Student Book. Describe where you would go to see a live volcano, why you might want to see it, what you would do, etc.

Student B: Look at the photo of the outdoor campfire on page 24. Describe where you would like to go camping, who you would go with, for how long, etc.

Part 3 (4–5 minutes)

With your partner, discuss what types of vacations the following people might want to take.

Consider the following: cost, activities available, entertainment, location, distance, etc.

UNIT 4
Oral Evaluation

Part 1 (4–5 minutes)

Ask your partner what parents and teens can do to improve communication in families.

Part 2 (1 minute each)

Student A: Look at the photo and illustration on pages 48 and 49 of the Student Book. You do not need to refer to the listening activity. Describe the differences between the men (Philip p. 48 and Johann p. 49) in each picture. Contrast the characters' facial expressions, emotions, and personality as they appear in the picture.

Student B: Look at the photo and illustration on pages 48 and 49 of the Student Book. You do not need to refer to the listening activity. Describe the differences between the women (Maureen p. 48 and Marianne, the woman with the green hat p. 49) in each picture. Contrast the characters' facial expressions, emotions, and personality as they appear in the picture.

Part 3 (4–5 minutes)

Use a cluster map to brainstorm as many characteristics of an effective communicator as you can in 2 minutes. Then categorize your characteristics into logical headings.

EFFECTIVE
COMMUNICATOR

UNIT 5
Oral Evaluation

Part 1 (4–5 minutes)

Ask your partner what he or she thinks is the most important technological development in his or her lifetime and why.

Part 2 (1 minute each)

Student A: Look at the pictures on pages 30–31 of your Student Book. Choose one of the pictures and talk for approximately one minute about the technological advances the picture represents and what impact these advances have had on our society.

Student B: Look at the same pictures. Choose a different picture from Student A. Talk for about one minute on the same topic.

Part 3 (4–5 minutes)

Work together to determine the two most significant and the two least significant discoveries from the pictures below.

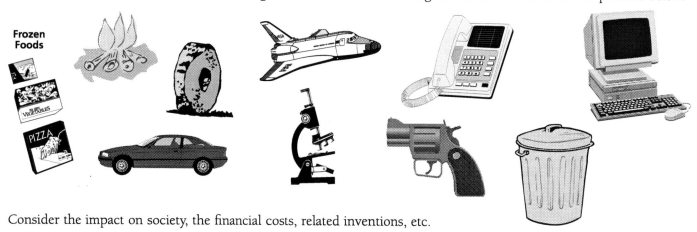

Consider the impact on society, the financial costs, related inventions, etc.

UNIT 6
Oral Evaluation

Part 1 (4–5 minutes)

Ask your partner to identify his or her hero. Find out about this hero's life and work. Find out why this person is your partner's hero.

Part 2 (1 minute each)

Student A: Look at the pictures on page 1 in your Student Book and discuss the effects of natural disasters on a community.

Student B: Look at the pictures on page 133 in your Student Book and discuss what causes eating disorders among young people.

Part 3 (4–5 minutes)

With your partner, look at the four items and discuss how life in our world would be different if these items hadn't been invented.

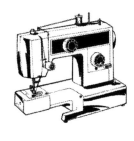

UNIT 7
Oral Evaluation

Part 1 (4–5 minutes)

Ask your partner about his or her favourite actor. Find out what films, television programs, or stage productions this actor has been in and why your partner admires this person's work.

Part 2 (1 minute each)

Student A: Look at the fashion photo (top right) on page 95 of your Student Book. Explain how fashion makes a statement about the person who wears it. What do today's fashions say about young people?

Student B: Look at the gangster movie photo (bottom right) on page 95 of your Student Book. Gangster movies were popular in the 1930s. They reflected concerns of North American society at the time. Choose one popular movie you have seen. Discuss the movie and tell how it reflects/reflected the times.

Part 3 (4–5 minutes)

Look at the illustrations below and discuss the appeal of each of these favourite pastimes. Why do people enjoy these activities?

UNIT 8
Oral Evaluation

Part 1 (4–5 minutes)

With a partner, ask each other about the role that sports plays in your lives. Has this role changed since your youth? Do you foresee changes in the future?

Part 2 (1 minute each)

Student A: Look at the pictures on page 50 of your Student Book. Talk for one minute discussing which picture appeals to you the most and why. Do you prefer individual or team sports? Why?

Student B: Look at the same pictures on page 50 and talk about which appeals to you the most and why. If you select the same picture as Student A, discuss how your opinion differs from or coincides with that of Student A.

Part 3 (4–5 minutes)

With your partner, discuss which two of the following sports you think are the most difficult and which two are the easiest.

UNIT 9
Oral Evaluation

Part 1 (4–5 minutes)

Ask your partner how he or she thinks eating habits are formed and what influences his or her food choices on a daily basis.

Part 2 (1 minute each)

Student A: Look at the picture of the flood on page 1 of the Student Book. Talk about the impact that flooding in an agricultural area can have on the rest of a country.

Student B: Look at the picture of the athletes on page 111 of the Student Book. Talk about the changes that athletes have to make in their diets to be in peak condition.

Part 3 (4–5 minutes)

Discuss the relevance of the following proverb in relation to countries where hunger is widespread and resources are scarce. What are three practical ways in which this idea could be applied?

"Give a man a fish and you feed him for a day. Teach him how to fish and you have fed him for life."

UNIT 10
Oral Evaluation

Part 1 (4–5 minutes)

Ask your partner to describe his or her adolescence, the transition years between childhood and adulthood. Ask about activities, interests, and experiences that impacted on your partner's adult life. Find out what predominant memories your partner has from these years.

Part 2 (1 minute each)

Student A: Look at the pictures of the children playing on page 50 of your Student Book. Describe how you relate or don't relate to these children based on your own childhood experiences.

Student B: Look at the picture of Roberta Bondar, the famous Canadian astronaut, and the children on page 45 of your Student Book. Discuss how you think adults, other than family, can influence children's lives. Who were some important adult role models in your own life?

Part 3 (4–5 minutes)

With your partner choose four of the stages of life depicted in the illustrations below and discuss what you think are the driving concerns and most important experiences of each generation. Discuss males and females separately.

Breakthroughs Advanced English Program
Oral Evaluation Grading Criteria

Criteria	1.0	2.0	3.0	4.0	5.0
Communication Management	Participation in the task is limited. Lacks ability to use conversation strategies to maintain the flow of discourse in unpredictable contexts, although may be able to do so in predictable contexts. Requires major prompting and assistance.	Some features of 1 and some features of 3 in generally equal measure **1.5 ↔ 2.5**	Participation in the task is moderate. Demonstrates ability to use conversation strategies to maintain the flow of discourse adequately in some unpredictable contexts. Requires only minimal assistance to perform the task.	Some features of 3 and some features of 5 in generally equal measure **3.5 ↔ 4.5**	Participation in the task is extensive. Demonstrates ability to use conversation strategies easily and effectively to maintain the flow of discourse in a variety of unpredictable contexts.
Expressiveness Competence	Accuracy and clarity of ideas are inadequately expressed for the task. Demonstrates limited ability to ask for clarification and probe for details.	Some features of 1 and some features of 3 in generally equal measure **1.5 ↔ 2.5**	Ideas are expressed sufficiently clearly for the task, although the ideas may not be expressed with precision. Can clarify meaning and probe for details adequately, using limited clarifying strategies.	Some features of 3 and some features of 5 in generally equal measure **3.5 ↔ 4.5**	Expresses thoughts and ideas clearly and accurately to enhance performance of the task. Uses a variety of strategies to clarify meaning and probe for details.
Grammar	Language forms are mostly inaccurate and inadequate for the task. Flexibility to manipulate structures not evident.	Some features of 1 and some features of 3 in generally equal measure **1.5 ↔ 2.5**	Language form is adequate for the task. Demonstrates limited flexibility to manipulate structures.	Some features of 3 and some features of 5 in generally equal measure **3.5 ↔ 4.5**	Language form is complex and mostly accurate. Flexible use and manipulation of structures.
Lexical Competence	Uses limited and inappropriate vocabulary and idiomatic phrases for the task.	Some features of 1 and some features of 3 in generally equal measure **1.5 ↔ 2.5**	Uses appropriate vocabulary and idiomatic phrases for the task, although forms may be inaccurate. Words and phrases are sufficiently varied for the task.	Some features of 3 and some features of 5 in generally equal measure **3.5 ↔ 4.5**	Uses appropriate and varied vocabulary and idiomatic phrases so as to enhance performance of the task.

Communication Management: ability to use various conversation strategies (initiating conversation, maintaining conversation, interrupting, changing the topic, bringing the topic back on track, etc.) to participate in and maintain the flow of discourse.

Expressiveness Competence: ability to express ideas and thoughts clearly and accurately and ability to use varied strategies to clarify information and probe for details.

Grammar: ability to use language structures appropriately and accurately. Ability to manipulate structures to handle task.

Lexical Competence: ability to use varied vocabulary and idiomatic phrases appropriate to the task. Ability to use words and phrases in accurate forms.

UNIT QUIZ NOTES/ANSWERS

Note: Criteria for grading students on all of the oral evaluations is provided on page 135.

• UNIT 1
Written Quiz
Answer Key

A. Vocabulary (5 marks)

1. whiteout / snowstorm / hard rain
2. aftershocks
3. tornado / twister
4. lava
5. drought

B. Grammar (10 marks)

Possible answers:

1. According to Native legend, the seasons are controlled by the winds.
2. The mountains were formed by the touch of the buzzard's wings.
3. Nature is not really being controlled by humankind.
4. Countless deaths have been caused by natural disasters.
5. Victims were rescued from the rubble by soldiers.

C. Writing (12 marks)

If your students are following the Process Writing Program in the Workbook, you may want to assign a different task to include only brainstorming and the topic sentence. If using the assigned task, the following grading criteria may be used.

presents events in step-by-step sequence	4	3	2	1
uses standard English grammar	4	3	2	1
uses standard punctuation and spelling	4	3	2	1

4 = accurate to a level that enhances communicative function

3 = adequately accurate

2 = needs improvement

1 = inaccurate to a level that interferes with communicative function

• UNIT 2
Written Quiz

Note: In section C of the quiz, you will need to read an account of the paranormal to the students. To ensure that all students begin section C together, you may wish to have them complete this section first.

Answer Key

A. Vocabulary (10 marks)

 1. poltergeist
 2. paranormal / supernatural / psychic
 3. cursed
 4. seance
 5. medium
 6. premonition
 7. telepathy
 8. subconscious
 9. reincarnated
10. telekinetic

B. Grammar (10 marks)

Give two marks for each question: one for using an appropriate tense in the reported speech and one for accuracy with pronouns and time words.

1. Brenda asked Walter if he believed / believes in the paranormal.
2. Jim said the apparition of the leopard could have been an optical illusion.
3. Alan ordered (told) Bianca not to move.
4. Karen said she had / has never had an encounter with the supernatural.
5. Peter said (claimed) that his neighbour Kurt had been / was clairvoyant.

C. Writing (16 marks)

If your students have completed the Process Writing Program section on narrative paragraphs in the Workbook, you may wish to expand the grading criteria. Otherwise, grade the paragraph using the following criteria.

includes main events and pertinent details	4	3	2	1
presents story in appropriate sequence	4	3	2	1
uses standard English grammar	4	3	2	1
uses standard punctuation and spelling	4	3	2	1

4 = accurate to a level that enhances communicative function

3 = adequately accurate

2 = needs improvement

1 = inaccurate to a level that interferes with communicative function

Read this story aloud.

SHE WARNED ME

Last month I visited a psychic whom a friend had recommended. I had never been to a psychic before and frankly I was a bit sceptical. On the other hand, I had been working a lot lately and hadn't been out in a while so I thought it might be fun to hear some mysterious person predict my future. My mother said, "Joanne, you're wasting your money. Go to dinner and a movie instead." But, as usual, I didn't follow my mother's advice.

I do drive, but I took the bus to the psychic's house that evening because my car was in the garage for repairs. Her house was two blocks from the bus stop, which I didn't mind because it was a beautiful fall evening and the night was crisp and clear.

I had just crossed the road and was approaching her house when I saw a strange light coming from the living room window. It wasn't a normal light from a lamp or candle, but a purple light that faded in and out. Finally the light rose and lifted from the house, swirling into the air and up to the sky where it eventually disappeared. I knew this must be the house of the psychic because — well — I somehow just knew. Although I found the light strange, I wasn't frightened. And so, I continued toward the house.

I arrived at the front door and rang the doorbell. I could hear a lot of panic inside the house and I thought I heard someone yelling into the phone. After several rings, an old woman answered the door. She was clearly upset and when I announced who I was and that I had an appointment with the psychic she broke into tears and announced that her daughter, the psychic, had just suffered a heart attack and had died just seconds before I arrived. The implication, I trust, is obvious.

Oral Evaluation

The three oral tasks are done with the same partner. In part 3, each partner is to use two of the objects on the bottom of the page in telling the story. It could be any story, or if you wish, a story about the paranormal. Let the first person speak until he mentions two of the objects or for about 2 minutes, then announce that the second person will finish the story, including the remaining objects.

• UNIT 3
Written Quiz

Parts A and B of the written quiz should take approximately 20 minutes. The optional part C will take an additional 20–30 minutes.

Answer Key

A. Vocabulary (5 marks)

1. blew it
2. on their last legs
3. play it by ear
4. give it my best shot
5. adventurous / brave / courageous

B. Grammar (10 marks)

1. large, cascading Canadian waterfalls
2. magnificent, hand-carved ice sculpture
3. exquisite, colourful Japanese gardens
4. mysterious old wood house
5. popular tourist destination
6. The man who lives next door went to Paris on business.
7. It's a cruise ship that goes to Alaska.
8. My father, who recently retired, is spending the winter in Florida.
9. The CN Tower is in Toronto, which is the capital of Ontario.
10. Tickets are still available for the train that departs at 1 p.m.

C. Writing (16 marks)

If your students are following the Process Writing Program in the Workbook, you may wish to create your own grading criteria based on the unit checklist for Descriptive Paragraphs or use the following grading criteria.

includes sufficient descriptive detail	4	3	2	1
picture is described in logical sequence (e.g., top to bottom)	4	3	2	1
uses standard English grammar	4	3	2	1
uses standard punctuation and spelling	4	3	2	1

4 = accurate to a level that enhances communicative function

3 = adequately accurate

2 = needs improvement

1 = inaccurate to a level that interferes with communicative function

• UNIT 4
Written Quiz
Answer Key

A. Vocabulary (10 marks)

Answers will vary. Give one mark for content that reflects the appropriate use of the word or expression and a second mark for satisfactory use of standard English grammar, spelling, and punctuation.

B. Grammar (10 marks)

Answers will vary. Give one mark for the correct use of an appropriate contrastive connector. Give a second mark if the sentence is joined correctly (grammar, punctuation, etc.)

C. Writing (16 marks)

If your students are following the Process Writing Program in the Workbook, you may wish to expand the grading criteria. Otherwise, grade the paragraph using the following criteria.

student has contrasted appropriate information	4	3	2	1
contrasts have been expressed accurately	4	3	2	1
uses standard English grammar	4	3	2	1
uses standard punctuation and spelling	4	3	2	1

4 = accurate to a level that enhances communicative function

3 = adequately accurate

2 = needs improvement

1 = inaccurate to a level that interferes with communicative function

Oral Evaluation

Part 3. Have students write their ideas on the cluster map to help them focus and see what characteristics they've already mentioned. You may also allow them to write when they are grouping their ideas into headings. Don't worry if they don't finish the task. It is their conversation that is important.

• UNIT 5
Written Quiz
Answer Key

A. Vocabulary (10 marks)

1. about / on
2. for
3. in
4. against
5. into / of
6. about / on
7. of
8. of
9. of
10. into / in / on

B. Grammar (5 marks)

1. Juan doesn't know what cloning is.
2. Kim wondered how much the new computer was.
3. Habib isn't sure if Jean does like science.
4. Martin is worried about what the future holds.
5. It seems probable that someone will try cloning.

C. Writing (16 marks)

If your students are following the Process Writing Program in the Workbook, you may wish to create your own grading criteria based on the unit checklist or use the following grading criteria.

clearly identifies main concerns	4	3	2	1
uses examples of individual concerns for support	4	3	2	1
uses standard English grammar	4	3	2	1
uses standard punctuation and spelling	4	3	2	1

4 = accurate to a level that enhances communicative function

3 = adequately accurate

2 = needs improvement

1 = inaccurate to a level that interferes with communicative function

• UNIT 6
Written Quiz
Answer Key

A. Vocabulary (15 marks)

Give 3 marks per answer: one mark for identifying the incorrect word, one mark for choosing an appropriate substitute, and one mark for using the substitute in the appropriate grammatical form.

1. worked towards — led to / resulted in / caused / brought about
2. opinion — analogy
3. figure out — bring about
4. spatial — source / causes / cause
5. argument — ingenuity

B. Grammar (10 marks)

Answers will vary. Give two marks for each answer: one mark for a contextually appropriate answer and one mark for using standard English grammar.

C. Writing (16 marks)

If your students are following the Process Writing Program in the Workbook, you may wish to expand the grading criteria. Otherwise, grade the paragraph using the following criteria.

student has addressed the "causes" or "effects" as required by the topic (not both)	4	3	2	1
student has supported his/her arguments	4	3	2	1
uses standard English grammar	4	3	2	1
uses standard punctuation and spelling	4	3	2	1

4 = accurate to a level that enhances communicative function

3 = adequately accurate

2 = needs improvement

1 = inaccurate to a level that interferes with communicative function

• UNIT 7
Written Quiz
Answer Key

A. Vocabulary (16 marks)

Give two marks for each answer: one for an appropriate word and one for the correct grammatical form of the word.

1. idol / god
2. gimmicks
3. trivia
4. condemn
5. dysfunctional
6. outlet / release
7. pretentious / stuck-up
8. hype

Note: Any word that supports the communicative function of the sentence should be accepted.

B. Grammar (15 marks)

Give one mark for correctly identifying the sentence as correct or incorrect. Five sentences are incorrect. Give one mark for each appropriate correction to the incorrect sentences.

1. C
2. C
3. I — to balance
4. I — to avoid
5. I — to appreciate

6. C
7. C
8. I — may not use
9. I — not to have known
10. C

C. Writing (20 marks)

If your students are working through the Process Writing Program in the Workbook and writing is an important part of your curriculum, you may wish to expand the marks to include effective topic sentences and supporting points. Otherwise, you may use the following criteria to mark the essay outline.

outline has essay title	4	3	2	1
topic has been narrowed	4	3	2	1
outline has thesis statement	4	3	2	1
outline has an introduction, body, and conclusion	4	3	2	1
each body paragraph supports thesis	4	3	2	1

4 = accurate to a level that enhances communicative function

3 = adequately accurate

2 = needs improvement

1 = inaccurate to a level that interferes with communicative function

Oral Evaluation

Have students work in pairs. In section C, have students alternate, each discussing one of the illustrations.

• UNIT 8
Written Quiz
Answer Key

A. Vocabulary (10 marks)

Give 2 marks for each sentence: 1 mark for an appropriate expression and 1 mark for appropriate grammatical form.

1. to go downhill
2. has beat us to the punch / beat us to the punch
3. a ballpark figure
4. clear sailing
5. was playing hardball / played hardball

B. Grammar (10 marks)

Give 2 marks each for the first 3 sentences. Give 1 mark each for 4 through 7.
1. Ice dancers enjoy skating to rhythmic music.
2. My son loves kicking the soccer ball with his dad.
3. The grass is cut short on the playing field.
4. Competing / to compete
5. to join
6. trying
7. losing

C. Writing (12 marks)

If your students are following the Process Writing Program in the Workbook, you may wish to assign them an introductory paragraph to an essay instead and modify the grading accordingly. For this assignment the following criteria may be used for grading.

presents opinion clearly and accurately	4	3	2	1
uses standard English grammar	4	3	2	1
uses standard punctuation and spelling	4	3	2	1

4 = accurate to a level that enhances communicative function
3 = adequately accurate
2 = needs improvement
1 = inaccurate to a level that interferes with communicative function

• UNIT 9
Written Quiz
Answer Key

A. Vocabulary (10 marks)

Answers will vary. Give 2 marks for the correct meaning of the word and 1 mark for using the word in a sentence with standard English grammar.

B. Grammar (8 marks)

1. followed
2. informed
3. concerned
4. misleading
5. starved
6. designed
7. suffering
8. driven

C. Writing (12 marks)

If your students are following the Process Writing Program in the Workbook, you may wish to modify this activity by assigning an essay instead and increasing the mark value. If using the suggested writing assignment, the following grading criteria may be used.

presents opinion clearly and accurately	4	3	2	1
uses standard English grammar	4	3	2	1
uses standard punctuation and spelling	4	3	2	1

4 = accurate to a level that enhances communicative function
3 = adequately accurate
2 = needs improvement
1 = inaccurate to a level that interferes with communicative function

• UNIT 10
Written Quiz
Answer Key

A. Vocabulary (15 marks)

Give one mark for each correct answer.
1. resolve
2. spanned
3. contemporary
4. revolutionary
5. apprenticed
6. development / maturity
7. flourish
8. turbulent / flaming
9. tryouts
10. flaming
11. serene
12. global
13. strive
14. matured / developed
15. Theoretically / In theory

B. Grammar (10 marks)

Give one mark for each appropriate answer.
1. was
2. thought
3. was
4. accepted
5. am
6. reject
7. will (probably) accept
8. reject *Note: the tense is future (will reject), but will is not repeated because the sentence is joined by a coordinating conjunction (yet) where the auxiliary for the verb before and after the conjunction remains the same.*
9. will have
10. will have had

C. Writing (16 marks)

If your students are following the Process Writing Program in the Workbook, you may wish to assign a narrative/descriptive essay topic instead and assign more marks. Otherwise, the following marking scheme is suggested.

includes introductory and closing remark	4	3	2	1
includes descriptive elements	4	3	2	1
uses standard English grammar	4	3	2	1
uses standard spelling and punctuation	4	3	2	1

4= accurate to a level that enhances communicative function

3= adequately accurate

2= needs improvement

1= inaccurate to a level that interferes with communicative function

MID-TERM ASSESSMENT NOTES

Total Time: 1 hour

Purpose: to assess students' ability to apply reading, listening, speaking, and writing strategies and skills to communicate competently in a communications task

Title: the Global Village

Topic: the effects of communications technology on the global village

Technique: jigsaw reading used as a springboard to completing a task

Materials: (1) POINT OF VIEW/PERSPECTIVE paragraphs (see following reproducible pages), (2) pencil and paper, (3) two copies (one for rough draft and one for final copy) of the PRESENTATION OUTLINE sheet (see reproducible pages following)

Process: Cut out the four POINT OF VIEW/ PERSPECTIVE paragraphs on the reproducible sheets and organize students into teams of three or four. Give each student one of the paragraphs to read (in teams of three, omit one of the paragraphs). Tell students that their task is to prepare an outline for a team presentation on *the impact communications technology is making on the global village*. The task is to be completed in four phases. (Before beginning, make sure students understand the term "global village.")

1. 15 minutes   Students read their paragraphs individually. Their task is to present a summary of the point of view given in the paragraph to their team. Before students join their team, the teacher collects the paragraphs. If students have questions about the reading, they may take notes and discuss these questions in their teams.

2. 15 minutes   Students present their summaries to the team.

3. 15 minutes   Students discuss what perspectives or information they wish to include in their presentation. This may include information from their readings and their own ideas, or their own ideas only. The POINT OF VIEW/PERSPECTIVE paragraphs are designed only as springboards to discussion and idea generation. Students need not agree with these perspectives nor include them in their presentations.

4. 15 minutes   Students work together to complete the team presentation outline sheet.

Collect one PRESENTATION OUTLINE sheet from each team.

Evaluation: Let students know in advance how they will be graded and what the criteria will be.

Evaluate students' performance in the group individually using the oral grading criteria on page 135 as a guide. (Each student should get an individual grade). As you circulate around the room, you may wish to ask probing questions or ask individual students to summarize their reading to check understanding.

Evaluate the team as a whole based on its completed Presentation Outline sheet. You may use the following grading criteria:

	1	2	3
Content	needs improvement to argue adequately for the main point	argues adequately for the main point	argues convincingly for the main point of the presentation
Vocabulary	needs to be improved to communicate the information adequately	adequate for presenting the information clearly and accurately	enhances the clarity and accuracy of the information presented in the outline
Grammar	needs to be improved to communicate the information adequately	adequate for presenting the information clearly and accurately	enhances the clarity and accuracy of the information presented in the outline

MID-TERM ASSESSMENT

POINT OF VIEW/PERSPECTIVE

While proponents of current communications technology and the media would have us believe that access and delivery of information today allows us to live more cohesively in a global village, the current information explosion does quite the opposite. Let's consider the value of information from a historical perspective. Before the introduction of railroads in North America in the 1830s and 1840s, information travelled only as fast as humans could carry it. With railroads that meant about 55 km/h. Clearly, people did not have access to mounds of information from far away places delivered at lightning speeds. But the news they received had relevance to their daily lives. The first town newspapers delivered information that was useful to the people in the community. The information was functional and contextual; it related to the problems and decisions readers had to make to manage their personal and community affairs. Readers could act on the information and therein lay its value. Today, information plays a very different role. Not only do we have access to unimaginable amounts of information, but we are bombarded with it — and most of it is useless. In *Amusing Ourselves to Death* (1985), Neil Postman invites us to ask, "How often does it occur that information provided you on the morning radio or television, or in the morning newspaper, causes you to alter your plans for the day, or to take some action you would not otherwise have taken, or provides some insight into some problem you are required to solve?" The answer, of course, is never or very rarely. Today's information gives us something to talk about, but doesn't lead us to any meaningful action. It is decontextualized — unrelated to the context of our daily lives. The value of news today lies in how much information it delivers, from how far away, and at what speed. It's presented to amuse us, to entertain us, and to divert us. Read a newspaper and you will notice that the information you read is not connected to what follows it, nor to what precedes it. It is fragmented. And information delivered on the Internet is even more fragmented and decontextualized. So, contrary to what the supporters of communications technology claim, namely that having hoards of information available and at warp speed results in a cohesive, global village, these technologies actually result in a fragmented and impotent world.

Source: Neil Postman, "The Peek-a-Boo World" in *Amusing Ourselves to Death* (New York: Viking Penguin, 1985)

POINT OF VIEW/PERSPECTIVE

When we analyze the effect of communications technology on the global village, we are often so concerned with the amounts and speed of information delivery that we forget about the revolutionary impact of photo images on delivering information. When William Henry Fox Talbot, an English mathematician and linguist, invented the process of preparing a negative from which several positives could be made, making the mass production of photographs possible, the way in which we viewed the world was changed forever. Ironically, although photography literally means "writing with light," photography and writing dwell in different universes of communication. Images speak only about particularities and concrete representation. Words and sentences, on the other hand, present ideas about the world. Images, by themselves, don't deal with the unseen, the internal, or the abstract. You can photograph a man, but not "man." You cannot photograph nature, only a fragment of nature. Abstract concepts such as courage and honour cannot be captured by images. Images only need to be recognized, whereas writing needs to be understood. Images present the world as a series of objects, but writing presents the world as ideas. Images present the world as fragmented slices of time and space without a context. They require no explanation or analysis and offer no opinions. There is nothing to dispute in the world of images, for images present the world as it appears. With language, on the other hand, we begin to understand the world by disputing and drawing conclusions about the facts. Understanding begins with not accepting things as they appear. It is said that a picture paints a thousand words, yet a picture really paints a moment in time and space that is unconnected to the world. Today's media, particularly television, are built around images, not words; images have replaced words rather than complemented them. As a result, rather than bringing us to a better understanding of our global village, today's media, including the Internet, offer up the world as a series of unconnected, fragmented images that require no understanding.

Source: Neil Postman, "The Peek-a-Boo World" in *Amusing Ourselves to Death* (New York: Viking Penguin, 1985)

MID-TERM ASSESSMENT

POINT OF VIEW/PERSPECTIVE

No matter what arguments the adversaries of communications technology feed us about the perils of the information revolution, no one can deny its positive effect in saving lives. In the not too distant past, information moved only as fast as a person could carry it. In rural areas especially that meant if a person needed medical assistance due to an accident or a farmer needed assistance with a sick animal, a doctor had to be summoned on foot or by carriage, sometimes with the result of arriving too late. Now, everything is just a phone call away. My father and I were recently vacationing in Québec when he suffered a second heart attack. At the hospital, doctors were sent his medical records from British Columbia within minutes of his arrival, providing the treating physician with critical information about his previous heart attack, the damage it caused, and his current medication — information I didn't have. Accessing that information had nothing to do with entertainment; it was useful, relevant, and potentially life-saving information the doctor could act on. On a global scale, communications technology is allowing doctors and researchers around the world to benefit from each other's experiences and findings. This sharing of information is especially beneficial for poorer countries where medical practitioners don't readily have access to this information. Professionals in all disciplines who don't know each other are not just accessing published information, they are chatting on-line, discussing important information, and building professional relationships that would not be possible without telecommunications technology. Not only is communications technology bringing people around the world together in ways never dreamt of before, it is saving lives around the world — all our lives.

POINT OF VIEW/PERSPECTIVE

One of the many positive effects that information technology is having on the global village is that it is generating an interest in people to find out about other parts of the world. Through Internet communications and television, people are finally able to see that the world is inhabited by many cultures and ideas, and that no one ideology and culture is at its centre. We cannot feel connected to people and places we have never seen — out of sight, out of mind. Most of us will never have the opportunity to visit the jungles of Ecuador or the deserts of the Kalahari, but through images from television and other media we can finally glimpse how people in far away places live. These visual images foster a tie between us, and for the first time we may be emotionally drawn to other people and places. Some will argue that the world as presented in television and other media is a biased version of who we are and what is important. I agree. But at least it invites us to find out more about each other. The mega success of the film *Braveheart*, shot in the Scottish highlands, fostered a resurgence of interest in Gaelic music, and tourism in Scotland rose by leaps and bounds. Of course the film didn't depict life in Scotland as it is in reality, but had the film not been seen by millions of movie-goers, the predominant image of Scotland as a land where men play bagpipes and wear kilts would remain today. It is true that we shouldn't accept the information we are fed from any source as truth, but that doesn't mean that we should stop the flow of information. We simply need to learn what to do with the information that bombards us. Keeping people ignorant of each other, denying them information about what is happening in other parts of the world, and starving them of knowledge is what breeds dictatorship and inevitably anarchy. Much of our current apathy — our lack of interest in acting — is a result of ignorance. If we aren't aware of human rights violations in the world, we can't act to change them. If we don't know about global warming and its causes, we can't act to change our ways of interacting with the environment. If we don't know who our neighbours are and why they live the way they do, we can't respect them or live peacefully with them. Information liberates us from the confines of our own views and as such, communications technologies that provide us with information liberate us and strengthen the bonds within our global village.

MID-TERM ASSESSMENT
ORAL PRESENTATION OUTLINE

Names: _____
_____
_____
_____

Write in complete sentences.

Topic of the presentation: _____
_____

Main point of the presentation: _____
_____

Introductory remarks: _____
_____
_____

Argument: _____

Supporting points:
a) _____
b) _____
c) _____

Argument: _____

Supporting points:
a) _____
b) _____
c) _____

Argument: _____

Supporting points:
a) _____
b) _____
c) _____

Concluding statement:
_____
_____
_____

FINAL TERM ASSESSMENT

Name: _____ Date: _____

Read the following essay and then answer the questions that follow.

The Evolution of the English Language

The English spoken in the 6th century bears little resemblance to today's banter heard in classrooms and business meetings. Of the 750 000 words in the English language, half are Germanic in origin and half come from the romance languages (French, Spanish, Italian, and Latin), along with generous inclusions from other languages such as Greek, Dutch, Arabic, Hindi, and Russian. The changes that have taken place are both external (as new words are adopted from other cultures) and internal (as the structure of the language itself changes). English underwent three major periods of development — Old English, Middle English, and Modern English — and continues to evolve with each generation as cultural influences recreate the living language.

Marked by repeated invasions and resulting settlements, the period from AD 449–1100 formed the base of Old English. The first invasion by the Jutes, Angles, and Saxons from northern Germany and southern Denmark in AD 449 and the settlement by these invading tribes was the beginning. Old English had a very complicated system of grammatical changes to indicate case, number, person, and tense. Many of the most basic terms in our language can be traced back to this period. Nouns such as man, wife, father, brother, ground, land, tree, grass, and summer all have Germanic origins, as do verbs such as come, get, hear, meet, see, sit, stand, and think. During the period from the 6th to the 8th centuries, Christianity had a strong influence on the Anglo-Saxons. As a result, the language of religion, Latin, had a major impact on the English language. It is from this period that words such as angel, candle, church, and school became part of the language. From the 8th to the 10th centuries, the coastal regions of Britain were plundered by the Vikings who eventually settled in the area. Traces of their language, "Old Norse," are still evident in words such as give, law, skin, sky, and take. The Old English period drew to a close with the arrival of the Norman French in England.

In the Norman Conquest of 1066, the Norman French invaded England and proceeded to conquer the entire island. For the following 200 years, French became the language of the ruling class: all issues related to government, law, and nobility were conducted in French. It is from this period that words dealing with politics such as president, parliament, congress, and constitution became part of the English language. London became the centre of culture and French was the language of prestige. English peasants who worked the land and raised sheep, cows, and swine continued to speak English, however. The French-speaking nobility ate the mutton, beef, and pork that the peasants raised and the French gave English the terminology for living animals as opposed to animals being served for meals. These borrowed words were examples of external change in the language; however, the changes that took place from Chaucer's time in the 1400s to Shakespeare's time in the 1600s were the fundamental internal changes that formed the basis of Modern English.

The movement toward the development of Modern English occurred swiftly at the dawn of the 16th century. The printing of some key literary works helped standardize the language. In 1525 Tyndale published a translation of the New Testament. The next 90 years were the golden age of literature culminating in the plays of Shakespeare. The printing of a dictionary in 1755, Lindly Murray's "English Grammar" in 1795, and an English Spelling book in 1804 cemented internal changes in the English language. Significant changes in pronunciation and word order are marked differences between Modern and Old English. Many words, common in Old English such as lo, verily, and egad have ceased to be used, while new words borrowed from other cultures continue to enrich Modern English. From the Greeks we got many science and technology terms such as geometry, geology, pathology, and biology. Words such as alcohol, sugar, and syrup are Arabic in origin. Canyon, tornado, and mosquito have Spanish origins. Words like coffee, robot, ketchup, and pajamas are all borrowed from cultures around the world. These adoptions to our language continue to this day as we become exposed to new and influential cultures.

As the exposure to many cultures increases and borders become relics of the past, language will continue to adapt to the needs of modern living. As each new generation attempts to make a statement through its use of the language, it reshapes the living word. The words popularized by a generation's parents bear little resemblance to the popular words of that generation. Language is an ever-changing entity that has altered a great deal since its beginnings and will continue to evolve.

A. READING COMPREHENSION (20 marks)

Part I. Scan the essay "The Evolution of the English Language" to answer the following questions. (10 marks)

1. Which culture gave English many of its political terms? _____
2. Which culture gave English many of its scientific terms? _____
3. Which period did Chaucer belong to? _____
4. Which period did Shakespeare belong to? _____
5. What are two significant differences between Old and Modern English? _____ and _____
6. What are two major external influences on the evolution of language? _____ and _____
7. Name two important literary works that helped standardize Modern English. _____ and _____

Part II. Write a short answer in response to the following questions. (10 marks)

1. Why did the Vikings originally come to England?

_____

2. Describe an example of how language can reflect a class difference.

_____

3. What would the major difference be in words found in modern English that also existed in Old English?

_____

4. What is a major difference between the ways cultures initially influenced the English language and how they now influence the language?

_____

5. When did the French control of England end?

_____

B. VOCABULARY (20 marks)

Part I. Find the words in the reading that mean the same as the following words. (10 marks)

1. chatter _____
2. the point where it starts _____
3. to develop naturally _____
4. small amounts _____
5. victory in battle _____
6. respect based on good reputation _____
7. technical terms used in a particular subject _____
8. ended _____
9. made popular _____
10. traditions from the past _____

Part II. Define the following terms in your own words. (10 marks)

1. invasion _____
2. period _____
3. fundamental _____
4. adapt _____
5. reshape _____

C. WRITING (20 marks)

Write a paragraph in response to one of the following. Your response will be graded on content, vocabulary, style, and grammar.

1. In your opinion, what have been the major influences on the evolution of the English language in the past 50 years?

2. How does your usage of the language differ from that of your parents' generation?

3. How do you think real changes (internal or external) in the English language take place?

D. SPEAKING

Working in pairs or small groups of three or four, discuss what you think the English of the future will be like.
Consider:

> technological influences
> cultural influences
> language needs (What will we use English for?)
> social influences

FINAL TERM ASSESSMENT NOTES

Total Time: 2 hours (written)
            10 minutes (oral)

Total Marks: 60 (for written component)

Answer Key
A. READING COMPREHENSION

Part I. (10 marks)

1. French
2. Greek
3. Middle English — 1400s
4. Modern English — 1600s

5. pronunciation and word order
6. culture and social change
7. Dictionary of English Grammar and English Spelling Book or translation of the New Testament

Part II. (10 marks)

1. The Vikings first came to plunder the coastal areas of England.
2. During the Middle English period, the nobility spoke French and the working peasants spoke English.
3. The way the words are pronounced.
4. Initially the influence was due to war or invasion, now the influences are peaceful.
5. Approximately 1266

B. VOCABULARY

Part I. (10 marks)

1. banter
2. origin
3. evolve
4. traces
5. conquest
6. prestige
7. terminology
8. ceased
9. popularized
10. relics

Part II. (10 marks) Answers will vary.

C. WRITING (20 MARKS)

Mark only for grammar that has been covered in the text.
The following grading criteria may be used.

content addresses the question	4	3	2	1
support for main idea	4	3	2	1
uses standard English grammar	4	3	2	1
uses standard spelling and punctuation	4	3	2	1

4 = enhances communicative function

3 = adequate

2 = needs improvement

1 = inadequate to a level that seriously interferes with communicative function

D. SPEAKING

Use the oral evaluation criteria on page 135 to evaluate this section.

Call students out to work together in teams while others are completing the written test. This can be done in the hall or a neighbouring room. Allow students a half hour before calling out the teams to ensure all students have read the essay. One and a half hours allows you to engage six teams of four students each comfortably in the speaking activity.

TAPESCRIPT

• UNIT 1 The Calm Before the Storm

Listening 1 Tapescript 1.a

Sure-Fire Ways to Predict the Weather

When I was a boy my grandfather taught me how to predict the weather for the upcoming year. Every year on Christmas Day (December 25th) my grandfather and many other people living in his region of France would follow the same carefully prescribed ritual to determine what the weather would be like for the next twelve months. He would take his time and select twelve big round onions. Then he would line them up in a row. The first onion would represent January, the second February, the third March, and so on until the twelfth onion which represented December. He would then meticulously place a generous pinch of salt on the top of each onion. For the next twelve days, known as the "Days of Fate," no one was allowed to touch the onions. Finally on the Epiphany (January 6th) he examined the onions. If the salt remained intact on top of the onion, it meant that the month that onion represented would be dry. If the salt melted on the onion, that particular month would be wet.

Nature has its own way of letting us know that she is about to unleash her fury. I have weathered many a fierce hurricane in my time — never have they come unannounced. Usually the humidity gets unseasonably high and the atmosphere has a hazy quality to it as a strong storm approaches. Those who live by the ocean keep a sharp eye on the tide. If they see unusually high tides at the shore or deep ocean swells they know that trouble is brewing and it's high time to batten down the hatches and brace themselves for nature's antics. Those are probably the most common indicators that we're in for a spot of trouble. My way of predicting a hurricane, however, may be considered a little unnatural to some. Every time a hurricane is in the making, my swans fly against the wind. When I see the swans fighting the strong air current, I know that a hurricane will occur within 24 hours, but usually within 12 hours. Nature seldom acts without sending us her warning first — it is the fool that ignores her warning.

You know, no other representation of nature's power comes with so little warning as a tornado. It seems to me that tornados tend to follow certain paths. My neighbour, Glen's grandfather, lost his barn to a tornado in 1927. Luckily no one was killed, but some of the animals were picked up by the funnel and flung kilometres away. The barn was unrecognizable — nothing left except parts of the foundation. The neighbours all pitched in and rebuilt the barn on the foundations of the old one. In 1993, two twisters wound their way through the neighbourhood taking the roofs off houses, uprooting trees, and once more destroying that same barn. Needless to say, when Glen rebuilt the barn he changed the location — no sense tempting fate. In these parts we know that if the sky turns an emerald green, a tornado is forming and the smartest thing we can do is get to the basement and get under a sturdy table. Whatever you do, don't try to outrun those death clouds — they are as unpredictable as a high-strung horse.

I really like the winter because it's so fun to go tobogganing, skating, and skiing. My mom likes winter for the first few months, but then she starts talking about spring. I think she doesn't like chasing my little brother around the house trying to get him to put on his winter coat, hat, and mittens. In Canada and the United States, we do this thing on February 2nd. It's Groundhog Day. All the news stations show a groundhog coming out from the ground. They say if the groundhog sees its shadow, it will go back in the ground to sleep and winter will last six more weeks. If the groundhog doesn't see its shadow, spring is almost here. I hope we get six more weeks of snow!

Everyone who lives here knows all too well about earthquakes. Scientists think that they can predict when an earthquake is going to happen, but I know the most sure-fire predictor — it's the animals. It's almost as though they have a sixth sense. They behave very strangely just before a tremor hits — maybe they hear it coming before we do. Pets really can save your life.

Listening 2 Tapescript 1.b

The following is a reenactment of the original interview between Farley Mowat and David Suzuki. Farley Mowat speaks first.

Farley Mowat: Perhaps we can only know nature by becoming a part of it, which is what our ancient ancestors did, and what the survivors of the hunter-gatherer tribes still try to do.

David Suzuki: But science doesn't recognize that kind of knowledge. I have come to appreciate the limitations of the scientific method and the arrogance that comes with it. It's an arrogance that comes from the intellectual insights we gain, which seem to give us such power but are actually restrictive. Extrapolating from little bits of knowledge to a whole ecosystem or to the whole planet seems to me to be fundamentally wrong.

When I hear foresters tell me they know enough to be able to clear-cut an old-growth watershed and then replace it with the likes of what they cut down, I think that this is the absolute height of arrogance and stupidity. They know so little about the enormously complex interacting components in an ecosystem that they can't possibly reproduce it. It's the arrogance of modern man to think that we, viewing the world through our tiny windows of science, can control, dominate, and direct the natural world.

Farley Mowat: What can we do to bring us back to some semblance of sanity in our relationship with the rest of life?

David Suzuki: I don't know of a strategy for how to do that. I think we are saddled with incredible blinders, which are historic. Ninety-nine point nine percent of human existence has been spent as small numbers of hunter-gatherers or very primitive agriculturalists. Nature during that period was always vast and endlessly renewing. Then our numbers exploded. In 1830 we reached a billion people; in 150 years we have doubled twice to reach 4 billion; we are going to double again to reach 8 billion in another 30 or 40 years. The explosive growth in numbers, combined with the acquisition of technology, has given us a power far beyond anything any organism has ever had in the history of life on earth. But we continue to use a mind that says, "We've got to cut down those trees; we've got to kill those animals; we've got to do all of this for our own safety." We are attacking the environment as if we were still puny, but we've got all this incredible technological power. Now, instead of bouncing back, natural structures are falling down under our attacks. Our mind-set just hasn't realized the overwhelming power of our species in terms of numbers and technological prowess.

Source: From *Rescue the Earth: Conversations with the Green Crusaders* by Farley Mowat. Used with permission from Farley Mowat Limited.

• UNIT 2 Strange But True

Listening 1 *Tapescript 2.a*

The House of My Dreams

When I was a young Canadian lad of about 8 or 12 years old, I had frequent dreams, some good and some bad. But there was one dream that kept recurring. The dream came back so many times that it seemed real to me at the time. Even now, many years later (I am now 66 years old), I can still remember the dream as a very pleasant experience, and I can remember the appearance of the house in my dream, both inside and outside.

As I approached, I could see it was a very large house, two stories in height and quite wide. Then, as I entered the front door, I stepped into a large sitting room with a high, cathedral-type ceiling which ran right up to the roof. Then there was a stairway on the left which rose to a balcony that ran all round the inside, with doors leading off into various rooms.

But there was one room at the back of the house into which I was always sent to play. In this room, I had a secret compartment where I could hide all my valuable toys, so that other kids could not play with them or take them from me. Also, this room had a large window looking out over a vineyard and an orchard of some unknown kind of trees.

Then, many years later, when I was about 19 or 20 years old, I was in the Canadian army in Italy. We were marching along a country road after the Germans had retreated to the north. Our unit commander called for a rest break (or a "smoke break," as we called it then). So I sat down at the side of the road beside a buddy, and just as I was lighting my cigarette, I looked across the road at a house, and stared at the house of my boyhood dreams. A cold chill ran up my spine.

I told my buddy about those dreams of long ago, and then talked him into going inside with me to investigate. I told him, in advance, just exactly what I expected to find and, sure enough, everything was just as it was in my dreams, even to the vineyard. Outside that backroom window there was a grove of olive trees, the orchard in my dreams.

Everything was there except the secret panel where I hid my toys in my dream. I was so disturbed by this one thing being different that I was prompted to check the room's dimensions from the door to the wall and then do the same in the room next door. Thereby I discovered an area of four to six feet [approx. one to two metres] that was unaccounted for in the room size. I then took my bayonet and punched a hole in the plaster wall, exposing a hidden compartment where the Italian family (before retreating from the war zone) had hidden all their worldly treasures, things that they could not carry while retreating, things like linens, silverware, dishes, etc.

Now the mysterious questions.

1. I had those dreams long before the war, so how did I know there would be a secret room?

2. Why did I dream the same dream over and over, when there was nothing in my present life to relate the dream to?

3. What caused me to remember those dreams so vividly, when most dreams are forgotten as soon as a person wakes up?

4. Had I lived in that house in some previous life, before being reincarnated to a Canadian life?

5. Or was there someone sending me messages through mental telepathy?

6. What quirk of fate caused our unit to stop in exactly the right spot to have me placed exactly opposite the house?

7. Has some mysterious soul from the past been put to rest by my finding that house?

Another mystery that I forgot to mention was that while in Italy I had no trouble talking Italian, and since I found the house I have never had the dream again, and I have forgotten most of the Italian language that I knew then.

Source: From *Mysterious Encounters: Personal Accounts of the Supernatural in Canada*, edited by John Robert Colombo. Copyright © Harry Stevens, 1990.

Listening 2 *Tapescript 2.b*

The Above Is Strange Enough in Itself

In the summer of 1976, I took my wife and three daughters to Camp Oconto on Eagle Lake, northwest of Kingston, for a vacation (for them) and a working holiday (for me). I was the "camp doctor."

In the middle of the afternoon, several days later, I was sitting in an easy chair, reading a book on the verandah of our small bungalow. The chair was sideways-on, so that in the corner of my eye I could see the living room through the open door. Quite suddenly, but at the same time with no sense of dramatic suddenness, I could see our pet cat walking slowly across the room, apparently quite unconcerned, calmly looking straight ahead. It took me a couple of seconds to realize that she was walking along a foot and half [approx. half a metre] or so above the floor level. She ambled across to the other side of the room and, just short of the far wall, disappeared — not quite instantly, but within a fraction of a second.

The "apparition" had been present, I suppose, for about 15 seconds. I would like to emphasize, however, that there was nothing about what I saw to suggest any form of apparition. The cat was normal in every detail, completely opaque and moving in her accustomed fashion. She was not surrounded by any dark aura, or glow, and I have to say that in every way, apart from being a foot and a half off the floor, appeared absolutely normal. At the time of the "apparition" I had no sense of dread, or fear, no sensation of cold or heat, or any other unusual sensation whatsoever.

My first thought, within a second or so of her appearing, was the following: How did she manage to travel all the way from Hamilton? Then I realized that she was, in fact, a foot and a half off the floor, and it couldn't be her. By this time she was about one-third of the way across the room, and for the remainder of her walk I just watched her with my mind blank. My sense of blankness persisted for maybe a minute or so after she had disappeared. Then I began to "re-run the tapes," and take a closer look at the living room to see if, by any faint chance, it could have been some sort of optical illusion and that a cat very like ours had in fact been walking on something which I hadn't perceived. However, I couldn't find anything to substantiate this.

I called two of my children from nearby to tell them what I had seen and to give me a hand to see if we could find any cat anywhere in or near the bungalow, just in case I was losing my mind. We couldn't. During this exercise I began to wonder not whether or how I had seen this, but why. Immediately, of course, I was reminded of having read of similar sightings and that the associations were usually bad. Half an hour later, telling my wife and my other child of the occurrence, the only strong impression I had of the whole event was a feeling of the absolute reality of this "apparition."

This is strange enough in itself, but the real impact came about two and a half hours later, when we went into supper and I was told that there had been a telephone message for me at the Camp Telephone

Office from our neighbours in Hamilton. I went across and, on the way, the uneasy suspicion that something bad had indeed happened recurred. I telephoned our neighbour, and she told me that our cat had been run over by a car about three hours before, which was pretty near the time I saw the "apparition." She also added that the cat had not been killed instantly but had lived for a few minutes after being hit. I immediately wondered whether I would have seen the apparition had the cat died instantly — the implication I trust is obvious.

This is the only experience that I have had that I would really call paranormal, although I have had other experiences such as "some places give me the creeps," and on two occasions I have been overwhelmed by a fainting sensation when somebody nearby was, unbeknown to me, in the process of fainting.

Source: From *Mysterious Encounters: Personal Accounts of the Supernatural in Canada*, edited by John Robert Colombo. Copyright © Thos. J. Muckle, 1990.

• UNIT 3   The Road Less Travelled

Listening 1 *Tapescript 3.a*

Women of the World

Women travellers have left countless trails through history. Some of them were religious pilgrims who ventured far from home to see the shrines and holy places of their faiths. One of the first of these was Etheria (or Egeria), a nun from Spain or southern France. In the late fourth century AD she not only travelled to Jerusalem and Egypt to visit places mentioned in the Bible, but also wrote a brief account of her journey to guide other pilgrims. Her description of the view from atop Mount Sinai is one of the earliest pieces of travel writing by a woman.

Some early women travellers made journeys with foreign explorers. The best-known of these is Sacagawea, a Native American woman of the Shoshone people. She was one of the guides and interpreters for the Lewis and Clark expedition that crossed western North America in 1805 to 1806. Sacagawea joined the expedition in North Dakota, along with her French-Canadian husband, Toussaint Charbonneau. She accompanied Lewis and Clark west to the Pacific Ocean and back again to North Dakota, carrying her infant son, Jean Baptiste, on her back the whole way.

Sacagawea's most important contribution to the expedition took place when Lewis and Clark entered the Rocky Mountains and met a group of Shoshone warriors. Because she was able to communicate with the Shoshone, the warriors treated the white explorers as friends and gave them food, horses, and information about the country ahead. Sacagawea appears to have been a brave and level-headed traveller. Unfortunately, we know little about her — just a few details recorded by Lewis and Clark in their expedition notes. Her own thoughts and recollections were not preserved.

Another way that women became travellers was through family relationships. The wives, sisters, and daughters of soldiers and diplomats sometimes accompanied their menfolk to far-off places. Emily Eden, for example, was an Englishwoman who spent six years in India in the 1830s as part of the household of her brother, Lord Auckland, the governor-general of Britain's India colony. Her book, *Up the Country*, about an 18-month trip into the tiger-infested foothills of the Himalayan Mountains, was published in 1866 and became a classic of travel writing. Yet Eden thoroughly disliked travelling. She came to India only out of a sense of duty to her brother, and she eagerly counted the days until she could return to England.

A fourth type of women traveller was the emigrant who left her homeland to live in another country. Emigrant women may not have been explorers in the strict sense of the word, but they often felt like explorers when they left the known and familiar world behind to begin a new life in a strange land. One emigrant woman who kept a record of her experiences was Susanna Moodie. She and her husband left England for Canada in 1832 to settle in the backwoods of Ontario. *Roughing It in the Bush: Or, Life in Canada*, published in 1852, tells the story of their first years as homesteaders, during which they suffered from bitter weather in winter, swarms of mosquitoes in summer, and lean times while they learned to live off the land. Eventually, though, the Moodies adapted to their new home. When she died at age 81, Susanna Moodie was one of Canada's most respected novelists, but her best-known book was her tale of emigrant life in the back country.

Thousands of women travelled in the roles of pilgrims, guides, family members, and emigrants. But in the 19th century a new class of woman traveller appeared in Europe and the United States. These women left home not to be with their men or out of necessity, but simply to please themselves, and they ventured beyond the destinations that were considered safe and respectable for travellers. They went to places where no other woman from the Western world had gone before — and sometimes to places where no man had gone. The more distant and dangerous the destination, the more eager these women were to make the trip. They claimed the right to see the world on their own terms, and they also laid claim to the title "explorer."

Women travellers and explorers emerged at a time when women in Europe and America were reaching toward emancipation, or freedom, in many aspects of life. Women were regarded by the law, by their churches, and by society in general as not having the same rights and responsibilities as men. Their opportunities to study and work were limited; the household was their domain, not the larger world of ideas and events. Women were expected to be good wives and mothers. If they did not marry, they were expected to keep house for their male relatives or quietly earn a living in some genteel way, perhaps by giving drawing lessons or doing embroidery.

Not all women accepted this view of things. Many of them began to challenge the rules. They demanded the right to vote, they sought recognition in the arts and sciences, and they looked for a new sense of liberty in their lives. Some of them found that liberty in travel and exploration.

The women travellers of the 19th century were exploring more than just geography. They were also exploring women's place in the world. By showing that a woman could survive the snows of Tibet or the jungles of Borneo as well as any man, they enlarged the world's awareness of what all women can do. They helped prepare the way for the later achievements of women in every field, not just in exploration.

Source: Excerpt from *Women of the World: Women Travelers and Explorers*. Copyright © 1992 by R. Stefoff. Used by permission of Oxford University Press, Inc.

Listening 2 *Tapescript 3.b*

The following is a reenactment of the original interview between Roberta Bondar and five 10-year-olds.

Michael: How long does it take to get out of Earth's gravity?

Bondar: It depends on how high you want to be. You have to achieve a certain speed to get into an orbit around Earth. For our particular flight — for the orbit we wanted to achieve of 163 nautical miles [262 km] — we had to travel at a terminal speed of 17,500 miles an hour [28 163 km\h], and we achieved that at the end of eight and a half minutes.

Crystal: How did it feel being weightless?

Bondar: It's kind of fun sometimes, because you're able to be like Peter Pan and go down a tunnel and not touch any surface.

You just propel yourself off; you keep that energy all the way through. Sometimes you can just turn around like an airplane and sort of roll from one side to another. You really become an airplane yourself, within the spaceship. It was actually better than being a bird because I didn't have to flap my wings to fly!

Jenny: How did being in space change your views about the environment?

Bondar: I had very strong feelings about the environment before I flew, and it certainly deepened that commitment inside me. Seeing this wonderful planet of ours from space filled me with a very great sense of protection towards the Earth. I really couldn't wait to get back to explore it more and to tell people that when we look out into the black of the universe, the nearest star is not very near. We really need to get along with each other and along with our environment, because it's part of us.

Sarah: Did you ever dream about being an astronaut when you were a kid?

Bondar: I dreamed about being an astronaut, I guess, from the time I can remember dreaming. I remember when I was about seven or eight I was putting models together. So probably at that point, I had decided I'd like to become an astronaut.

When you're young, sometimes you don't realize that some dreams are more difficult than others. I was very pleased eight years ago when Canada decided to have a program for astronauts. I was very lucky.

Jonathan: How did being in space change your views about life and God?

Bondar: Well, to tell you the truth, I don't often get into religious discussions, because there are many religions on this Earth. But it seems that a common thing is that people believe we have a spirit in ourselves. And somehow we all feel, regardless of the religion, that there is part of us that is very special, that is good, our soul. I believe the space flight — when I looked down at the planet — helped me feel so much closer to the people on the Earth. It didn't feel like there were borders in the whole world.

There seems to be this one common thing with all religions, and that is to be the best you can. That would be the spiritual experience for me.

Source: From 'The view from outer space,' *The United Church Observer*, September 1992, pp. 34–35.

• UNIT 4   That's Not What I Meant

Listening 1 Tapescript 4.a

Excerpt 1

Maureen: The only weekend we seem to have free is October tenth.

Philip: That's the opening of hunting season.

Maureen: Well, let's do it Saturday or Sunday evening.

Philip: Okay, make it Saturday.

Maureen: Wouldn't you want to be able to hunt later on the first day of hunting?

Philip: I said Saturday, so obviously that's the day I prefer.

Maureen: I was just trying to be considerate of you. You didn't give a reason for choosing Saturday.

Philip: I'm taking off Thursday and Friday to hunt, so I figured I'll have had enough by Saturday night.

Maureen: Well, why didn't you say that?

Philip: I didn't see why I had to. And I found your question very intrusive.

Maureen: I found your response very offensive!

Excerpt 2

Ingmar Bergman's film *Scenes from a Marriage* opens with a couple being interviewed for a magazine by a woman named Mrs. Palm. Marianne and Johan respond very differently to Mrs. Palm's question: "How would you describe yourselves in a few words?" Listen to Johan's answer.

Johan: It might sound conceited if I describe myself as extremely intelligent, successful, youthful, well-balanced, and sexy — a man with a world conscience, cultivated, well-read, popular, and a good mixer. Let me see, what else can I think of . . . friendly. Friendly in a nice way even to people who are worse off. I like sports. I'm a good family man. A good son. I have no debts and I pay my taxes. Is this enough or do you want more details?

Announcer: This is Marianne's answer:

Marianne: Hmm, what can I say . . . I'm . . . I'm married to Johan and I . . . I have two daughters.

[Even with prodding Marianne doesn't add much information]

Marianne: That's all I can think of for the moment.

Mrs. Palm: There must be something . . .

Marianne: I think Johan is rather nice.

Johan: Kind of you, I'm sure.

Marianne: We've been married for ten years.

Johan: I've just renewed the contract.

Marianne: [with slight sarcasm] I doubt if I have the same natural appreciation of my own excellence as Johan. But to tell the truth, I'm glad I can live the life I do. It's a good life, if you know what I mean. Well, what else can I say . . . Oh dear, this is difficult!

Johan: She has a nice figure.

Marianne: You're joking. I'm trying to take this thing seriously. I have two daughters, Karin and Eva.

Johan: You've already said that.

Excerpt 3

Even if they grow up in the same neighbourhood, on the same block, or in the same house, girls and boys grow up in different worlds of words. People talk to them differently and expect and accept different ways of talking from them. But more than that, children learn how to talk, how to have conversations, not only from their parents but from their peers. If you know any children whose parents have a foreign or regional accent, for example, you've probably noticed that the children don't have it; they learn to speak with the pronunciation of the region where they grow up.

Here is a summary of research by anthropologists such as Marjorie Harness Goodwin and sociologists such as Annette Weaver showing that boys and girls have very different ways of talking to their friends. Although they often play together, boys and girls spend most of their time playing with other children of the same sex. And, although some of the activities they play at are similar, their favourite games are different, and their ways of using language in their games are separated by a world of difference.

Boys tend to play outside, in large groups that are hierarchical. Their groups have a leader who tells others what to do and how to do it, and who resists doing what other boys propose. So one way high status is achieved is by giving orders and making them stick. Another way is to take centre stage by telling stories and jokes, and by sidetracking or challenging the stories and jokes of others. Boys' games have winners and losers and elaborate systems of rules that are frequently the subject of arguments. Finally, boys are frequently heard to boast of their skill and argue about who is best at what.

Girls, on the other hand, play in small groups or in pairs; the centre of a girl's social life is a best friend. Within the group, intimacy is all important. Standing in the group is measured by relative closeness. In their most frequent games, like jump rope and hopscotch, everyone gets a turn. Many of their activities don't have winners or losers, for example, playing house. Although some girls are more skilled than others, and all the girls may be aware of this, girls who excel are expected not to boast about it, or to show that they think they're better than others. Girls don't give orders; they express their preferences as suggestions, and suggestions are likely to be accepted. Whereas boys say, "Gimme that!" and "Get outta here!," girls are more likely to say, "Let's do this," and "How about doing that?" Anything else is put down as "bossy." Girls don't grab centre stage — they don't want it — and so they don't challenge each other directly. And much of the time, they simply sit together and talk. Girls aren't accustomed to jockeying for status in an obvious way; they're much more concerned about being liked.

Source: Excerpts from *You Just Don't Understand* by Deborah Tannen, 1990.

• UNIT 5   The Cutting Edge

Listening 1 *Tapescript 5.a*

Kalil: Wasn't that a great episode of *Star Trek* last night? I love those old shows — they're classics.

Aline: I wonder how many times Scotty said: "I can't push the engines any further captain. They'll blow."

Kalil: He always manages to push the impulse engines just far enough to get them out of the scrapes though.

Aline: Michael, you're kinda quiet. Did you watch the show last night?

Michael: No. I don't like science fiction shows — they're a complete waste of time and an insult to my intelligence.

Kalil: How can you say that?

Michael: Oh, come on. Shows like *Star Trek* are complete fantasy — I might as well be daydreaming. I'd rather watch a show that's based on some sort of reality.

Aline: You're wrong Michael. *Star Trek* is one of the best science fiction shows on television.

Michael: You expect me to believe that things like androids and impulse engines are real?

Kalil: Well, maybe advanced androids like Mr. Data are not possible yet, but there are many cybernetic researchers who are convinced they are within our capabilities in the near future.

Aline: [jumping right in] And the impulse engine isn't so unrealistic either. It's based on a fusion reaction, so I'll bet it's only a matter of time before one's developed.

Michael: So what you're saying is that things like androids and impulse engines don't exist now, but they really could in the future.

Kalil: For sure. Soon we'll be using transporters to beam ourselves from one side of the world to the other in a manner of seconds — no more 14-hour plane rides.

Aline: [cutting in] Wait a minute — you don't really believe that do you? The transporter that breaks people into molecules

and beams them through space is complete fiction. There's nothing in physics that even comes close to that. The closest we'll ever come to saying "Beam me up, Scotty" is when we order a drink called that at a bar.

Michael: Now that's the kind of science fiction I can relate to. I'd rather go on a date than watch Sci-Fi on TV anytime.

Kalil: Now the real Michael is coming out. Actually — I'll bet you can really identify with Captain James T. Kirk of the Starship *Enterprise*.

Michael: Why?

Aline: Let's put it this way — if they watched television on the Enterprise, he'd be watching *Baywatch*. That original *Star Trek* series was made in the sixties and Captain Kirk always ended up with a beautiful woman.

Kalil: Do you think that limits the show's appeal?

Aline: Actually, *Star Trek* appeals to a wide audience. The shows have cutting edge technology, fantasy, and a love interest for those incurable romantics — [jokingly] like you Michael. You really should watch it and give it a chance before saying it's a waste of time.

Michael: I guess it can't really hurt to give it a try. Hey, did you catch *Baywatch* last night?

Aline: [cutting in] Stop right there. If you two are going to sit here and discuss the virtues of that kind of show, I'm gone.

Kalil: [jokingly] Okay, see you later Aline. Hey Michael, what did you think of . . .

Listening 2 *Tapescript 5.b*

The Dolly Debate

She does not look like a circus freak or a monster or an omen of evil. Her eyes and ears have a pinkish hue — just like they are supposed to. She is seven months old and coated with fistfuls of woollen curls, a natural sweater against Scottish air so cold on this winter morning that her breath rises in puffs every time she bleats. Her white eyelashes blink sleepily despite the mania around her: the staccato popping of strobe lights and whirring of cameras as photographers elbow closer to her pen, whistling to get her attention and calling out "Dolly, Dolly, over here Dolly," as if she were someone's pet dog instead of a sheep. "Who's the freak here?," Dolly might well have wondered, gazing back at the pack of one-eyed humans. "As you see, she is a normal sheep," says Dr. Alan Colman, a redheaded 48-year-old scientist watching with a bemused smile from a few feet away. "She looks like a sheep, behaves like a sheep." But that does not mean that Dolly is just any old Finn Dorset from down on the farm. She was created by what Colman's research partners at the Roslin Institute just south of Edinburgh were calling — with some understatement — "an unusual method." For Colman is also a businessman and his business is biotechnology, an industry where the maxim is build a better mouse and the world will beat a path to your door. Judging by the worldwide interest in Dolly's coming out last week, he and his Roslin partners have done it.

In scientific language of the landmark paper Roslin's researchers published in the British science journal *Nature*, Dolly "was born after nuclear transfer from a mammary gland cell, the first mammal to develop from a cell derived from adult tissue." In everyday language, they did something that most people considered to be purely in the realm of pulp fiction. Taking a cell containing 98% of the DNA, or its genetic blueprint, from the udder of a six-year-old adult sheep, they fused it to the egg of another sheep to produce a lamb that is virtually an exact copy — an identical twin, six years younger — of the original animal. (Two percent of DNA is transmitted only through a mother's egg.) The lamb, Dolly, has the same hereditary characteristics as her genetic mother. And if they can do it with a cell from an adult animal, the researchers acknowledge it is "probable" that the same technique could be used to copy humans. "What Dolly shows, in principle, is that we can start again," says Ian Wilmut, the embryologist who headed the Roslin team.

Whether the discovery was of atom-splitting significance for science or just another step along the biogenetic road was debatable. But there was a convulsive popular reaction to breaking the barrier between the realms of science and fantasy. While many scientists welcomed any new understanding of biology's mysteries, religious leaders and many ethicists shuddered at this latest method by which science can now tamper with the fundamentals of life. The Vatican condemned it. The German media, hearing ugly echoes of Nazi eugenics experiments, brooded about it. And the British government, with an eye on the storm, announced an end to Roslin's funding.

Many people shared the unease of British Nobel Peace Prize winner Joseph Rotblat, who called for international ethical safeguards against abuses of biotechnology. Genetic engineering, said Rotblat, "was a threat to humankind." One set of humans clearly in danger: the Roslin researchers themselves, who were openly nervous that their discovery would prompt animal rights activists to seek revenge for their experiments with sheep. The scientists would not divulge where they lived, and camera crews were told not to take pictures of the staff. Animal rights activists vowed to take revenge anyway.

While Dolly allowed late-night-show gag writers to breathe easier for a week, she also spawned widespread speculation about how the technique might be used — and abused. The institute was quickly swamped with appeals from the wacky and the sad, people from around the world desperately begging the researchers to regenerate dead husbands and children. Talk shows touched on outlandish scenarios. Was it now possible for people ill with terminal diseases to produce a twin they could tap for "spare parts?" Could musicians clone themselves to continue creating for eternity, or supermodels provide designers with an endless supply of bony look-alikes? And would megalomaniac dictators be tempted to populate the world with copied versions of their evil selves?

The reality, of course, is that even if human cloning took the enormous leap from the theoretical to the practical, personalities are shaped by an array of factors beyond genetics. But that vision of multiple Hitlers troubled even Colman's wife, who asked her husband at home one night whether "some tin-pot dictator somewhere in the world could use unscrupulous means to clone himself." Colman told her it would be exceedingly difficult but technically possible. "I'm not absolutely sure that reassured her," he said dryly last week. His 14-year-old son also questioned what his dad was unleashing on the world. "I knew then," said Colman, squirming slightly as he reluctantly divulged his own family's misgivings, "that we were going to have a problem with the general public."

Source: Excerpt from 'The Dolly Debate' from *Maclean's* Magazine, Maclean Hunter Publishing Ltd., 10 March 1997, pp. 54-55.

• UNIT 6   It Stands to Reason

Listening 1 *Tapescript 6.a*

The following is a short excerpt from the speech Martin Luther King Jr. delivered on December 5th, 1955. After the excerpt and for clarity, an actor will read segments of the speech.

[Following the taped original excerpt, the speech is read twice by an actor: first straight through and then in segments.]

Actor's reading:

(First Segment) We're here this evening for serious business. We're here in a general sense because first and foremost, we are American citizens, and we are determined to acquire our citizenship to the fullness of its meaning. We are here also because of our deep-seated belief that democracy transformed from thin paper to thick action is the greatest form of government on earth.

(Second Segment) There comes a time that people get tired. We are here this evening to say to those who have mistreated us so long that we are tired — tired of being segregated and humiliated; tired of being kicked about by the brutal feet of oppression.

There comes a time my friends when people get tired of being plunged across the abyss of humiliation, when they experience the bleakness of nagging despair. There comes a time when people get tired of being pushed out of the glimmering sunlight of last July and left standing amid the piercing chill of an Alpine November.

(Third Segment) We had no alternative but to protest. For many years, we have shown amazing patience. We have sometimes given our white brothers the feeling that we liked the way we were being treated. But we come here tonight to be saved from that patience that makes us patient with anything less than freedom and justice.

One of the great glories of democracy is the right to protest for right.

(Fourth Segment) These organizations (White Citizens' Councils and the Ku Klux Klan) are protesting for the perpetuation of injustice in the community; we are protesting for the birth of justice in the community. Their methods lead to violence and lawlessness. But in our protest there will be no cross burnings. No white person will be taken from his home by a hooded Negro mob and brutally murdered. There will be no threats and intimidation. We will be guided by the highest principles of law and order.

Our method will be that of persuasion, not coercion. We will only say to the people, "Let your conscience be your guide." Our actions must be guided by the deepest principles of our Christian faith. Love must be our regulating ideal. Once again we must hear the words of Jesus echoing across the centuries ("Love your enemies, bless them that curse you, and pray for them that despitefully use you"). If we fail to do this our protest will end up as a meaningless drama on the stage of history, and its memory will be shrouded with the ugly garments of shame. In spite of the mistreatment that we have confronted we must not become bitter, and end up by hating our white brothers. As Booker T. Washington said, "Let no man pull you so low as to make you hate him."

(Fifth Segment) We are not wrong in what we are doing. If we are wrong, the Supreme Court of this nation is wrong. If we are wrong, the Constitution of the United States is wrong. If we are wrong, God Almighty is wrong. If we are wrong, Jesus of Nazareth was merely a Utopian dreamer who never came down to earth.

(Sixth Segment) If you will protest courageously, and yet with dignity and Christian love, when the history books are written in future generations, the historians will have to pause and say, "There lived a great people — a black people — who injected new meaning and dignity into the veins of civilization." This is our challenge and our overwhelming responsibility.

Source: Martin Luther King Jr. 'There comes a time when people get tired.' Licence granted by Intellectual Properties Management, Atlanta, Georgia, as Manager for the King Estate.

SIDE 2

• UNIT 7   All the Rage

Listening 1 *Tapescript 7.a*

Narrator: From the moment the Boeing Stratocruiser taxied up to the International Air Terminal at Idlewild, James Bond was treated like royalty.

Bond followed the other passengers through the wire fence towards the door marked US HEALTH SERVICE.

Halloran: "Mr. Bond?"

Narrator: A pleasant-looking nondescript man in plain clothes had stepped forward from the shadow of the Health Service building.

Halloran: "My name's Halloran. Pleased to meet you!"

Narrator: They shook hands.

Halloran: "Hope you had a pleasant trip. Would you follow me please?"

Narrator: Directly outside a black Buick waited, its engine sighing quietly. They climbed in. Bond's two light suitcases were in front next to the driver. Bond couldn't imagine how they had been extracted so quickly from the mound of passengers' luggage he had seen only minutes before being trolleyed over to Customs.

Bond: "Well, that's certainly one of the reddest carpets I've ever seen. I expected to be at least an hour getting through Immigration. Who laid it on? I'm not used to VIP treatment. Anyway, thanks very much for your part in it all."

Halloran: "Oh you're very welcome, Mr. Bond."

Narrator: Halloran smiled and offered him a cigarette from a fresh pack of Luckies.

Halloran: "We want to make your stay comfortable. Anything you want, just say so and it's yours. You've got some good friends in Washington. I don't myself know why you're here but it seems the authorities are keen that you should be a privileged guest of the Government. It's my job to see you get to your hotel as quickly and as comfortably as possible and then I'll hand you over and be on my way. May I have your passport a moment, please?"

Narrator: Bond gave it to him. Halloran opened a briefcase on the seat beside him and took out a heavy metal stamp. He turned the pages of Bond's passport until he came to the US Visa, stamped it, scribbled his signature over the dark blue circle of the Department of Justice cipher and gave it back to him. Then he took out his pocketbook and extracted a thick white envelope which he gave to Bond.

Halloran: "There's a thousand dollars in there, Mr. Bond."

Narrator: Bond eyed him narrowly and then grinned. He put the envelope away in his notecase.

The driver chose the Triborough Bridge and they soared across the breathtaking span into the heart of uptown Manhattan, the beautiful prospect of New York hastening towards them until they were down amongst the hooting, teeming, petrol-smelling roots of the stressed-concrete jungle.

They drew up at the best hotel in New York, the St. Regis, at the corner of Fifth Avenue and 55th Street. A saturnine middle-aged man in a blue overcoat and black homburg came forward behind the commissionaire. On the sidewalk, Halloran introduced him.

Halloran: "Mr. Bond, meet Captain Dexter."

Narrator: He was deferential.

Halloran: "Can I pass him along to you now, Captain?"

Captain Dexter: "Sure, sure. Just have his bags sent up. Room 2100. Top floor. I'll go ahead with Mr. Bond and see he has everything he wants."

Narrator: Bond turned to say goodbye to Halloran and thank him. For a moment Halloran had his back to him as he said something about Bond's luggage to the commissionaire.

Bond looked past him across 55th Street. His eyes narrowed. A black sedan, a Chevrolet, was pulling sharply out into the thick traffic, right in front of a Checker cab that braked hard, its driver banging his fist down on the horn and holding it there. The sedan kept going, just caught the tail of the green light, and disappeared north up Fifth Avenue.

It was a smart, decisive bit of driving, but what startled Bond was that it had been a negress at the wheel, and through the rear window he had caught a glimpse of a single passenger — a huge grey-black face which had turned slowly towards him and looked directly back at him, Bond was sure of it, as the car accelerated towards the Avenue.

Bond shook Halloran by the hand. Dexter touched his elbow impatiently.

Captain Dexter: "We'll go straight in and through the lobby to the elevators. Half-right across the lobby. And would you please keep your hat on, Mr. Bond."

Narrator: As Bond followed Dexter up the steps into the hotel he reflected that it was almost certainly too late for these precautions. And the giant shape in the back seat? Mister Big?

"Hm," said Bond to himself as he followed the slim back of Captain Dexter into the elevator.

Source: Excerpt from *Live and Let Die* by Ian Fleming © Glidrose Publications, 1954.

Listening 2 Tapescript 7.b

"Superman's Song" by Crash Test Dummies

Tarzan, wasn't a ladies' man,
He'd just come along and scoop 'em up under his arm,
Like that, quick as a cat in the jungle
But Clark Kent, now there was a real gent
He would not be caught sittin' around in no
Junglescape, dum as an ape, doing nothing

Chorus
Superman never made any money
For saving the world from Solomon Grundy,
And sometimes I despair the world can never see
Another man like him

Hey Bob, Supe had a straight job
Even though he could have smashed through any bank
In the United States, he had the strength, but he would not
Folks said, his family were all dead
Their planet crumbled but Superman, he forced himself
To carry on, forget Krypton, and keep going

Repeat Chorus
Tarzan was king of the jungle and lord over all the apes
But he could hardly string together four words: "I Tarzan, You Jane."

Sometimes when Supe was stopping crimes
I'll bet that he was tempted to just quit and turn his back
On man, join Tarzan in the forest
But he stayed in the city, and kept on changing clothes
In dirty old phonebooths till his work was through
And nothing to do but go on home

Repeat Chorus

• UNIT 8   It's How You Play the Game

Speaking 1 Tapescript 8.a

1. He shoots. He scores.

2. Going, going, gone — it's a home run.

3. The horses are neck and neck. Silver Streak has just taken the lead by a nose.

4. Shots up. What a rejection by Jones!

5. We have just witnessed the fastest 100 metres ever.

6. Schneider lines it up and lasers it at the goalie.

7. Goal — a great finish on that shot.

8. Another ace! Sampress has his big gun going today.

9. A great dig, but an even bigger spike!

10. Smith punches it into the end zone. Touchdown!

Listening 1 Tapescript 8.b

Reporter: Why are you at the arena on this cold wintery day at 6 a.m.?

Roger: Well, see that girl in the net and the tall girl playing left forward — those are my daughters.

Reporter: Is your whole family playing?

Roger: My son's game starts at 10 a.m. The kids really enjoy playing hockey, even if it means getting up at 5 a.m.

Reporter: I always thought that hockey was a male sport.

Roger: It used to be, but not any more. The girls still don't get as much ice time as the boys' teams; but, every year they are moving toward a more equal footing.

Reporter: Why do you think it's important to have your children involved in hockey?

Roger: Hockey is an excellent way for kids to learn about hard work and commitment. They have to attend several practices and games every week. Their participation and effort affect the whole team, so they quickly learn the importance of being a team player. I think these are all lessons that help them out later in life.

Reporter: Being a hockey dad must mean a certain amount of sacrifice on your part.

Roger: It's a commitment for the whole family. My wife helps out getting the kids to their practices and games, as well as with fundraising activities for the teams and the Hockey Parents Association. The children recognize that we're willing to sacrifice a lot in order to have them involved. Hockey really is a whole family activity in our house and it helps to keep us together as a family.

Reporter: Is it expensive to have your children play hockey?

Roger: In fact, it does involve quite a financial commitment, much more than a sport like baseball or soccer. Usually in the little leagues there are team uniforms that you borrow for the season; but, as the kids get older you have to outfit them head-to-toe in specific approved hockey gear. If bought new, it would cost well over a thousand dollars to outfit a kid, but usually you can find used equipment for about $500. The worst part is that the kids keep growing and you have to change their equipment every year. Doing that for three children can get really pricey. On top of that you have to figure in all the expenses from driving them around to their practices and games. When there's a weekend tournament in a distant town, we often rent a hotel room because it's too far to drive every day. On top of that there are meals for the family. You get the picture. It really does cost quite a bit.

Reporter: Living in a small farming community, do you think hockey plays an important role in tying that community together?

Roger: Absolutely. It's a common purpose that brings the whole community together. In hockey there are no politics or racial issues involved. Everyone comes for the game. My wife and I have met some really great parents that we might not have met otherwise and we've developed some lasting friendships. Likewise, the children have met lots of kids from neighbouring schools, which will really help them out when they get to high school because in small communities like ours, each community has a public school, but there is only one local high school. Our kids will have established many friendships before they ever get there and that should take some of the pressure off when starting at a new school.

Reporter: Well, it sounds as if you are committed to your family and to the value of hockey.

Roger: Absolutely. I know that keeping my kids active will help keep them out of trouble. Hopefully, they will be able to apply their knowledge of being a team player when they join the workforce.

Reporter: It looks as if your girls are just about finished their practice. I'd better let you go. Thanks for filling me in on the benefits of playing hockey.

Roger: No problem.

Vocabulary 2 Tapescript 8.c

booted	slammed	dribbled	smashed
slices	slap	roar	tap
groaned	pop		

Listening 2 Tapescript 8.d

Excerpt 1

Today's game of tenpins has German roots that have been traced back to about 300 AD. It was the custom for all males of Germanic tribes to carry clubs or *kegels* to settle any arguments that might come up with man or beast. A club in the hands of a hothead was a serious threat for the priests and missionaries who struggled to Christianize Germany.

The priests ordered that all clubs be stacked at the door whenever the men entered a place of worship. The club, the priests said, was evil, and leaving it at the door was an act of faith and peace. To carry the symbolism a step further, the priests invented a game. When a man came to church, he was given a round stone to roll at his club. If the man could knock down the "evil club," the priest praised him for his virtue. If the man failed to knock the club over, he was warned to correct his sinful ways.

The game at first was undoubtedly taken quite seriously, but eventually *kegling*, as bowling is still sometimes called today, was pursued for fun, with religious overtones forgotten.

Excerpt 2

In the late 1930s in the ruins of Khafaje, a city that was built 5000 years ago, archaeologists came upon a bronze casting of two wrestlers. Khafaje stood near present-day Baghdad. The castings and a stone carving of a boxing match were found close to an altar dedicated to the Sumerian god of fertility. The location suggests that boxing and wrestling matches had been part of ancient religious rites. Second, both works of art looked as if they could have been modelled after modern athletes. The styles of both wrestling and boxing have changed little since 3000 BC.

Excerpt 3

In China during the Han Dynasty, which lasted from 207 BC to 220 AD, there were two kinds of ball-kicking games. In one, players took turns kicking a ball at a target. In the other, players took turns showing off their skill in juggling, dribbling, and passing the ball without touching it with their hands, similar to today's practice drill for soccer.

Excerpt 4

A ball and stick is a natural combination for play. It was such a popular combination in North America that it would have been fair at one time to have called it a "national sport." Native Americans from coast to coast had refined the ball and stick game to a high level long before the first European explorers arrived. European settlers converted the native game into what we now know as lacrosse.

The modern game, however, is quite different from the native sport. For one thing, the native game seemed to be remarkably free from rules. Although 70 players on a side was the average number, there were times when teams of 2000 or more took to the field. The field itself might be a mile or more long, and dimensions might change during a game.

Excerpt 5

The Egyptians developed a very powerful bow more than 3000 years ago. The bow and arrow was used to hunt game along the Nile and as a weapon in war. It may be that archery was a skill borrowed from neighbouring tribes. Some inscriptions speak of bordering tribes as the "bow people." Possibly the bowmen who marched with Egypt's armies were imported mercenaries, foreigners who gave archery an alien character.

Excerpt 6

Basketball was dreamed up by a Canadian-born minister, Dr. James A. Naismith. In the winter of 1891 he devised a new indoor game in the hope of attracting more youth off the streets and into the YMCA. Dr. Naismith wanted goals to be scored more through skill than by speed or muscle. He fastened two empty peach baskets to the balconies at the ends of the gymnasium.

Excerpt 7

Golf, as it is played today, originated on the eastern shore of Scotland. In fact, the Scots called the rolling stretches of shoreland *links*, a word now applied to golf courses. Another Scottish word, *divot*, means "piece of turf." The most likely story of how the game started, golf historians believe, is that in some ancient time Scottish shepherds became bored sitting out on hillsides with no one to talk to but flocks of sheep. So, to break the monotony, they used their crooked sticks to knock pebbles around. To make a game of this knock-about diversion, they dug small holes and aimed pebbles at them.

Source: Excerpts from *The Games They Played: Sports in History* by Richard B. Lyttle. Used by permission of the author.

• UNIT 9 Food For Thought

Listening 1 Tapescript 9.a

Compulsive Eating: The Culture, the Family, the Individual

Food can be a source of sustenance and pleasure. It does more than satiate hunger; it is the main event at celebrations like birthdays, baptisms, even funerals. For many people, growing food in the backyard garden and cooking are enjoyable hobbies.

Sometimes people use food to cope. When a person feels sad or depressed, a scoop of ice cream or some potato chips can be soothing. When anxiety strikes, cookies may serve as a way to reduce the tension. Once the uncomfortable feeling passes, the individual resumes normal eating patterns.

For some people, however, normal eating does not resume. The good feelings from eating reinforce its use time and time again. A love-trust relationship is established; food initially fills a need that is not being met. This behaviour usually results in weight gain or a fear of weight gain. Consequently, the individual may turn to dieting or other means to regain control and to lose weight.

A change in the body occurs. When a person diets, the body adjusts to a lower calorie intake; the metabolic rate slows down, and it becomes easier to gain more weight. So the more times a person diets, the harder it becomes to lose weight. This can lead to more bingeing and purging, an activity marked by a tremendous intake of food followed by ridding the body of calories or weight, usually through inducing vomiting, use of laxatives, or even excessive exercise. For the compulsive eater, food is an addiction and, as with any addiction, it becomes the major focus in the person's life.

For example, compulsive eaters often avoid social engagements that involve eating if they are on a diet. Or they may binge before or after a social event, coming late or leaving early. In daily conversations with people, they are often mentally absent because they are thinking about what they have eaten or what they will be eating.

There are many similarities between compulsive eating and alcoholism. Compulsive eating can be as addictive as alcohol; it is a chronic, progressive disease and, like alcohol, not only harms the victim but everyone around her.

Compulsive eaters consume huge quantities of food rapidly and secretly. For example, a binge might consist of two dozen cookies, a pint or two of ice cream, and several candy bars. This binge feels pleasurable while the person is gorging. Once the person stops eating, however, she is consumed with overwhelming feelings of guilt, remorse, and self-hate. She has a strong urge to gain control and does so by purging her body (fasting, rigid dieting, laxative abuse, or vomiting).

Compulsive eaters are driven by a desire to be thin. This obsession makes compulsive eaters easy prey for fad diets or "miracle" weight loss schemes. Buying books, consuming pills, and going to weight loss programs which require special foods are ways that compulsive eaters search for a miraculous cure. Compulsive eaters are forever dieting, forever counting calories, and forever battling their feelings about food.

They feel deprived much of the time. They are resentful and angry because they aren't like other people when it comes to food. They feel there is something radically wrong with them and try to hide their problems with food from others. They feel a deep sense of shame and embarrassment.

Compulsive eaters equate thinness with success and being in control. Consequently, they think in terms of "if only's." "If only I were thinner, then I would get that promotion." "If only I were thinner, then I would be married." Being thin is the dream of dreams; it means everything will be wonderful.

Compulsive eaters, regardless of weight, generally share the following traits:
- they feel worthless and powerless;
- they have a strong need to control their world;
- they have difficulty expressing feelings, especially anger;
- they have confused feelings about their sexuality;
- they have difficulty in intimate relationships;
- they have a distorted body image; and
- they are perfectionistic.

Surveys among college women reveal that 75% or more describe themselves as binge eaters, and 4 to 8% admit that they have vomited on at least one occasion to deal with overeating.

Over 50 million Americans exceed by 10% or more their ideal body weight and therefore can be considered obese; 15 million Americans are so obese that their health is seriously at risk. It has always been assumed that overweight people have merely been unable to control themselves. It has been especially difficult in the last ten years for overweight people to deal with cultural expectations, as fitness has become the norm.

For decades, women have tried to be small and petite. They have sacrificed their well-being to be more acceptable. In the 1900s, for example, women suffered immense pain when wearing whalebone corsets, which sometimes caused broken ribs. These undergarments allowed women to have the feminine hourglass figure popular during that cultural period. Some of them even had surgery to remove lower ribs so they could be even more acceptable and admired.

American women were not the only ones to endure physical pain for the cultural vision of beauty. The Chinese bound little girls' feet to stunt growth and give the appearance of delicacy.

The message is clear; "You are not acceptable as you are. You should look like . . ." In the fifties, it was Marilyn Monroe; in the sixties and seventies, it was Jackie Kennedy and Twiggy; in the eighties, it was Jane Fonda. The culture and media keep brainwashing us with images of thin, beautiful women who seem to have it all. Women get trapped into believing that their physical appearance and their beauty and kindness will ensure that their needs will be met and life will be wonderful. Compulsive eating results from struggling to live up to an ideal of femininity.

Source: Excerpts from *Feeding the Empty Heart: Adults, Children and Compulsive Eating* by Barbara McFarland and Tyeis Baker-Baumann. Copyright © 1988 by the Hazelden Foundation. Used by permission of the authors.

Listening 2 *Tapescript 9.b*

Interviewer: Today we are talking about poverty and hunger — problems that affect people around the world and even in our country. With us today is Dr. Barbara Manders, a leading expert on world poverty. Welcome to the show Dr. Manders.

Dr. Manders: Thank you for inviting me to discuss such an important topic today.

Interviewer: How many people suffer from hunger worldwide? Millions?

Dr. Manders: Would you believe that over one billion people suffer from a chronic lack of food?

Interviewer: How can that be when we hear on the news that the prices of grains are plummeting due to surplus supplies?

Dr. Manders: Unfortunately there is no one simple solution to world hunger. Solutions include grassroots movements, effective government policies, and the implementation of knowledge already available.

Interviewer: There are so many organizations and attempts to relieve hunger worldwide. Why have we seen so little progress?

Dr. Manders: Poverty is a mighty large obstacle to overcome. The poor lack the assets, resources, and the knowledge to produce change. In addition, there are people in powerful positions who profit from the wide gap between the rich and the poor, and they have a vested interest in ensuring that the gap between the "haves" and the "have nots" continues.

Interviewer: You're referring to Third World countries where powerful people use violence and power to maintain the current situation.

Dr. Manders: In fact, powerful regimes in Third World countries are not the only culprits. We need to look no further than in our own backyard.

Interviewer: We don't have powerful regimes in Canada.

Dr. Manders: You're right; however, we do have chronic hunger amongst our poorest people. That's part of the reason food banks are so frequently used.

Interviewer: Despite being one of the best places in the world to live, Canada has an income gap between the rich and the poor that is nearly twice that of other industrial countries. Food banks are a way of life for many people in Canada. Why are they such an integral part of the survival of our nation's poorest?

Dr. Manders: The media constantly contrast the chronic suffering of the poor in underdeveloped nations such as Asia, Africa, and Latin America and the king-like lifestyle led by the rich in those countries. It's easy for the average Canadian to distance himself or herself from the hunger over there, but it is much harder to distance yourself from the reality of what is happening in our own country. It doesn't garner the same media attention as hunger in Third World countries because people don't want to be reminded that this situation exists in such a rich country. We like to believe that with a few charitable donations to food banks the problem will go away.

Interviewer: Are food banks the answer?

Dr. Manders: No. Food banks are no different than providing temporary relief for starving people around the world. There's a proverb which states: "Give a man a fish and you feed him for a day. Teach him how to fish and you feed him for life." In other words, temporary food relief is not the solution for world hunger — it's merely a temporary stop-gap measure.

Interviewer: How do people who operate food banks feel about government policies?

Dr. Manders: People who work with food banks will tell you that our government chooses to have hunger in the country through its policies. During tough economic times, it continues to cut back social programs but still finds money to spend on its pet projects. In fact, government relies on food banks and people's charity to make up for its lack of commitment to alleviating poverty. Caseworkers regularly refer their customers to food banks when their welfare cheques run out.

Interviewer: What can we do about the hunger problem in Canada and worldwide?

Dr. Manders: We have to work together and lobby governments worldwide to make a strong and ongoing commitment to eliminating world hunger. Commitment is the key.

• UNIT 10 The Circle of Life

Listening 1 Tapescript 10.a

Your Children Are Not Your Children

Your children are not your children,
They are the sons and daughters of Life's longing for itself.
They came through you but not from you.
And though they are with you yet they belong not to you.
You may give them your love but not your thoughts,
For they have their own thoughts.
You may house their bodies, but not their souls,
For their souls dwell in the house of tomorrow, which you cannot visit, even in your dreams.
You may strive to be like them, but seek not to make them like you,
For life goes not backward nor tarries with yesterday.
You are the bows from which your children as living arrows are sent forth.

Source: From *The Prophet* by Kahlil Gibran, 1923.

Listening 2 Tapescript 10.b

[A = interviewer]

Interview 1 Christopher

A: Hi. I'm going to ask you a few questions. Let me start by asking you your name.

Chris: My name is Christopher

A: And how old are you Christopher?

Chris: I'm eight years old.

A: And what grade are you in?

Chris: I'm in grade three.

A: Christopher, what do you enjoy doing in your spare time?

Chris: Reading.

A: Reading?

Chris: Yes.

A: Anything else?

Chris: Thinking.

A: What do you like to think about?

Chris: Sonic jets . . . um . . . and really neat airplanes.

A: What kinds of things frighten you or worry you?

Chris: And I like to play with my friends.

A: You like to play with your friends?

Chris: Yes.

A: And, what kinds of things frighten you or worry you?

Chris: Monsters, from a certain show called *Goosebumps*.

A: Anything else?

Chris: GHOSTS!

A: What kinds of things do you worry about?

Chris: Um . . . if somebody's going to beat me up after school. Mmm . . . like . . . if I don't do my math and I have to stay in after school. Like those things.

A: What's the best thing about being a child?

Chris: Mmm . . . You're young and you can play and run.

A: And what's the worst thing about being a child?

Chris: You always get bossed around by grown-ups!

A: What is the most important thing and who are the most important people in your life?

Chris: My mother, my father, my brother, my aunt, my uncle, and my grandmother and grandfather and me. Me.

A: OK. What do you want younger people to know about what it's like to be your age?

Chris: Well . . . sometimes people are harsh on you. Sometimes they scream at you when you really didn't do it. But sometimes people are smooth . . . like when you've been really good and you get a reward.

A: And, what do you want older people to remember about being your age?

Chris: That you were a lot better runner when you were a child than when you're a grown-up.

Interview 2 Serene

A: OK. Let's begin. First of all, can you tell me your name?

Serene: My name is Serene.

A: How old are you Serene?

Serene: I'm seventeen.

A: Can you tell me what you enjoy doing in your spare time?

Serene: Spending time with friends, going to fun places, going to dances.

A: And what kinds of things frighten you or worry you at this stage in your life?

Serene: (pause) Well, what frightens me the most is thinking about death. Death really scares me because I don't want to die. I think about it sometimes. But I'm mostly concentrating on my education and getting into university so I want to do good in school. I worry about if I'm going to make it and how my grades are going to be.

A: What's the best thing about being a person your age?

Serene: The best thing is that it's supposed to be the best time of your life. You get to do fun and crazy things and you don't have to have a reason. And you don't have a lot of responsibility yet like a family and stuff.

A: And what's the worst thing about being a person your age?

Serene: The pressure you get from your parents — not letting go and not letting you go out when you want to go out.

A: What is the most important thing for you and who are the most important people in your life right now?

Serene: Right now the most important people in my life are my friends because I spend most of my time with them. But also, the most important thing is to try to get a good education so that I can get into a good university.

A: OK. What do you want to tell younger people about people your age?

Serene: Um . . . Well, although it's really fun and you always want to do fun stuff, you have to be patient with your parents and concentrate on school because it's really important at this stage.

A: What do you want to tell older people about people your age?

Serene: That we might do things that annoy you, and we might do stupid things but we're just learning. Sometimes we'll make mistakes but we are trying. So maybe just be patient.

A: Thank you very much Serene.

Serene: You're welcome.

Interview 3 Martha

A: Thank you for speaking with me. Perhaps we can start by you telling us your name.

Martha: My name's Martha.

A: Martha. And how old are you?

Martha: I turned 40 this year.

A: What do you enjoy doing in your spare time?

Martha: Well I do a lot of gardening and I do a lot of reading and I guess I'd love to have the chance to travel, but that's an impossibility right now.

A: What kinds of things frighten you or worry you at this stage in your life?

Martha: I think it's totally involved with my health. I would be scared to become a quadriplegic — or have a brain injury. I worry about losing the capability of taking care of my family.

A: What's the best thing about being a person your age?

Martha: I think when you reach your forties, hopefully you have the confidence and experience to make decisions that won't leave you with regrets.

A: What's the worst thing about being a person your age?

Martha: Um . . . if you have small children, you're responsible for them. If you work you're doubly responsible for your family and your work. But also, at this point in life your parents are getting older and you find yourself responsible for them too. So, I'd say it's the tremendous responsibility.

A: What is the most important thing in your life and who are the most important people in your life at the moment?

Martha: My children and my husband. The most important thing? Well, I don't know. I guess I'd love to win the lottery because then we'd have more options.

A: What do you want to tell younger people about people your age?

Martha: It's so different for everyone because where you're at at 40 depends on the decisions you make when you're young. But you know I'd say to young people: "Having grey hair is not bad. Starting to sag a little is not bad. Going up a dress size or a shirt size is not bad. The only thing you have to learn is to age gracefully."

A: What do you want to tell older people about people your age?

Martha: That sometimes you have to make choices that don't seem logical to other people (I go through this with my father-in-law), but you still have to have the right to make your own choices. So I'd say to them, "Let us make our own choices and don't treat us like children."

Interview 4 Konrad

A: I appreciate that you agreed to do this interview. Before we begin, can you tell us your name and how old you are?

Konrad: My name is Konrad and I'm 86 years old.

A: Here's the first question. What do you enjoy doing in your spare time?

Konrad: In my spare time? I would honestly say it's work.

A: And what kind of work do you do?

Konrad: I'm in the catering business. I work usually 20 to 30 hours a week. It keeps me young.

A: What kinds of things frighten you or worry you at this stage in your life?

Konrad: Well . . . that I have to go one day. Other than that, I don't really worry about anything from day to day.

A: What's the best thing about being a person your age?

Konrad: Well. That's not an easy question . . . that you're still alive!

A: What's the worst thing about being a person your age?

Konrad: I can't say that there is anything really bad about being old. You see nothing is really that important. When you are young you think money is important, but it's true when they say money can't buy happiness.

A: What is the most important thing or who are the most important people in your life at this time?

Konrad: My health. And the most important person is my wife. At my age there aren't many other people left. I have no children. So, my wife.

A: What do you want to tell younger people about people your age?

Konrad: Younger people shouldn't be rude to old people. When you are old, you are not stupid or unimportant. Treat us with respect.